Advance Praise for
The New Meaning of Educational Change, **Fourth Edition!**

"For many years the first edition of *The New Meaning of Educational Change* was my 'bible' for understanding how to improve teaching and learning for all students within complex school systems. The book's fourth edition continues and deepens that tradition by featuring a knowledge-base that Michael Fullan describes as 'more profound and accessible' and that blends the achievement of meaning with an action orientation. As with earlier editions, I particularly appreciate Fullan's recognition of the important roles played in the change process by students, parents, community members, teachers, principals, and district administrators."

—**Dennis Sparks**, Emeritus Executive Director,
National Staff Development Council

"This new edition of a classic and highly influential text significantly extends Fullan's remarkable efforts to synthesize and make useful what is known about successful educational change processes."

—**Ken Leithwood**, Professor, Policy Studies,
OISE/University of Toronto

"When the third edition was published in 2001, I wrote that 'Those who seek to understand the last decade will find no better source. Those seeking a view of the terrain for the next will find no surer guide.' I reiterate these views for the fourth edition with even stronger conviction. Michael Fullan is at the peak of his knowledge and influence on change and reform in education. He has been a master of the field for the quarter century in which *The New Meaning of Educational Change* has been published. No writer can draw on developments in so many countries, and he has no peer in his command of the links between research, policy, and practice. There is a sense of urgency in the fourth edition because a system-wide breakthrough has not been made at the level of the student and classroom, even though the knowledge of how to do it is at hand. Those who seek to achieve such a breakthrough must read this book."

—**Brian J. Caldwell**, Managing Director,
Educational Transformations Pty Ltd,
Professorial Fellow, University of Melbourne,
and Deputy Chair of Board,
Australian Council for Educational Research (ACER)

"Twenty five years ago I was privileged to read the first edition of *The New Meaning of Educational Change* in manuscript form. It changed my professional life. As a neophyte change worker, Michael Fullan's knowledge of the educational change landscape, his ability to add value through analysis, and his unique skill in forecasting the future through reflecting on the past, whilst remaining pragmatically in the present, enabled me to take some (minimal) control over the world of educational change that I was entering. To his great credit, Fullan as the archetypical action-oriented intellectual has pulled off the same trick with each successive edition of the book. In this fourth edition, however, Fullan has excelled himself. Although following a similar structure to previous editions, this is no mere updating of a tried and tested formula. Here Fullan is in full flow: He offers us a view of educational change as comprehensive as the first edition, but with a depth and understanding of the complexities that are unsurpassed in their authority, vision, and passion."

—**David Hopkins**, HSBC iNet Chair of International Leadership,
Institute of Education, University of London,
and Formerly Chief Adviser to the
Secretary of State for Education, England

"*The New Meaning of Educational Change*, first published in 1982, has provided insights that have informed and inspired thousands of educators. Never one to 'stand in place,' Fullan offers new thinking and perspectives in the fourth edition. There is a new emphasis on 'capacity building with a focus on results.' Among many things, Fullan explains the promise and pitfalls of 'going deeper,' creating shared meaning, reculturing, using tri-level reform, and bringing change to scale. Fullan, once again, centers his work on motivation, relationships, and the human dynamics involved in all change efforts. As usual, each concept is built on much research and the field experience of others; each is clear and resonates with plain common sense; each draws from Fullan's own work as a change facilitator on the national, state, and district levels. Michael Fullan's acclaimed work is aptly titled. Change ever changes and we need to understand its ever evolving meaning if we are to make a difference in schools."

—**Lew Smith**, Director,
National Principals Leadership Institute,
and National School Change Awards,
Fordham University Graduate School of Education

The NEW Meaning of Educational Change

FOURTH EDITION

MICHAEL FULLAN

TEACHERS COLLEGE PRESS

Teachers College, Columbia University
New York and London

Published by Teachers College Press, 1234 Amsterdam Avenue, New York, NY 10027

Library of Congress Cataloging-in-Publication Data

Fullan, Michael.
  The new meaning of educational change / Michael Fullan.—4th ed.
    p. cm.
  Includes bibliographical references and index.
  ISBN 978-0-8077-4765-0 (pbk. : alk. paper)
  ISBN 978-0-8077-4766-7 (cloth : alk. paper)
    1. Educational change—Canada. 2. Educational change—United States.
  3. Education and state—Canada. 4. Education and state—United States.
  I. Title.
LA412.F85 2007
370.971—dc22
                            2006038077

ISBN-13: 978-0-8077-4765-0 (paper)
ISBN-13: 978-0-8077-4766-7 (cloth)

Printed on acid-free paper
Manufactured in the United States of America

14 13 12 11 10 09 08 07   8 7 6 5 4 3 2 1

To four boys and a girl

Contents

Preface

This fourth edition of *The New Meaning of Educational Change* is different in that it is more action-based and contains more of my own assessment and interpretation of what is happening. I start with a key paragraph from each of the prefaces of the three previous editions. This gives an idea of how the core message has evolved in the past quarter of a century.

In the original edition (1982) I wrote:

> The issue of central interest in this book is not how many new policies have been approved or how many programs have been developed, but rather what has actually changed in practice—if anything—as a result of our efforts and how do we know when change is worthwhile? What can teachers, administrators, or policymakers do when they know something is wrong in our schools? Can rejecting a proposed educational program be more progressive than accepting it? Why are we so often unclear about how to put a new program into practice?

In the second edition (1991):

> It is essential to understand both the small and the big pictures. We have to know what change looks like from the point of view of the teacher, student, parent, and administrator if we are to understand the actions and reactions of individuals; and if we are to comprehend the big picture, we must continue to aggregate knowledge of those individual situations with an understanding of organizational and institutional factors that influence the process of change as government departments, universities, teacher federations, school systems, and schools interact.

In the third edition (2001):

> An enormous amount has happed in the decade since the last
> edition. If anything, "the meaning hypothesis" has been deeply
> confirmed. . . . Advances in cognitive science make meaning the
> foundation for the new pedagogy of constructivism. Chaos or
> complexity theory leads us inevitably to the conclusion that
> working on "coherence" is the key to dealing with the frag-
> mented demands of overloaded reform agendas.

What is new in 2007? More has happened to further our understanding of educational change in the 6 years since the previous edition than in the 20 years spanning the first and third editions. Meaning has always been about doing. The work that we
are now engaged in has a strong knowledge base *because* it is
deeply grounded in action. The initiatives are more ambitious,
more comprehensive, and more demanding. Because of the strong
applied nature of this work, the insights are more robust and
more precise. Theory and practice are becoming more fused, to
the benefit of both.

   We still have not cracked the code of getting beyond the classroom door on a large scale, but the questions are more penetrating
and the forces being mobilized in this quest are more powerful
and increasingly harder to ignore.

   The core question in this edition is how to combine "meaning" and "action" to achieve continuous improvement on a sustainable scale never before experienced. What is "new" are strong,
actionable concepts in combination: capacity building, learning in
context, lateral capacity building, sustainability, and systems leaders in action—leaders at all levels engaged in changing the system, changing their own context. All of these new and powerful
concepts will become clearer in the course of this book.

   What is "bad" is the overdosing on standards and assessment
(the failure to get the balance right between assessment and capacity building); the inability to get inside the classroom; superficial professional learning communities; and the failure in many
countries to reduce the gap between lower- and higher-achieving
students and schools. Indeed, widening of the income and education gap is occurring in some of the richest countries—a sure danger sign that society is worsening.

   The work on the meaning of educational change has benefited greatly from the growing number and variety of academics, policymakers, and practitioners who are partnering to bring about substantial improvement, as they understand how to go even further. I have the privilege of being in a worldwide network of people who are morally and intellectually committed to educational improvement. This is great work, made all the more meaningful by the collective effort underway in all quarters of the globe. I wish here to thank the literally hundreds of co-workers and friends who have been and continue to be on this journey. What I have learned is contained in the myriad of actions and interactions I have had over the past 40 years.

   In this book I plan to show that the knowledge base of change is becoming more profound and accessible, and that it is absolutely indispensable to leading within the relentless ubiquity of innovation and reform. The answer to endemic social complexity is for individuals, especially in interaction with others, to arm themselves with knowledge of the change process, to engage in reflective action, and to test what they know against the increasingly available knowledge in the literature on change.

   The meaning of change will always be "new" because it is a human endeavor that is perpetually dynamic. Educational change has meaning because it pursues moral purpose and does so by bringing best knowledge to bear on critical issues of the day. Above all, when it works, it does so because it motivates "a million change agents" to find meaning in collective action to improve humankind. Meaningful work, action-based, never finished— one could spend a lifetime!

PART I

UNDERSTANDING
EDUCATIONAL CHANGE

CHAPTER 1

A Brief History of Educational Change

Everything must change at one time or another or else a static society will evolve.
— Anonymous first-year university student on an English language proficiency test

One person claims that schools are being bombarded by change; another observes that there is nothing new under the sun. A policymaker charges that teachers are resistant to change; a teacher complains that administrators introduce change for their own self-aggrandizement and that they neither know what is needed nor understand the classroom. A parent is bewildered by a new practice in reading and by the relevance of education to future jobs. Some argue that restructuring schools is the only answer, while others decry that this too is just a pipe dream diverting our attention from the core curriculum changes that are desperately needed. One university professor is convinced that schools are only a reflection of society and cannot be expected to bring about change; another professor is equally convinced that schools would be all right if only superintendents and principals had more "vision" as educational leaders, and teachers were more motivated to learn new approaches to improving the curriculum. A governor works hard to get major new legislation passed to reform education; a principal thinks, "this too shall pass." Charter schools are hailed simultaneously as saving the day and destroying the public education system. Commercial entities take over school districts and claim that they can do a better job. States pass dramatic legislation to serve notice to "failing schools" and "failing school districts" with corresponding invasive interventions intended to

3

make things right. Standards-based reform is held up as the answer to our woes.

Amid all this turmoil, agents at all levels wonder how to get more and more programs institutionalized, while teachers think that it is these same promoters of change who should be institutionalized, not their programs. Students are too distracted by a host of other matters to pay much attention to all the uproar.

What are we learning from these mostly aborted and confused attempts at reform? Remarkably, the history of intensive educational change is little more than half a century old. I won't say much about the 1950s. It was relatively quiet for most of the decade. The big initial development, as Miles (1993) has noted, was the National Training Laboratories' (NTL) training in group skills, shared reflection, diagnosis, and action. For the most part, these experiences were laboratory-based, detached from the day-to-day instructional issues and function of schools.

To say that NTL and related projects had limited impact is not to say that they were on the wrong track. Today, for example, it is abundantly clear that one of the keys to successful change is the *improvement of relationships* (Fullan, 2001)—precisely the focus of group development. In any case, as it turned out, these early attempts represented mere tinkering. There were much larger fish to fry if education was to play a leading role in societal development.

THE FIRST ATTEMPT FALLS FLAT

One doesn't have to believe that Sputnik was the literal cause of large-scale reform in the United States post-1957, or that all new ideas started in the 1960s, or that the United States was the only country engaged in national educational reform, to know that something very different was in the air in the 1960s. Elmore (1995) comments on the pre-1950s "progressive period":

> What is most interesting about the progressive period, as compared with other periods of educational reform, is that its aims included explicit attempts to change pedagogy, coupled with a relatively strong intellectual and practical base. Noted intellec-

tuals—John Dewey, in particular—developed ideas about how schools might be different. (p. 7)

Progressive reformers believed, according to Elmore, that for the most part "good ideas would travel of their own volition" into schools and classrooms (p. 18). The strategy, noted Elmore, "turned inward, toward the creation of exemplary settings" (p. 11), particularly over time. The result:

> We can produce many examples of how educational practice could look different, but we can produce few, if any, examples of large numbers of teachers engaging in these practices in large scale institutions designed to deliver education to most children. (p. 11)

Despite these failures, and indeed ignoring their lessons, the U.S. federal government launched a large-scale national curriculum reform series of initiatives in the late 1950s and throughout the 1960s. I previously have labeled this the "adoption era" of reform because the goal was to get innovations out there, as if flooding the system with external ideas would bring about desired improvements. Huge sums of money were poured into major curriculum reforms like PSSC Physics, BSCC Biology, and MACOS Social Sciences, and organizational innovations such as open-plan schools, flexible scheduling, and team teaching.

By the early 1970s, there was mounting evidence that the yield was minuscule, confined to isolated examples. Goodlad, Klein, and associates' *Behind the Classroom Door* (1970), Sarason's *The Culture of the School and the Problem of Change* (1971), and Gross, Giacquinta, and Bernstein's *Implementing Organizational Innovations* (1971) all attested to the absence of change at the classroom level. The term *implementation* (or more accurately, *failed implementation*) came into the vocabulary of reform, and in the first major review of research, Fullan and Pomfret (1977) documented the massive failure of reform. Putting ideas into practice was a far more complex process than people realized.

Elmore (1995) states that what these models missed was

> the complex process by which local curricular decisions get made, the entrenched and institutionalized political and com-

mercial relationships that support existing textbook-driven curricula, the weak incentives operating on teachers to change their practices in their daily work routines, and the extraordinary costs of making large scale, long-standing changes of a fundamental kind in how knowledge is constructed in classrooms. (p. 15)

There was actually great pressure and incentives to become innovative, and this resulted in many schools adopting reforms that they did not have the capacity (individually or organizationally) to put into practice. Thus, innovations were adopted on the surface, with some of the language and structures becoming altered, but not the practice of teaching.

Another major force for reform around the Western world in the 1960s was the various forms of civil rights movements, pinpointing scores of inequities. Numerous national initiatives across the world focused on the disadvantaged. The education system was thought to be one of the major societal vehicles for reducing social inequality. To the intrinsic complexity of changing one's practice was added the enormous difficulty of tackling the existing power structure and overcoming the prejudice and ignorance of ethnic, class, gender, and special differences of all kinds. Nor is there much evidence that the lives of the disadvantaged have improved, even in cases where sincere efforts to do so are in evidence (Oakes, Quartz, Ryan, & Lipton, 1999; Oakes & Lipton, 2002). And where gains have been achieved, it has been in isolated cases, seemingly guaranteed not to go to scale.

Not much progress has been made since the 1960s, despite renewed interest in the 1980s in large-scale reform focusing on accountability. The *pressure* for reform has increased, but not yet the reality. The good news is that there is a growing sense of urgency about the need for large-scale reform, more appreciation of the complexity of achieving it, and even some examples of partial success. The bad news is that in some countries, such as the United States, we are losing ground—the economic and education gap has been widening at least since the year 2000 (Berliner, 2005; Education Trust, 2005; Fullan, 2006). At this point we know what needs to be done, but there is neither the sense of urgency nor the strategic commitment to do the hard work of accomplishing large-scale, sustainable reform.

The urgent reasons for reform are now familiar. The global society is increasingly complex, requiring educated citizens who can learn continuously, and who can work with diversity, locally and internationally. Although the source of blame varies, it is now an undeniable conclusion that the education system and its partners have failed to produce citizens who can contribute to and benefit from a world that offers enormous opportunity, and equally complex difficulty finding one's way in it. Rohlen (1999) makes this case convincingly in his analysis of "social software for a learning society," in which he argues:

> In essence, the message is that our schools need to teach learning processes that better fit the way work is evolving. Above all, this means teaching the skills and habits of mind that are essential to problem-solving, especially where many minds need to interact. (pp. 251–252)

We also are beginning to see the large-scale consequences of failed reform—health and well-being costs rise, economic prosperity becomes jeopardized, and the social cohesion of society weakens to dangerous levels.

For these reasons, we have witnessed a growing intensity in the efforts at large-scale reform in the 1990s, and even more so now. We can now conclude accurately, as I will illustrate throughout this book, that large-scale reform has returned. We are now less naive than the last time we had such an opportunity, although society and therefore the problem of reform have become more complex.

The factors reinforcing the status quo are systemic. The current system is held together in many different cross-cutting ways. Confronting the isolationism and privatism of education systems is a tall order. It requires intensive action sustained over several years to make it possible both physically and attitudinally for teachers to work naturally together in joint planning; observation of one another's practice; and seeking, testing, and revising teaching strategies on a continuous basis. Reform is not just putting into place the latest policy. It means changing the cultures of classrooms, schools, districts, universities, and so on. There is much more to educational reform than most people realize. This book honors that complexity but also identifies the most powerful levers for reform at our disposal. These levers must have the strength to influence complex webs of factors, while having the virtue of clarity, if not simplicity. We need powerful usable strategies for powerful recognizable change.

If a healthy respect for and mastery of the change process do not become a priority, even well-intentioned change initiatives will continue to wreak havoc among those who are on the firing line. Careful attention to a small number of key details during the change process can result in the experience of success, new commitments, and the excitement and energizing satisfaction of accomplishing something that is important. More fundamentally, reducing the number of failures and realizing new successes can lead to the revitalization of teaching and learning that is so desperately needed in the lives of educators and students today.

The problem of meaning is central to making sense of educational change. In order to achieve greater meaning, we must come to understand both the small and the big pictures. The small picture concerns the subjective meaning or lack of meaning for individuals at all levels of the education system. Neglect of the phenomenology of change—that is, how people actually experience change as distinct from how it might have been intended—is at the heart of the spectacular lack of success of most social reforms. It is also necessary to build and understand the big picture, because educational change, after all, is a sociopolitical process. This book will have succeeded or failed to the extent that people who are involved in education can read the account and conclude that it makes sense of their individual context, enables them to understand the broader social forces influencing change, and—above all—points to some action that they and others around them can take to improve their immediate situation.

In the process of examining the individual and collective settings, it is necessary to contend with both the "what" of change and the "how" of change. Meaning must be accomplished in relation to both these aspects. It is possible to be crystal clear about what one wants and totally inept at achieving it. Or to be skilled at managing change but empty-headed about which changes are most needed. To make matters more difficult, we often do not know what we want, or do not know the actual consequences of a particular direction, until we try to get there. Thus, on the one hand, we need to keep in mind the values and goals and the consequences associated with specific educational changes; and on the other hand, we need to comprehend the dynamics of educational change as a sociopolitical process involving all kinds of individual, classroom, school, local, regional, and national factors at work in interactive ways. The problem of meaning is one of how those involved in change can come to understand what it is that should change, and how it can be best accomplished, while realizing that the what and how constantly interact with and reshape each other.

We are not only dealing with a moving and changing target; we are also playing this out in social settings. Solutions must come through the development of *shared meaning*. The interface between individual and collective meaning and action in everyday situations is where change stands or falls.

Large-scale reform failed in the 1960s because it focused primarily on the development of innovations and paid scant attention to the culture of schools and districts in which innovations would reside. During the 1970s, large-scale change went underground as the field focused on effective schools, and innovative schools, which turned out to be sporadically placed. Growing pressure on education systems to improve in a context of global competition led most countries to introduce "accountability schemes" in the 1980s without much attention to capacities that would be required at all levels of the systems to actually do the work of improvement.

As the 1990s unfolded, some countries, most notably England, started to pay greater attention to continuing "pressure and support." In a National Literacy and Numeracy Strategy (NLNS), England focused on a few core priorities, stepped up the requirements for schools and local authorities to concentrate on the daily teaching of literacy and numeracy in relation to ongoing student achievement, used external inspection and assessment to buttress the effort, and invested heavily in the instructional materials, professional development, and use of "change agents" (consultants, lead literacy and numeracy teachers) at all levels of the system. Although the causes and detailed meaning of the results are still being debated, England had considerable success (to a point). From 1977–2001 the percentage of 11-year-olds achieving proficiency in literacy and numeracy on national assessments moved from a little over 60% to about 75% (Earl, Fullan, Leithwood, & Watson, 2003). This represents an impressive accomplishment given that almost 20,000 primary schools over 150 local authorities were involved. Aside from the fact that 75% success is still not good enough, the results "plateaued" in England for several years following 2001—an issue that is now being addressed.

So, comprehensive systemwide reform, such as the case in England, is promising but not yet the answer. In the United States, large-scale reform was addressed in a different way in the 1990s through the development of comprehensive school reform (CSR) models, sometimes called whole-school reform (WSR) models. Whole-school reform models are intended to provide proven school-wide innovations that would be adopted by schools in order to improve student achievement, especially among more disadvantaged and low-performing schools. The most prominent sponsor of WSR models over the past decade has been New American Schools (NAS)—a private, nonprofit organization whose mission is to help schools and districts raise student achievement. Since its inception, NAS has been involved in a development phase (1992–1993), a demonstration phase (1993–1995), and a scale-up phase (1995–2002).

The decade-long experience (1991–2001) with whole-school reform models has been well evaluated by the Rand Corporation (Berends, Bodilly, & Kirby, 2002; Berends, Chun, Schuyler, Stockly, & Briggs, 2002), and by independent researchers such as Datnow and her colleagues (Datnow, Hubbard, & Mehan, 2002; Datnow & Kemper, 2003). The main conclusion from the Rand research was that "the initial hypothesis, that by adopting a whole-school design a school could improve its performance was largely unproven" (Berends, Bodilly, & Kirby, 2002, p. xxxvi).

As policymakers realized that WSR models were not the answer, they gravitated to more direct methods of changing the system. Much of this new work is contained in the chapters of this book, so I will not dwell on the post-2000 strategies here. In most jurisdictions, this work involves stepping up the ante through intrusive accountability-based interventions. The United States' No Child Left Behind (NCLB) is a prime example, as is England's Every Child Matters (ECM) legislation. In the words of this book, by and large the policies and strategies employed have not yet inspired widespread "meaning" on the part of the scores of people that would be necessary for success to occur. Let me frame the problem.

The main dilemmas in large-scale reform are all a variation on what I call the too-tight/too-loose problem. Top-down change doesn't work because it fails to garner ownership, commitment, or even clarity about the nature of the reforms. Bottom-up change— so-called let a thousand flowers bloom—does not produce success on any scale. A thousand flowers do not bloom, and those that do are not perennial! The strategies that are needed have a "bias for action" and pursue this by reconciling and combining top-down and bottom-up forces for change. In our work, we call this strategy *capacity building with a focus on results* (Fullan, 2005, 2006; Fullan, Hill, & Crévola, 2006). We will see many practical, large-scale examples of this strategy throughout the chapters.

The search, then, for large-scale reform that is successful continues. In this brief history of educational change, let me make one final point. There is an important distinction to be made between *innovation* and *innovativeness*. The former concerns the content of a given new program, while the latter involves the capacities of an organization to engage in continuous improvement. Both are of interest to us. One can productively focus on a particular innovation and trace its path of success or failure. One also can start with the culture of a school, district, or other level of the system, and examine how innovative it is. We will do both in this book, although I would place the emphasis on how institutions can become innovative on a sustainable basis. Indeed, there is a shift over the four editions from innovation to innovativeness, and this current edition continues and deepens the trend.

The meaning of change is one of those intriguing concepts that seems like so much common sense, but eludes us when we pursue it on a large scale. The reason that it is so difficult to pin down is that at the end of the day large-scale reform is about *shared* meaning, which means that it involves simultaneously individual and social change. Socially meaningful change in complex times will always be intrinsically difficult to accomplish.

THE PLAN OF THE BOOK

I do not attempt to survey the content or substance of all the latest educational innovations and reforms. I do, however, use a wide range of specific innovations to explain the practical meaning of educational change. Included in the studies on which I draw are changes in various curriculum areas (e.g., literacy, mathematics, science, social studies), computers, cooperative learning, special education, school restructuring, teacher education, school-wide innovations, district reform, state and national policies, and so on. Locally initiated changes are well represented along with those sponsored at the provincial/state and national levels.

The book is divided into three main parts. Part I: Understanding Educational Change (Chapters 1 through 6) provides a detailed overview of how educational change works. We started in this chapter with a brief history of change in order to get a sense of the territory. We continue this journey in Chapter 2, which deals with the subjective reality of coping with change, both involuntary and desired change, and makes explicit the objective reality of what we mean when we refer to something as having changed. This chapter defines what change is. Chapter 3 is brand-new to this book. It introduces the dynamics of change and offers key new insights into the inner workings of successful and unsuccessful change processes—ideas essential for all remaining chapters in the book.

Chapter 4 identifies the main factors that relate to adoption or decisions to initiate change. There are a variety of reasons why individuals or groups decide to embark on a change—personal prestige, bureaucratic self-interest, political responsiveness, and concern for solving an unmet need. This chapter raises questions about how and why decisions about particular educational changes are made. The way in which these decisions are made strongly influences what will happen at the follow-up or implementation stage.

Implementation and continuation (or the extent to which change actually occurs and is sustained) are the focus of Chapter 5. Since implementation refers to what really happens in practice (as distinct from what was supposed to happen), it is a central theme that runs through the whole book. The history of implementation research is not pleasant. It shows that planned change attempts rarely succeed as intended. As some old sayings go, "There's many a slip 'twixt the cup and the lip," "the proof is in the pudding," and "the road to hell is paved with good intentions." Honorable motives are even more problematic when we attempt to get others to heaven as well as ourselves—when social rather than individual change is at stake. In fact, I will show that, ironically, in many ways the more committed an individual is to a specific form of change, the less effective he or she will be in getting others to implement it. While the above sayings have been around a long time, it is only in the past 30 years that educators have come to realize that "the proof is in the 'putting'": The way in which change is put into practice determines to a large extent how well it fares. As we shall see, some of the most recent evidence indicates that we may be getting better at planning and implementing not only specific innovations, but also more complex policy reforms. Certainly there is greater clarity about what factors need to be addressed and how to address them.

Chapters 4 and 5 cover the process of change: from how changes become initiated to how or whether they get put into practice and become institutionalized. What happens at one stage has powerful consequences for subsequent stages. In the final analysis, Chapter 5 provides an overview of the dynamics of how educational changes get implemented/nonimplemented and institutionalized/discontinued.

It is one thing to know the events and situations that cause change or prevent change from happening; it is an entirely different question to know what to do about it. Chapter 6 delves into the complex issues of planning and coping with educational change. Paradoxically, and entirely consistent with the message of this book, planning is more about doing (reflective doing) than it is about pre-action planning. I endorse a bias for action not just because I am committed to change on the ground, but equally because it is only through action that we come to understand and develop the skills and clarity to actually make change successful. Chapter 6 addresses the perplexing question of "the pathways problem"—that knowing what constitutes success is not the same thing as achieving it in a new situation. Many attempts at change fail because no distinction is made between theories of change (what causes change) and theories of changing (how to influence those causes). And when solutions are attempted, they often create their own problems, which are more severe than the original ones. Chapter 6 contains examples of both failure and success at planned change.

Part I, then, provides the overall framework for thinking about and doing something about educational change. It shows, incidentally, that "rationally planned" strategies are not that rational when it comes to dealing with people and the problem of meaning. Part I does not differentiate in detail what it all means for the everyday teacher, principal, parent, and so on. This is the purpose of Part II, Educational Change at the Local Level, which consists of five chapters (7 through 11) in which I examine what is known about the role of people in different positions at the local school and school district levels. In each case, I bring to bear the body of research knowledge (particularly concrete, experiential evidence) on a given role in order to address two sets of questions. The first set concerns the meaning of change for people in the role under discussion—what their experience is in relation to the process of educational change. Then, when we have some understanding of the meaning of change for given role incumbents, the second set of questions is directed at generating ideas for what they could or should do about it. These guidelines will range from general suggestions to specific steps to be taken, depending on the circumstances.

The five chapters in Part II are designed so that individuals within these roles can gain greater understanding of their place in the context of changes around them. These chapters also enable individuals in one role to gain an understanding of the realities of participants in other roles and thereby a clearer view of the sociology of educational change in the society as a whole.

Chapters 7 to 9 examine change within the school by analyzing the roles of key participants and their organizational relationships. As implementation is the essence of change, it follows that the teacher as implementer is central. Chapter 7 examines the concrete situation of the teacher and shows that change is only one among many problems the teacher faces—it turns out that the conditions for change as well as strategies employed by central policymakers and administrators provide many more disincentives than benefits. Sociologically speaking, few of us, if placed in the current situation of teachers, would be motivated or able to engage in effective change. Obvious strategies do not seem to work. Professional development of teachers has been ineffective and wasteful more times than not. Building on earlier chapters, Chapter 7 explains why many approaches to change do not work for teachers and suggests some remedies. There have been great new advances in knowledge in the past few years in understanding professional learning communities and the role they play in "reculturing" the teachers' role in improvement.

More lip service than mind service has been given to the pivotal role of the principal as gatekeeper or facilitator of change. However, the research evidence is mounting, and we have much to go on in sorting out the role of school leadership. Chapter 8 describes the situation of the principal and his or her current role in facilitating or inhibiting change. As before, to understand what is, we examine specific evidence and situations. It is only through specificity that we can go beyond the generalities of leadership qualities found in much of the literature. In deriving implications for what the role of the principal could or should be, the emphasis will be on the formulation of specific guidelines that deal with the total reality faced by the principal. The principal is absolutely key when it comes to developing the "school capacity" to manage change. Ironically, the more that we have recognized the vital importance of the principal, the more we have overloaded the principalship. Today the problem is to figure out how principals can be supported to become the lead change agent.

People think of students as the potential beneficiaries of change. They think of achievement results, skills, attitudes, and the need for various improvements for the good of the children. They rarely think of students as *participants* in a process of change. Consequently, there is limited evidence regarding what students think about changes and their role regarding them. It is interesting and worthwhile to attempt to develop the theme of what the role of students is and what it could be. Naturally there will be differences according to the age of students, but Chapter 9 will elaborate on the possible meaning of change for children and adolescents. Fortunately, growing attention is being paid to the "voice" and participation of students in school reform.

The remaining two chapters of Part II address the local context of schools, namely, parents/community and district infrastructure. In Chapter 10 the roles of parents, communities, and school boards are examined. The problem of meaning is especially acute for these groups, which are vitally concerned with and responsible for educational decisions but which often have limited knowledge. Case-study materials and other research evidence will be used to clarify what communities do vis-à-vis questions of initiating, rejecting, supporting, or blocking particular changes in their schools, and will illustrate the dilemma that schools face about whether to involve parents in decisions about change. I will take up especially questions regarding the role of the individual parent in instruction, decision making, and otherwise relating to the school and to the education of his or her child.

A considerable amount of evidence exists that the superintendent and other district administrators are as crucial for determining change within the district as is the principal within the school. Again it will be necessary to examine evidence that will allow us to determine in which ways this is specifically true. What is it that the district administrator does? What is the actual process of events, and what are the results? As interest in large-scale reform has increased, the role of districts has received greater attention. The goal is to engage *all* schools in the district in ongoing reform, not just a few. Case studies of school districts doing this are discussed in Chapter 11.

As Part II analyzes what happens at the local level, the four chapters in Part III turn to the regional and national levels. If we are to understand the realities of change at the local level, we must discover how societal agencies, for better or worse, influence change in schools. The role of government agencies represents another dilemma for understanding educational change. On the one hand, important social reforms would not be launched without federal or state/provincial impetus. On the other hand, external reforms frequently are not successful and are seen as interfering with local autonomy. We now have enough evidence from governmental change efforts since 1960 to understand why this source of reform is necessary, why it often doesn't work, and what the implications are for altering the approach. Common principles and research findings will be used to analyze how national and state agencies function in the realm of education. Chapter 12 assesses these issues and formulates guidelines for governmental action. Compared with the previous edition of this book, we now are able to be much more precise about the role of governments in large-scale successful reform. We have examples underway that represent deliberate use of the knowledge base in change in order to accomplish major reforms.

In Chapters 13 and 14 the education and continuing professional development of school personnel are examined. Nothing is more central to reform than the selection and development of teachers and administrators. The initial preparation of teachers, including induction, is the purview of Chapter 13. The preservice education of teachers does not prepare them at all for the complexities of educational change. And until recently, the plight and the potential of the beginning teacher have been ignored. While reversal of these traditions is not yet in evidence, I will present considerable data to demonstrate that teacher education is receiving some of the critical attention it deserves.

Career-long professional development for teachers and administrators, which I take up in Chapter 14, has not fared much better. Inservice education or ongoing staff development explicitly directed at change has failed, in most cases, because it is ad hoc, discontinuous, and unconnected to any plan for change that addresses the set of factors identified in earlier chapters. Factors affecting change function in interaction and must be treated as such; solutions directed at any one factor in isolation will have minimal impact. Chapters 13 and 14 analyze recent developments in the area of preparation and development of educators, and make the case that these developments must be linked to other strategies that focus on changing the cultures or working conditions of educators.

In the final chapter of the book (Chapter 15) I reflect on the problem of change in the context of future trends and expectations for educational change. In many ways we now know what works. Unfortunately this formulation itself is partly a theory of change rather than of changing—to know what works in some situations does not mean we can get it to work in other situations. The basis for hope, however, lies somewhere beyond the naivete of the 1960s, the cynicism of the 1970s, the partial successes of the 1980s and 1990s, and the sobering realization in the 2000s that this is going to be a lot harder than we thought. Going beyond hope, this book will identify and point to action steps that each and every one of us can take to bring about significant improvements.

PROSPECTS FOR REFORM

We have learned over the past decade that the process of educational reform is much more complex than had been anticipated. Even apparent successes have fundamental flaws. For example, in our development work we have been interested in how long it takes to turn around a poorly performing school or district to become a well- or better-performing system. In the third edition, I concluded that you can turn around an elementary school in about 3 years, a high school in about 6 years, and a school district (depending on size) in about 8 years (Fullan, 2001). Six years later, we can safely say, based on our recent experience, that by using the latest change knowledge we can cut these rates in half. Nonetheless, we are still not talking about changing the whole system.

The main reason that change fails to occur in the first place on any scale, and is not sustained when it does, is that the infrastructure is weak, unhelpful, or working at cross-purposes. By the infrastructure I mean the next layers above whatever unit we are focusing on. In terms of successive levels, for example, a teacher cannot sustain change if he or she is working in a negative school culture; similarly, a school can initiate and implement successful change, but cannot sustain it if it is operating in a less than helpful district; a district cannot keep going if it works in a state that is not helping to sustain reform.

It is for this reason—the need for whole-system, sustainable reform—that we recently have turned our attention to tri-level reform: what has to happen at the local school and community level as one of the "tri's;" at the district level as the mid "tri;" and at the state or national level as the final "tri" (Barber & Fullan, 2005; Fullan, 2005).

We also are engaged currently in attempts to realize tri-level reform. In Ontario, Canada, for example, we are directly involved in using the knowledge base to transform the entire school system, starting with literacy and numeracy up to the age of 12 (Fullan, 2006). In related work, Fullan, Hill, and Crévola (2006) have mapped out a comprehensive design for achieving break-through results (95%+) for all students. I also have raised more fundamental questions naming income and education gaps as the real reform agenda (Fullan, 2006). In *Turnaround Leadership* I argue that most attempts at turning around failing schools achieve, at best, superficial, nonsustainable results.

I believe that we are closer than ever in knowing what must be done to engage all classrooms and schools in continuous re-form. Knowing what must be done, as this book amply demon-strates, is not the same thing as getting it done. Meaning is key, but only if it is shared. And you cannot get shared meaning with-out purposeful action on many fronts.

CHAPTER 2

The Meaning of Educational Change

If there is no meaning in it, that saves a world of trouble, you know, as we needn't try to find any.
—King of Hearts in *Alice in Wonderland*, after reading the nonsensical poem of the White Rabbit

We have become so accustomed to the presence of change that we rarely stop to think what change really means as we are experiencing it at the personal level. More important, we almost never stop to think what it means for others around us who might be in change situations. The crux of change is how individuals come to grips with this reality. We vastly underestimate both what change is (the topic of this chapter) and what factors and processes account for it (Chapters 4 and 5).

The clarification process that I propose to follow in this chapter has four parts. The first task is to consider the more general problem of the meaning of individual change in society at large, not just confined to education. Second, I elaborate on the *subjective* meaning of change for individuals in education. Third, I organize these ideas more comprehensively to arrive at a description of the *objective* meaning of change, which more formally attempts to make sense of the components of educational change. The test of the validity of this objective description will indeed be whether it orders and makes sense of the confusion and complexity of educators' subjective realities. Fourth, and as a forward link to much of the rest of the book, I take up the critical related issues of shared meaning and program coherence. Finally, let me stress at the outset that meaning has both moral and intellectual dimensions. Making a difference in the lives of students requires care, commitment, and passion as well as the intellectual know-how to do something about it. Moral purpose and knowledge are the two main change forces that drive success.

THE GENERAL PROBLEM OF THE MEANING OF CHANGE

The titles of some of the more general accounts of individual and organizational change and reality in modern society provide us with as succinct an introduction to the problem as any: *Loss and Change* (Marris, 1975), *Beyond the Stable State* (Schön, 1971), *The Social Construction of Reality* (Berger & Luckmann, 1967), *Thriving on Chaos* (Peters, 1987), *Riding the Waves of Change* (Morgan, 1989), *The Fifth Discipline* (Senge, 1990), *Only the Paranoid Survive* (Grove, 1996), *Competing on the Edge* (Brown & Eisenhardt, 1998), *Leadership on the Line* (Heifetz & Linsky, 2002), *Change without Pain* (Abrahamson, 2004), and *Hard Facts, Dangerous Half-Truths and Total Nonsense* (Pfeffer & Sutton, 2006).

While there is a difference between voluntary and imposed change, Marris (1975) makes the case that *all* real change involves loss, anxiety, and struggle. Failure to recognize this phenomenon as natural and inevitable has meant that we tend to ignore important aspects of change and misinterpret others. As Marris states early in his book, "Once the anxieties of loss were understood, both the tenacity of conservatism and the ambivalence of transitional institutions became clearer" (p. 2).

According to Marris, "Whether the change is sought or resisted, and happens by chance or design; whether we look at it from the standpoint of reformers or those they manipulate, of individuals or institutions, the response is characteristically ambivalent" (p. 7). New experiences are always reacted to initially in the context of some "familiar, reliable construction of reality" in which people must be able to attach personal meaning to the experiences, regardless of how meaningful they might be to others. Marris does not see this "conservative impulse" as incompatible with growth: "It seeks to consolidate skills and attachments, whose secure possession provides the assurance to master something new" (p. 22).

Change may come about either because it is imposed on us

(by natural events or deliberate reform) or because we voluntarily participate in or even initiate change when we find dissatisfaction, inconsistency, or intolerability in our current situation. In either case, the meaning of change rarely will be clear at the outset, and ambivalence will pervade the transition. Any innovation "cannot be assimilated unless its *meaning* is shared" (Marris, 1975, p. 121, emphasis added).

I quote at some length a passage from Marris (1975) that is most revealing and fundamental to our theme.

> No one can resolve the crisis of reintegration on behalf of another. Every attempt to pre-empt conflict, argument, protest by rational planning, can only be abortive: however reasonable the proposed changes, the process of implementing them must still allow the impulse of rejection to play itself out. When those who have power to manipulate changes act as if they have only to explain, and when their explanations are not at once accepted, shrug off opposition as ignorance or prejudice, they express a profound contempt for the meaning of lives other than their own. For the reformers have already assimilated these changes to their purposes, and worked out a reformulation which makes sense to them, perhaps through months or years of analysis and debate. If they deny others the chance to do the same, they treat them as puppets dangling by the threads of their own conceptions. (p. 166)

Schön (1971) has developed essentially the same theme. All real change involves "passing through the zones of uncertainty . . . the situation of being at sea, of being lost, of confronting more information than you can handle" (p. 12). "Dynamic conservatism" in both Marris's and Schön's formulation is not simply an individual but a social phenomenon. Individuals (e.g., teachers) are members of social systems (e.g., schools) that have shared senses of meaning.

> Dynamic conservatism is by no means always attributable to the stupidity of individuals within social systems, although their stupidity is frequently invoked by those seeking to introduce change. The power of social systems over individuals becomes understandable, I think, only if we see that social systems provide a framework of theory, values and related tech-

nology which enables individuals to make sense of their lives. Threats to the social system threaten this framework. (Marris, 1975, p. 51)

The implications of the principles and ideas described by Marris and others are profound in relation to our understanding of educational change in two senses—one concerning the meaning of change, and the other regarding the process of change. In the rest of this chapter, I will begin to apply these principles to specific examples of the meaning of educational change by introducing concepts pertaining to different dimensions and degrees of change. In Chapters 4 through 6, the implications for the management of change will be documented in an examination of a large body of evidence on the causes and processes of change.

Real change, then, whether desired or not, represents a serious personal and collective experience characterized by ambivalence and uncertainty; and if the change works out, it can result in a sense of mastery, accomplishment, and professional growth. The anxieties of uncertainty and the joys of mastery are central to the subjective meaning of educational change and to the success or failure thereof—facts that have not been recognized or appreciated in most attempts at reform.

THE SUBJECTIVE MEANING OF EDUCATIONAL CHANGE

The details of the multiple phenomenologies of the different roles engaged in the educational enterprise will be taken up in each of the relevant chapters in Parts II and III. Here, my purpose is to establish the importance and meaning of the subjective reality of change. For illustration I will use examples taken from the world of the teacher, but the reader should refer to Chapter 7 for a more complete treatment of the teacher's situation, and to other chapters for the various relevant realities of other participants.

The daily subjective reality of teachers is very well described by Cohen and Hill (2001), Huberman (1983), Lortie (1975), Rosenholtz (1989), Ball and Cohen (1999), Spillane (1999, 2004), and Stigler and Hiebert (1999). The picture is one of limited development of technical culture: Teachers are uncertain about how to influence students, and even about whether they are having an influence; they experience students as individuals in specific circumstances who are being influenced by multiple and differing forces for which generalizations are not possible. Teaching decisions often are made on pragmatic trial-and-error grounds with little chance for reflection or thinking through the rationale. Teachers must deal with constant daily disruptions, both within the classroom, such as managing discipline and interpersonal conflicts; and from outside the classroom, such as collecting money for school events, making announcements, and dealing with the principal, parents, and central office staff. Teachers must get through the daily grind; the rewards are having a few good days, covering the curriculum, getting a lesson across, and having an impact on one or two individual students (success stories). Teachers constantly feel the critical shortage of time. And there are few intensive, ongoing learning opportunities for teachers individually or in concert to deeply acquire new learning concepts and skills.

Based on his own investigations and reviews of other research, Huberman (1983) summarizes the "classroom press" that exerts daily influences on teachers.

- The press for *immediacy and concreteness*: Teachers engage in an estimated 200,000 interchanges a year, most of them spontaneous and requiring action.
- The press for *multidimensionality and simultaneity*: Teachers must carry out a range of operations simultaneously, providing materials, interacting with one pupil and monitoring the others, assessing progress, attending to needs and behavior.
- The press for *adapting to ever-changing conditions or unpredictability*: Anything can happen. Schools are reactive partly because they must deal with unstable input—classes have different "personalities" from year to year; a well-planned lesson may fall flat; what works with one child is ineffective for another; what works one day may not work the next.
- The press for *personal involvement with students*: Teachers discover that they need to develop and maintain personal relationships and that for most students meaningful interaction is a precursor to academic learning. (pp. 482–483, emphasis in original)

This "classroom press," according to Huberman, affects teachers in a number of different ways: It draws their focus to *day-to-day effects* or a short-term perspective; it *isolates them from other adults,* especially meaningful interaction with colleagues; it *exhausts their energy;* and it *limits their opportunities for sustained reflection.*

In addition to these day-to-day factors that inhibit learning on the part of teachers, most strategies for reform focus on structures, formal requirements, and event-based activities involving, for example, professional development sessions. They do not struggle directly with existing cultures within which new values and practices may be required. As I have said elsewhere (Fullan, 1993, 1999), *restructuring* (which can be done by fiat) occurs time and time again, whereas *reculturing* (how teachers come to question and change their beliefs and habits) is what is needed.

Six recent studies, among many I could have selected, show that going deeper into reculturing is proving far more difficult than previously realized (Ball & Cohen, 1999; Cohen & Hill, 2001; Cross City Campaign for Urban School Reform, 2005; Oakes et al., 1999; Stigler & Hiebert, 1999; Timperley & Parr, 2005).

Ball and Cohen (1999) and Cohen and Hill (2001) talk about the persistent superficiality of teacher learning: "Although a good deal of money is spent on staff development in the United States, most is spent on sessions and workshops that are often intellectually superficial, disconnected from deep issues of curriculum and learning, fragmented and noncumulative" (Ball & Cohen, 1999, pp. 3–4). Teachers do not fare much better on the job, argue Ball and Cohen: "Teacher learning is usually seen as either something that just happens as a matter of course from experience or as the product of training in particular methods or curricula" (p. 4).

Cohen and Hill's (2001) study of California's decade-long effort to change and improve mathematics teaching is another case in point. Their conclusion is stated up front.

> The policy was a success for some California teachers and students. It led to the creation of new opportunities for teachers to learn. Teachers were able to work together on serious problems of curriculum teaching and learning in short-term professional communities. The policy also helped to create coherence among elements of the curriculum, assessment, and learning opportunities for certain teachers. Such coherence is quite rare in the blizzard of often divergent guidance for instruction that typically blows over U.S. public schools. Only a modest fraction of California elementary teachers—*roughly only 10 percent*—had the *experiences summarized.* (p. 9, emphasis added)

Cohen and Hill also found that norms of collaboration among teachers were weak, and that collaboration per se did not necessarily result in improvement. It had to be focused and sustained—a case we make in detail in *Breakthrough* (Fullan et al., 2006). The result for the vast majority of teachers is lack of consistency and coherence, with few opportunities for what Ball and Cohen, and Cohen and Hill, call practice-based inquiry and teaching for understanding, in which assessment, curriculum, and opportunities for teachers to learn about connecting assessment and instruction are evident on an ongoing basis.

Stigler and Hiebert's *The Teaching Gap* (1999) is even more revealing, as it is based on videotapes of an international sample of 8th-grade mathematics teachers. Mathematics lessons were videotaped in 231 classrooms: 100 in Germany, 50 in Japan, and 81 in the United States. Experienced mathematicians and mathematics teachers examined mathematical content with regard to its potential for helping students understand mathematics as judged in a blind test. The results showed that 89% of U.S. lessons contained low-level content, compared with 34% in Germany and 11% in Japan. Looking further into U.S. classrooms, Stigler and Hiebert found U.S. teachers said that they were familiar with the National Council of Teachers of Mathematics's (NCTM) *Professional Standards for Teaching Mathematics* (which is a well-developed vision of how teaching of mathematics should change in order to raise student understanding). Despite teachers' apparent familiarity with the NCTM *Standards*, Stigler and Hiebert report:

> When we looked at the videos, we found little evidence of reform, at least as intended by those who had proposed the reforms . . . [moreover], reform teaching, as interpreted by some teachers, might actually be worse than what they were doing previously in their classrooms. Teachers can misinterpret reform and change surface features—for example, they include more group work; use more manipulatives, calculators, and real-world problem scenarios; or include writing in the lesson—but fail to alter their basic approach in teaching mathematics. (pp. 106–107)

Next, consider Oakes and associates' (1999) study of middle schools implementing Carnegie's Turning Points agenda intended to create caring, intellectually productive schools for young adolescents. Oakes and associates observe that educators often rush to adopt new structures and strategies without considering their deeper implications. As one local leader observed:

> People jump on the practices. [They say], *"Turning Points* is having teams." Well, why are we having teams? What is the purpose of teams? "Well it's just having teams." Interdisciplinary curriculum? "Ok, let's do interdisciplinary curriculum." But why are we doing it? What are the purposes of it? What is our belief system about why we have interdisciplinary [curriculum]? They'll never have those discussions unless you've got somebody asking questions to prompt that dialogue. They haven't had an inquiry approach to making decisions. I think that we've said, "These are the good practices for middle grades." So everybody kind of jumps on the bandwagon and does them without really thinking about the process of change and how do we make that change happen? And then some people think that because they've changed the structure, they're there. (p. 242)

The Cross City Campaign for Urban School Reform's (2005) case studies of district-wide reform in Chicago, Milwaukee, and Seattle substantially corroborate the theme in this section. The change strategies put in place seem to have all the trappings of success: a large influx of new money; a focus on curriculum and instruction (especially related to literacy, math, and science); substantial professional development for teachers and principals; and major political support from the mayor and other community leaders. What transpired was discouraging. The bottom-line conclusion of the three case studies in the words of the authors:

> The three districts we studied had decentralized resources and authority to the schools, and had undergone significant organizational changes to facilitate their ambitious instructional improvement plans. The unfortunate reality for many principals and teachers we interviewed is that the districts were unable to change and improve practice on a large-scale. (p. 4)

To put it another way, the strategies employed, despite reflecting in many ways the state of the art of the knowledge base about change, were not powerful enough to create new shared meaning, skills, and commitment across large numbers of educators.

A particularly revealing problem of meaning, or more accurately different worlds of meaning, is contained in Timperley and Parr's (2005) research on the national literacy initiative in New Zealand. The essence of change, they say, revolves around three concepts (which will be familiar to readers of *The New Meaning of Educational Change*): beliefs and values; knowledge and skills; and outcomes. What their study demonstrates is that the government's "theory of change" relative to generating new beliefs, knowledge, and outcomes was different than the schools' conceptions. Most problematic was that the strategy of change employed failed to engage these two different worlds, and hence failed to produce positive outcomes. All of this is less a criticism of teachers and more a problem of the way in which change is introduced, and especially the lack of opportunity for teachers to engage in deeper questioning and sustained learning. As a result, *meaningful* reform escapes the typical teacher, in favor of superficial, episodic reform that makes matters worse.

In short, there is no reason for teachers to believe in the value of proposed changes, and few incentives (and large costs) to find out whether a given change will turn out to be worthwhile. House's (1974) observation over 30 years ago still holds.

> The personal costs of trying new innovations are often high . . . and seldom is there any indication that innovations are worth the investment. Innovations are acts of faith. They require that one believe that they will ultimately bear fruit and be worth the personal investment, often without the hope of immediate return. Costs are also high. The amount of energy and time required to learn the new skills or roles associated with the new innovation is a useful index to the magnitude of resistance. (p. 73)

Other studies of attempted change show that not all teachers experience even the comfort of false clarity. Both Gross and associates (1971) and Huberman and Miles (1984) found that abstract goals, combined with a mandate for teachers to operationalize them, resulted in confusion, frustration, anxiety, and abandonment of the effort. Thus, false clarity occurs when people *think* that they have changed but only have assimilated the superficial trappings of the new practice. Painful unclarity is experienced when unclear innovations are attempted under conditions that do not support the development of the subjective meaning of the change.

Lack of focus and clarity represents what I referred to earlier as the "too-loose" problem. Directly addressing this problem, as many jurisdictions have done, with standards-based reform gets us into the dysfunctions of the "too-tight" solution. Witness, for example, McNeil's (2000) devastating account of the impact of standardized testing in Texas, or Popham's (2004) equally trenchant dissection of the toxic effects of NCLB in its current form.

We will get to solutions later, but suffice it to say here that existing strategies fail to get at the day-to-day meaning and motivation of teachers. At this stage I draw two basic conclusions. First, change will always fail until we find some way of developing infrastructures and processes that engage teachers in developing new knowledge, skills, and understandings. Second, it turns out that we are talking not about surface meaning, but rather deep meaning about new approaches to teaching and learning. Meaning will not be easy to come by given this goal and existing cultures and conditions.

THE OBJECTIVE REALITY OF EDUCATIONAL CHANGE

People do not understand the nature or ramifications of most educational changes. They become involved in change voluntarily or involuntarily and in either case experience ambivalence about its meaning, form, or consequences. I have implied that there are a number of things at stake—changes in goals, skills, philosophy or beliefs, behavior, and so forth. Subjectively these different aspects are experienced in a diffuse, incoherent manner. Change often is not conceived of as being *multidimensional.* Objectively, it is possible to clarify the meaning of an educational change by identifying and describing its main separate dimensions. Ignorance of these dimensions explains a number of interesting phenomena in the field of educational change: for example, why some people accept an innovation they do not understand; why some components of a change are implemented and others not; and why strategies for change neglect certain essential components.

The concept of objective reality is tricky (see Berger & Luckmann, 1967). Reality is always defined by individuals and groups. But individuals and groups interact to produce social phenomena (constitutions, laws, policies, educational change programs), which exist outside any given individual. There is also the danger that the objective reality is only the reflection of the producers of change and thus simply a glorified version of *their* subjective conceptions. As Berger and Luckmann (1967) put it, we can minimize this problem by following the practice of posing double questions: "What is the existing conception of reality on a given issue?" Followed quickly by, "Says who?" (p. 116). With this caution in mind, I would now like to turn to the possibility of defining educational change.

What Is Change in Practice?

The implementation of educational change involves "change in practice." But what exactly does this mean? Although change in practice can occur at many levels—for example, the teacher, the school, the school district—I will use as an illustration the classroom or teacher level because this level is closest to instruction and learning. When we ask which aspects of current practice would be altered, if given educational changes were to be implemented, the complexity of defining and accomplishing actual change begins to surface. The difficulty is that educational change is not a single entity, even if we keep the analysis at the simplest level of an innovation in a classroom. Innovation is *multidimensional*. There are at least three components or dimensions at stake in implementing any new program or policy: (1) the possible use of new or revised *materials* (instructional resources such as curriculum materials or technologies), (2) the possible use of new *teaching approaches* (i.e., new teaching strategies or activities), and (3) the possible alteration of *beliefs* (e.g., pedagogical assumptions and theories underlying particular new policies or programs).

All three aspects of change are necessary because together they represent the means of achieving a particular educational goal or set of goals. Whether or not they do achieve the goal is another question depending on the quality and appropriateness of the change for the task at hand. My point is the logical one that the change has to *occur in practice* along the three dimensions in order for it to have a chance of affecting the outcome. As Charters and Jones (1973) observe, if we do not pay careful attention to whether change in practice has actually occurred, we run "the risk of appraising non-events" (n.p.).

It is clear that any individual may implement none, one, two, or all three dimensions. A teacher could use new curriculum materials or technologies without altering the teaching approach. Or a teacher could use the materials and alter some teaching behaviors without coming to grips with the conceptions or beliefs underlying the change.

Before we turn to some illustrations of the dimensions, three difficulties should be noted. First, in identifying the three aspects of change, there is no assumption about who develops the materials, defines the teaching approaches, and decides on the beliefs. Whether these are done by researchers, or an external curriculum developer, or a group of teachers is an open question (see Chapters 4 and 5). Second, and partly related, there is a dilemma and tension running through the educational change literature in which two different emphases or perspectives are evident: the fidelity perspective and the mutual-adaptation or evolutionary perspective. The fidelity approach to change, as the label indicates, is based on the assumption that an already-developed innovation exists and the task is to get individuals and groups of individuals to implement it faithfully in practice—that is, to use it as it is "supposed to be used," as intended by the developer. The mutual-adaptation or evolutionary perspective stresses that change often is (and should be) a result of adaptations and decisions made by users as they work with particular new policies or programs, with the policy or program and the user's situation mutually determining the outcome. Third, we can see that it is very difficult to define once and for all exactly what the objective dimensions of change are with respect to materials, teaching approach, and beliefs, because they may get transformed, further developed, or otherwise altered during implementation. Nonetheless, there is value in conceptualizing change (in order to define it over time) in terms of the three dimensions. Some examples illustrate this point.

In considering examples, it should be recognized that individual innovations or programs vary in terms of whether they entail significant change on the three dimensions in relation to the current practices of particular groups of individuals, but I suggest that the majority of educational innovations extant in the field involve substantial changes with regard to these criteria. In fact, innovations that do not include changes on these dimensions are probably not significant changes at all. For example, the use of a new textbook or materials without any alteration in teaching strategies is a minor change at best. Put in terms of the theme of this book, real change involves changes in conceptions and behavior, which is why it is so difficult to achieve.

Numerous examples could be used to illustrate the objective reality of the dimensions of change. I will draw on three examples—one on a provincewide curriculum for language arts, one on open education, and one pertaining to new developments in cognitive science. Considering these innovations in the light of the dimensions puts us in a better position to argue the desirability of the content of change because we can argue concretely.

Simms (1978) conducted a detailed study in one of the provinces in Canada on the use of an elementary language arts program. A few of the main objectives of the program are stated as follows:

- developing students' competencies in receiving information (critically) through listening, reading, viewing, touching, tasting, smelling;
- understanding the communication process as well as their role as receivers, processors or expressers in that process. (quoted in Simms, 1978, p. 96)

The three dimensions of potential change can be illustrated by reference to the basic document. For example, implications for pedagogical *beliefs* are contained in the following passage:

The basic focus is on the child as a flexible user of language. If language is to be truly useful (functional) we must begin with the present experience and competence of the child and fit our teaching into the natural language situation, which is an integrated, whole situation. It should be emphasized that the developing philosophy is one of total integration of all aspects of language arts. In this sense, integration refers to the treatment of all the communication skills as closely interrelated. (pp. 90–91)

References to possible alterations in *teaching approaches* are stated throughout the document. Recommended teaching methodologies include providing opportunities for active involvement of the child, using a variety of resources and techniques (viewing, reading, speaking, informal drama, mime, photography), and using "the inductive method frequently in small groups and individual teaching situations" (pp. 366–367). We need not describe the content of *curriculum materials and resources*—the third dimension—but the difficulties of clarifying and accomplishing changes in practice involving the interrelationship of beliefs, teaching approaches, and resources should be clear.

By employing the distinction between surface curriculum and deep structure in analyzing open education, Bussis, Chittenden, and Amarel (1976) have played right into our theme. They found that open-education teachers differed fundamentally in their use of open-education dimensions. Some teachers operated at the level of surface curriculum, focusing on materials and seeing that students were "busy." They tried to address open-education goals *literally*, but they did not comprehend the underlying purpose. For example, they wanted to ensure that children were "learning to share materials, to take turns, to respect the property of others, and so on—with the focus of concern being the manifestation of these behaviors rather than concomitant attitudes and understanding" (p. 59). It was these teachers who reacted to the problem of ambiguity by requesting further guidance on "what exactly has to be covered." Other teachers developed a basic understanding of the principles of open education and concrete activities that reflected them. They were "able to move back and forth between classroom activities and organizing priorities, using a specific encounter to illustrate a broader concern and relating broader priorities back to specific instances" (p. 61). Reflectivity, purposefulness, and awareness characterized these teachers, but not in a linear way; for example, they would do something out of intuition and then reflect on its meaning in relation to overall purpose. Assumptions about and orientations to children varied similarly. Teachers ranged from those who felt that children's ability to choose was unreliable and idiosyncratic (some could, others couldn't) to those who assumed and experienced that *all* children have interests and who were able to relate individualized interests to common educational goals across the curriculum.

In the pages of quotes from teachers and in their own analysis, Bussis and associates clearly demonstrate (although not using the same words) the nature of the dimensions of change at work. Some examples: teachers who saw open education as literally covering subject content but who had no underlying rationale; those "who were reasonably articulate in indicating priorities for children [but] were more vague in describing concrete connections between these priorities and classroom activities" (p. 69); still others who "may provide the classroom with rich materials *on the faith* that they will promote certain learning priorities" (p. 74, emphasis in original).

In the words of our dimensions, it is possible to change "on the surface" by endorsing certain goals, using specific materials, and even imitating the behavior *without specifically understanding* the principles and rationale of the change. Moreover, with reference to beliefs, it is possible to value and even be articulate about the goals of the change without understanding their implications for practice: "Action based on valuing and faith is not very likely to lead to an enlargement or strengthening of the teacher's own understanding. The potential informational support available in feedback to the teacher is not received because it is not recognized" (Bussis et al., 1976, p. 74).

The third example concerns the deep and expanding work in cognitive science. We have seen earlier in this chapter that the conditions for teachers coming to grips with this new knowledge are severely constrained (Ball & Cohen, 1999; Cohen & Hill, 2001; Stigler & Hiebert, 1999; see also Spillane, 1999). The best single source of these new theories is the companion volumes published by the National Academy Press under the title *How People Learn* (Bransford, Brown, & Cocking, 1999; Donovan, Bransford, & Pellegrino, 1999). Donovan and associates summarize the key findings with respect to students and teachers. With respect to students:

1. Students come to the classroom with preconceptions about how the world works. If their initial understanding is not engaged, they may fail to grasp the new concepts and information that are taught, or they may learn them for purposes of a test but revert to their preconceptions outside the classroom.
2. To develop competence in an area of inquiry, students must: (a) have a deep foundation of factual knowledge, (b) understand facts and ideas in the context of a conceptual framework, and (c) organize knowledge in ways that facilitate retrieval and application.
3. A "metacognitive" approach to instruction can help students learn to take control of their own learning by defining learning goals and monitoring their progress in achieving them.

Concerning teachers:

1. Teachers must draw out and work with the preexisting understandings that their students bring with them.
2. Teachers must teach some subject matter in depth, providing many examples in which the same concept is at work and providing a firm foundation of factual knowledge.
3. The teaching of metacognitive skills should be integrated into the curriculum in a variety of subject areas.

Needless to say, the implications for sorting out the beliefs, pedagogical practices, and learning materials from a meaning perspective are absolutely staggering given our starting point. We could take other educational changes to illustrate the significance of the different dimensions of change. Virtually every program change states or implies all three aspects, whether we refer to literacy, science, school–work programs, technology, early childhood, special education, restructuring, or standards-based reform. Working on the meaning and definition of change is all the more important these days because larger-scale and more complex reforms are being attempted, and thus more is at stake. The point is that educational change programs have an objective reality that may be more or less definable in terms of which beliefs, teaching practices, and resources they encompass.

Why worry about all three aspects of change? Why not be content to develop quality innovations and provide access to them? The answer is simply that such an approach does not adequately recognize how individuals come to confront or avoid behavioral and conceptual implications of change. The new policy or innovation as a set of materials and resources is the most visible aspect of change, and the easiest to employ, but only literally. Change in teaching approach or style in using new materials presents greater difficulty if new skills must be acquired and new ways of conducting instructional activities established. Changes in beliefs are even more difficult. They challenge the core values held by individuals regarding the purposes of education. Moreover, beliefs are often not explicit, discussed, or understood, but rather are buried at the level of unstated assumptions. And the development of new understandings is essential because it provides a set of criteria for overall planning and a screen for sifting valuable from not-so-valuable learning opportunities. The ultimate question, of course, is how essential are all three dimensions of change. The use of new materials by themselves may accomplish certain educational objectives, but it seems obvious that developing new teaching skills and approaches and understanding conceptually what and why something should be done, and to what end, represents much more fundamental change, and as such will take longer to achieve but will have a greater impact once accomplished.

McLaughlin and Mitra (2000) draw a similar conclusion based on their study of three innovations in which they were concerned about what it would take to achieve "deep" reform.

> The experiences of these three theory-based reforms underscore the point that the relevant "it" that needs to be embedded in practice is not the particular activity structures, materials, or routines of a reform but rather the first principles. The problem for implementation then, is not only teachers "learning how to do it," but teachers learning the theoretical basis . . . absent knowledge about *why* they are doing what they're doing; implementation will be superficial only, and teachers will lack the understanding they will need to deepen their practice or to sus-

tain new practices in the face of changing context. (p. 10, emphasis in original)

In other words, changes in beliefs and understanding (first principles) are the foundation of achieving lasting reform. Put differently, the changes referred to by Ball and Cohen, the National Research Council, Stigler and Hiebert, and McLaughlin and Mitra are revolutionary because they are based on fundamental changes in conception, which in turn relate to skills and materials. I will leave the whole matter of strategies of change until later chapters. How best to deal with conceptions (e.g., beliefs) and behavior (e.g., teaching approaches) is complicated, but some of the implications include the need for addressing them on a *continuous* basis through communities of practice and the possibility that beliefs can be most effectively discussed *after* people have had at least some behavioral experience in attempting new practices.

In summary, the purpose of acknowledging the objective reality of change lies in the recognition that there are new policies and programs "out there" and that they may be more or less specific in terms of what they imply for changes in materials, teaching practices, and beliefs. The real crunch comes in the relationships between these new programs or policies and the thousands of subjective realities embedded in people's individual and organizational contexts and their personal histories. How these subjective realities are addressed or ignored is crucial for whether potential changes become meaningful at the level of individual use and effectiveness. It is perhaps worth repeating that changes in actual practice along the three dimensions—in materials, teaching approaches, and beliefs, in what *people do and think*—are essential if the intended outcome is to be achieved.

SHARED MEANING AND PROGRAM COHERENCE

So far I have understated the collective and organizational requirements related to meaning. Acquiring meaning, of course, is an individual act, but its real value for student learning is when *shared* meaning is achieved across a group of people working in concert.

We have long known about the value of collaboration and the debilitating effects of isolation (see Fullan & Hargreaves, 1992). Rosenholtz's (1989) study of teachers' workplace is a good case in point. Rosenholtz studied 78 schools in eight districts in Tennessee. She classified the schools as "stuck," "in-between," or "moving." Rosenholtz describes teachers' subjective construction of reality as part and parcel of their everyday activities. Her study indicates that schools in which teachers have a shared consensus about the goals and organization of their work are more likely to incorporate new ideas directed to student learning. In contrast, teachers that worked in "low-consensus schools" more commonly "skirted the edge of catastrophe alone," learning the lesson that they must shoulder classroom burdens by themselves, not imposing on one another. In Rosenholtz's study, "shared meaning" among teachers and others characterized those schools that were continually improving.

Oakes and associates (1999) remind us that teacher exchanges are likely to be weak unless they are coupled with moral commitments. Many teachers in her study welcomed opportunities to share ideas about students.

> But unless they were bound together by a moral commitment to growth, empathy, and shared responsibility, teachers were as likely to replicate the prevailing school culture as to change it. Unless they applied their collaboration to educative, caring, socially just, and participatory activities they continued to closely guard their classroom autonomy, be suspicious of the capacity of teaming to divide and balkanize their faculty, and distrust collaboration with those outside the school. (p. 285)

In addition to shared moral commitment, the pursuit of meaning involves constantly refining knowledge. Nonaka and Takeuchi (1995) talk about the critical importance of knowledge creation in successful organizations. They found that collaborative cultures constantly convert tacit knowledge into shared knowledge through interaction. We also will see in explicit detail in Chapters 7 and 8 how teachers and principals in some elementary and secondary schools go about creating and acting on best knowledge through the development of professional learning communities.

Finally, I return to the matter of how multiple, fragmented

initiatives compound the problem of meaning. Organizationally speaking, schools must figure out how to achieve *program coherence* among many pieces. I will address this vexing issue later at the school (Chapter 8), district (Chapter 11), and state (Chapter 12) levels.

What I have been saying has nothing to do with the *intentions* of promoters of change. No matter how honorable the motives, each and every individual who is necessary for effective implementation will experience some concerns about the meaning of new practices, goals, beliefs, and means of implementation. Clear statements at the outset may help, but do not eliminate the problem; the psychological process of learning and understanding something new does not happen in a flash. The presence or absence of mechanisms to address the ongoing problem of meaning—at the beginning and as people try out ideas—is crucial for success, because it is at the individual level that change does or does not occur. Of course, in saying that change occurs at the individual level, it should be recognized that organizational changes are often necessary to provide supportive or stimulating conditions to foster change in practice.

Perhaps the most important conclusion of this chapter is the realization that finding moral and intellectual meaning is not just to make teachers feel better. It is fundamentally related to whether teachers are likely to find the considerable energy required to transform the status quo. Meaning fuels motivation; and know-how feeds on itself to produce ongoing problem solving. Their opposites—confusion, overload, and low sense of efficacy—deplete energy at the very time that it is sorely needed.

So far I have dwelt on the problem of meaning in relation to the content of innovations. I have suggested that individuals and groups working together have to become clear about new educational practices that they wish (and/or someone else wishes them) to implement. This is meaning, if you will, about the content and theory of educational practice. Affecting the likelihood of obtaining meaning about the desirability and workability of specific educational practices is the question of *how* new practices are introduced. The latter concerns the theory of change as a complex social process in which people have just as many problems understanding what is happening and why. I mentioned in Chapter 1 that educational change involves two main aspects: what changes to implement (theories of education) and how to implement them (theories of change). There are dangers in separating these two aspects, because they interact and shape each other. But it is helpful to recognize this distinction in planning or analyzing specific reform efforts. In short, we have to understand *both* the change and the change process.

Once we enter the dynamics of change over a myriad of situations, things become complex. Over the years, as a result of increasingly grounded and ambitious change initiatives, we have been better able to identify some of the more detailed and insightful lessons of what makes for successful change processes as measured by positive impact on student learning. I distill these findings in Chapter 3. Whether one is dealing with a specific change project, or addressing a change in the culture of an institution; whether one is situated locally, regionally, or nationally—getting to understand the dynamics of change processes is absolutely crucial.

Too many reformers have failed because they "knew" the right answer. Successful change agents learn to become humble. Success is not just about being right; it is about engaging diverse individuals and groups who likely have many different versions about what is right and wrong. What I have tried to do in this new edition is to show how we can move through this complexity within a reasonable time frame. Change cannot be accomplished overnight, but it also cannot be open-ended. We need to experience substantial progress within one election period, so to speak. So, what have we learned over the past 6 years about successful change processes?

CHAPTER 3

Insights into the Change Process

Would you rather change or die?
—Deutschman (2005, p. 53)

Take any 100 books on change, and they all boil down to one word: motivation. If you want more words, the holy grail of change is to know under what conditions hordes of people become motivated to change (because we are talking about whole-system reform). The answer is not as straightforward as we would like.

We do know one thing: All successful change processes have a "bias for action." There is a reason for this, which is wrapped up in several related insights. Dewey mentioned it first when he said that people learn not by doing per se but by *thinking* about their new doing. Of course, this is right up our "meaning" alley. Ultimately it comes down to what is going on in one's head, but the stimulation comes from new experiences that give us something new to think and learn about.

All our insights are connected to this one fact—they stem from reflective action. This accounts for the related but counterintuitive findings that (1) behaviors and emotions change before beliefs—we need to act in a new way before we get insights and feelings related to new beliefs—and (2) the size and prettiness of the planning document are inversely related to the amount and quality of action, and in turn to student achievement (Reeves, 2006), and (3) shared vision or ownership (which is unquestionably necessary for success) is more of an *outcome* of a quality change process than it is a *precondition* for success. All of these insights are compatible with the pursuit of meaning through reflective action (see also Pfeffer & Sutton, 2000, and Mintzberg, 2004). The subjective meaning of change for individuals is at the heart of the matter—a point that Jellison (2006) makes as he comments on the early stages of a change process: "Leaders focus on the future and all the benefits that are going to flow to them and the organization. The rank and file locks into the present, focusing on the costs rather than the rewards of change" (p. 42).

THE MYSTERIES OF CHANGE

If people were given a literal choice of "change or die," do you think most people would choose change? If you said yes, think again. Deutschman (2005) writes, "What if a well-informed, trusted authority figure said you had to make difficult and enduring changes in the way you think and act, and if you didn't you would die soon." The scientifically studied odds that you would change, he writes, are nine to one against you. Medical research shows that 80% of the health care budget is consumed by five behavioral issues: smoking, drinking, eating, stress, and not enough exercise. Deutschman quotes Dr. Edward Miller, the dean of the medical school and the CEO of the hospital at John Hopkins University, who talks about patients with severe heart disease. Miller says, "If you look at people after coronary-artery bypass grafting, two years later, 90 percent of them have not changed their lifestyle. Even though they have a very bad disease and they know they should change their lifestyle, for whatever reason, they can't" (p. 2).

Deutschman quotes John Kotter of Harvard Business School as saying, "The central issue is never strategy or structure. [It] is always about changing the behavior of people." Then Deutschman observes: "The conventional wisdom says that crisis is a powerful motivator for change [think turnaround schools]. But severe heart disease is among the most serious of personal crises and it doesn't motivate—at least not nearly enough. Nor does giving people accurate analyses and factual information about their situations" (p. 2).

Back to our observation that people change their attitudes when they experience new things, which in turn touch their emotions. Kotter says, "Behavior change happens mostly by speaking to people's feelings. In highly successful change efforts, people find ways to help others see the problems or solutions in ways that influence emotions, not just thought" (p. 2). Deutschman then offers additional useful insights. Fear, as in fear of dying, turns out not to be a powerful motivator beyond an initial immediate effect. Similarly, in the United States, fear of not meeting "adequate yearly progress" in No Child Left Behind legislation, with its increasingly punitive consequences, is not much of a motivator—perhaps a little, but only in the very short run (see Fullan, 2006, for a full analysis of this point).

In "reframing change," Deutschman argues that we must figure out how to motivate people on the basis of their seeing and experiencing that they can feel better (not, in this case, just live longer). The key, then, is how to help people feel and be better.

If feelings and emotions are the key factors, one would think that an appeal to moral purpose in situations of terrible failure would be a great motivator. Not so. Even in extremely difficult circumstances, moral purpose by itself is insufficient. One also must feel and see that there is a means of moving forward.

Howard Gardner (2004) says that the most important thing to do in changing someone's mind is to connect to the person's reality as the point of departure for change. He warns: "Avoid egocentrism—being ensnared in one's own construal of events. The purpose of a mind-changing encounter is not to articulate your own point of view but rather to engage the psyche of the other person" (p. 163).

All change solutions, as I mentioned in the previous chapter, face the too-tight/too-loose dilemma. If a situation is loosely focused, as is the case, for example, with schools in need of turnaround, the natural reaction is to tighten things. Command-and-control strategies do get results in these circumstances, but only for a short time and only to a degree. If we then say that we need to give people more leeway—give them resources and trust them to do the right thing—the press for change is lost.

In general terms, the solution to motivating people is to establish the right blend of tightness and looseness, or more accurately to build both into the interactive culture of the organization. We will see practical examples of strategies based on these principles throughout the chapters in this book, but here I would like to pin down the basic ideas. These ideas are relevant to all change situations, but I particularly stress here how we might raise the bar and close the gap for all students.

THE ELEMENTS OF SUCCESSFUL CHANGE

Drawing on insights from our experience in the past 6 years, we can construct a more sophisticated set of practical strategies that mobilize the forces of change—strategies that do not choose between tightness and looseness but incorporate both. In my view, there are ten key ideas for focusing our efforts to achieve greater success on a large scale.

1. Define closing the gap as the overarching goal
2. Attend initially to the three basics
3. Be driven by tapping into people's dignity and sense of respect
4. Ensure that the best people are working on the problem
5. Recognize that all successful strategies are socially based, and action oriented—change by doing rather than change by elaborate planning
6. Assume that lack of capacity is the initial problem and then work on it continuously
7. Stay the course through continuity of good direction by leveraging leadership
8. Build internal accountability linked to external accountability
9. Establish conditions for the evolution of positive pressure
10. Use the previous nine strategies to build public confidence

A reminder before proceeding: My colleagues Hargreaves and Fink (2006) say that lists of this kind are a meal, not a menu. You need all ten, not any six or seven, because (to stick with the meal metaphor) they furnish a well-balanced reform agenda.

Define Closing the Gap as the Overarching Goal

Raising the bar and closing the gap cannot just be a slogan. It captures a host of issues that go to the very core of how a society

functions. The first thing is to realize that decreasing the gap between high and low performers—boys, girls; ethnic groups; poor,
rich; special education—is crucial because it has so many social
consequences. The remaining nine strategic focuses are all in the
service of gap closing.

The education component can and must be quite precise
work; it needs to focus on all categories of students and schools.
For example (as I take up in Chapter 12 on governments), of the
approximately 4,000 elementary schools in Ontario, 497 are classified as having 25% or more students from low-income homes; this
categorization is called low-income cutoff point (LICO) and is based
on Statistics Canada data. At the other end of the scale, there are
1,552 schools with 0–5% LICO. The province has a current target
of reaching 75% achievement in reading, writing, and mathematics for 6th-grade students. The questions one would want to delve
into include

- Of the 497 schools in the low-income category, how many
  are achieving 75% (beating the odds)? What are they doing,
  to be so successful? What can the other schools learn from
  them?
- Of the 1,552 schools in the high-income category, which
  schools are not achieving 75% (squandering the odds)?
  What can be done to push them upward? Remember, we
  are talking about raising the bar for all, not just closing the
  gap.
- What is the gap, comparing the performance of the low-
  income group with the high-income group, and other subgroups therein? Is it being reduced over time?

We need to remind ourselves that it is not just a matter of being
aware of the gap goal, but working on it diligently day after day,
monitoring progress, and taking corrective action.

Attend Initially to the Three Basics

You need to work on numerous parts of the problem at once, but
the one set of things you absolutely should specialize in is to get
the three basics right by age 12. The three basics are literacy, nu-

meracy, and well-being of students (sometimes called emotional intelligence, citizenship, character education, safe schools). These are the three legs of the improvement stool. Well-being serves double duty. It directly supports literacy and numeracy; that is, emotional health is strongly associated with cognitive achievement. It also is indirectly but powerfully part of the educational and societal goal of dealing with the emotional and social consequences of failing and being of low social status. In this sense, political leaders must have an explicit societal agenda of well-being, of which education is one powerful component.

Literacy is not just about reading the words on the page; it includes comprehension, and the skill and joy of being a literate person in a knowledge society. Being numerate is about reasoning and problem solving as much as about being good with numbers and figures. The knowledge base is such today (and is growing steadily) that there is no excuse in developed countries for not reaching 90%-plus proficiency. My colleagues Peter Hill and Carmel Crévola and I have written a book on how to do this, and many of us are working practically on this in entire provinces or states (see Fullan et al., 2006; Fullan, 2006).

The third basic, well-being, is one we all know about but do little to invest in, even though it unlocks just about everything else. A good concrete example of what I am talking about is the Roots of Empathy program, based in Toronto but spreading across the world (Gordon, 2005). Roots of Empathy brings a mother and her baby together with students in a classroom setting in order to teach children empathy. It is a structured program that has six strands (neuroscience, temperament, attachment, emotional literacy, communication, and social inclusion). A baby and its mother come into a class (led by a Roots of Empathy instructor and the regular classroom teacher) three times a month from September to June. Students are coached in how to observe the development of the baby. They are taught how to reflect and are engaged in interpreting the social and emotional learning of the baby. Children develop their empathetic capacity to care. In the course of 1 year, bullying and aggression decrease in the school, empathy and inclusion of other students increase, and literacy (reading and writing) increases—because the program works directly on discussion and writing assignments, and because indirectly emotional development increases motivation and engagement necessary for cognitive development.

Two independent external evaluations have found that Roots of Empathy helps children develop the ability to (1) identify others' emotions, (2) understand and explain others' emotions, and (3) be emotionally responsive to others. One external evaluation concluded that "Roots of Empathy program children, relative to comparison children, exhibited significant increases in emotional understanding and pro-social behaviors and significant decreases in aggressive behaviors [in fact, comparison children exhibited significant *increases* in aggression over the school year]" (Gordon, 2005, p. 247). Furthermore, "when changes were examined in only those children demonstrating some form of aggression at pre-test it was found that [in] 67 percent of Roots of Empathy program children [aggression] *decreased* at post-test, whereas [in] 64 percent of comparison children [aggression] *increased*" (p. 248, emphasis in original).

The focus on well-being requires more than Roots of Empathy, but my point is to elevate emotional safety and development as a crucial foundational goal meshed with cognitive achievement. Clearly, with respect to well-being, there are a host of non-schooling policies that must be pursued, ranging from early child care to improvements in housing, health care, parenting, neighborhoods, and jobs.

In a fundamental and integrated way, England has tackled the well-being of children through its Every Child Matters (2003) agenda. After wide consultation with the public, educators, and yes, children themselves, England formed its new policy around five basic goals for children: (1) being healthy, (2) staying safe, (3) enjoying and achieving, (4) making a positive contribution, and (5) economic well-being. Going beyond rhetoric, England replaced Local Education Authorities (school districts) with Local Authorities within which schools, health care services, and related social agencies are integrated. Directors (superintendents) of education were replaced with new CEOs called Directors of Children's Services. This is a radical and bold move to take well-being the full distance.

Within schools, my emphasis on the three basics—literacy, numeracy, and well-being—is not to say, "Do not work on other goals." But the three basics are a priority and can operate as a set. If you can get them right, a lot of other things will fall into place. In effect, the three basics are the essential foundations for living in the knowledge economy of the 21st century.

Be Driven by Tapping into People's Dignity and Respect

Some students and teachers do not deserve respect, but the reason I emphasize this goal is that it is the key to people's feelings and thus to their motivation. Again, the set of ten is a meal and not a menu. The ten strategies in concert will help turn disrespect around.

To take an extreme example, the research literature on violence clearly shows that the trigger to violent acts is people feeling they are disrespected and threatened with loss of face. Wilkinson's (2005) brilliant analysis of the impact of social equality on societies makes this point forcefully. Wilkinson quotes Gilligan (1996): "I have yet to see a serious act of violence that was not provoked by the experience of feeling shamed and humiliated, disrespected and ridiculed, and that did not represent the attempt to prevent or undo this 'loss of face'—no matter how severe the punishment, even if it includes death" (p. 110).

As Gilligan says, "disrespect" is so central to modern psychodynamics that it has been abbreviated into the slang term "he dissed me." Violence is at the extreme end of the dissing spectrum, but there can be no doubt that teachers and students in publicly named failing schools feel dissed; and it is not a motivator to do good things. Again we leave the detailed solutions until later chapters. The point in this chapter is what motivates large numbers of people to invest their energies in making improvements and working collectively with others.

An interesting and much neglected take on respect in the teaching profession is Elizabeth Campbell's (2005) original contribution in uncovering issues related to unethical behavior among teachers. Campbell interviewed teachers about their relationship with colleagues concerning ethical matters regarding treatment of students. With remarkable directness, she states that the purpose of her study was "to explore the ubiquitous norms of collegial loyalty, noninterference, and solidarity that foster school climates in which students' best interests are not necessarily supported" (p. 207). Ironically, she observes, with all the talk of professional learning communities, one of the most entrenched norms of collegiality "is one which equates ethical treatment of colleagues with a kind of unquestioned loyalty, group solidarity, and an essential belief that teachers as professionals should not interfere in the business of other teachers, criticize them or their practices, or expose their possibly negligent or harmful behavior even at the expense of students' well-being" (p. 209).

Campbell provides numerous examples of teachers witnessing unethical behavior on the part of colleagues but not doing anything about it. She talks about Roger, a middle school teacher who saw a colleague physically hurt a student intentionally and then lie about it afterward. Roger's fear of confronting a colleague inhibited him from addressing the matter. Campbell says that many teachers in her sample come to "accept that the best way to keep out of trouble in schools is to avoid challenging colleagues on matters of competence and ethical conduct and learn to live with the guilt over their inaction" (p. 214). Or the student teacher who recalled how her supervising teacher walked by a grade 5 student who had rather large ears that protruded; the teacher flicked the student's ear with a snapping motion that made it turn pink. The student was quietly sitting at his desk, and all the teacher said was, "I couldn't resist," as the rest of the class laughed in response. These norms of collegial loyalty serve "to close down collective and reflective dialogue rather than embrace it" (p. 215).

My argument here is subtle, so I will be explicit. This is about dignity and respect as a source of motivation. Clearly, students who are not respected are not motivated to learn. Jean Rudduck and her colleagues (1996; Rudduck, in press) consistently have found that students are more or less motivated according to whether they are treated with respect (see also Chapter 9). Note that I also am saying the same thing applies to teachers in terms of how they are treated by the outside.

This chapter is about motivation, so the solution is not to go around fingering badly behaved teachers (although in extreme cases that would be necessary). Like Campbell, I favor a socially based solution. The set of recommendations I am suggesting in this chapter serves to support the conditions for improvement. I also am saying, with Campbell, that fostering professional learning communities should include forums for teachers to collectively reflect on and collaborate on the ethical and moral dimensions of their work and behavior. Because these are collective forums not tied to the latest specific incident, they need not be threatening. Ethical behavior clearly fits with my emphasis on the moral imperative (Fullan, 2003). In fact, one of the three components of moral purpose that I identified is how we treat one another, including exhibiting "demanding respect" concerning mutual expectations to contribute to the betterment of the school (Fullan, 2005). The other two aspects of moral purpose concern a commitment to raise the bar and close the gap, and school leaders' commitment to improve the social environment by contributing to the development of other schools in their district.

Professional learning communities, in other words, should not be confined to latest ideas and innovations. And they should not be places for well-meaning superficial exchanges. Especially in schools, where emotions run high, these communities must foster an open exchange where teachers can explore elements of their own practice that they see as ethically responsive or problematic. The goal is to simultaneously show empathy with teachers in difficult circumstances while calling for and reinforcing higher ethical standards. Schools that promote trust in this way are more likely to motivate people all round, and in turn more likely to do better. Bryk and Schneider's findings in *Trust in Schools* (2002) are similar. Interestingly, they found that the higher the trust in the school, the more likely action would be taken in relation to teachers who were mistreating students.

Thus, it is not that you never disrespect a given teacher; rather, the point is that doing so is not a good motivational starting point. In extreme cases, formal disciplinary action is required. But for most teachers' daily motivation, good solid social support is essential. The ten strategic elements used in concert help sort out those teachers who truly deserve to be disrespected (see especially the one on positive pressure). The vast majority of teachers will respond to solutions in which they see students motivated and engaged for the first time. When they are working with colleagues who support them and have good ideas, all the better.

It is obvious that dignity and respect are crucial for relating to downtrodden parents and neighborhoods (see Chapter 10). As schools develop capacities using the elements described here, they extend their involvement with the outside. The school of the future is not autonomous; it will have many forms of engagement with the outside as part and parcel of improving the system as a whole.

Ensure That the Best People Are Working on the Problem

Minthrop (2004) and Kanter (2004) both show that when things go wrong and there is little constructive help from the outside, the more talented teachers and principals leave the scene. They have more options, and it is depressing to work in a failing school that has little chance of becoming good. We also have evidence that some of the most talented never show up in the first place because policies and practices work against the flow of teachers most appropriate for schools in difficulty (Levin, Mulhern, & Schunck, 2005). *The opposite must happen.*

The more talented teachers and principals are needed precisely because the challenges are greater. Governments and districts can foster incentives and other resources for principals and teachers to work in challenging circumstances. If the right combination of strategies and support is marshaled, problematic situations can become successful, and this could be where the best educators get their satisfaction. In England, for example, the government has just asked its National College of School Leadership to develop a proposal and program based on identifying effective school principals who would form a cadre of National School Leaders, to be given incentives and support to work in the most challenging circumstances. This approach also must furnish incentives for attracting the best teachers in numbers to work with school leaders. The idea is to make it prestigious in the profession to help improve the most difficult situations—getting the best people to work on the problem. I am not advocating this particular English solution, but the concept of getting the more talented principals and teachers on the scene rather than the less talented (the situation in many difficult schools) is critical. In other words, reverse the current incentive system.

It is obvious that leadership is crucial in all of this. Kanter (2004) captures this well when she says, "The fundamental task of leaders is to develop confidence in advance of victory, in order to attract the investments that make victory possible—money, talent, support, empathy, attention, effort, or people's best thinking" (p. 19). Once you start gaining on the close-the-gap problem, there will be fewer cases of extreme challenge. In countries where the gap is not as great as in others, circumstances are already more favorable. In Ontario, for example, there are only 497 (of 4,000) elementary schools with highly challenging circumstances as measured by percentage of students living in poverty, and some of these schools already are performing well. What if there was a concerted effort to get some of the best educators along with strong policy and resource support to tackle the situation? What is needed is to turn around momentum in a way that creates a new, continuous winning streak.

I need to make a more fundamental point here. Through use of the strategies I am suggesting, the overall talent in the system increases. The talent in the system improves as people's potential is unlocked; some may leave, and others are attracted to the profession. Motivated people get better at their work.

Recognize That All Successful Strategies Are Socially Based and Action Oriented

Wilkinson (2005) found that the most important determinants of health (and I should say motivation to do good things) include "the nature of early childhood experience, the amount of anxiety and worry we suffer, the quality of our social relationship, the amount of control we have over our lives, and our social status" (p. 9). A core strategy, then, must be to improve relationships. All successful change initiatives develop collaboration where there was none before. When relationships develop, trust increases, as do other measures of social capital and social cohesion.

This represents a difficult challenge, but again the set of ten elements working together makes it possible. The fact that all successful strategies are socially based is reinforced all the time when we develop professional learning communities (PLCs) that were not there before (Dufour, Dufour, Eaker, & Many, 2006; Dufour,

Eaker, & Dufour, 2005). This is why Kanter (2004) identifies collaboration as one of three key elements in confidence and winning streaks (the other two are accountability and initiative, both of which are reinforced by collaboration). Restoring people's confidence, says Kanter, requires four kinds of action:

1. Getting connected in new ways through conversation
2. Carrying out important work jointly
3. Communicating respect
4. Demonstrating inclusion (that everyone is part of the picture) (p. 241)

This is why Deutschman, in his "Change or Die" article (2005), found that the only situation under which heart patients improved was when the change process was "buttressed with weekly support groups" (p. 4). Socially based strategies can help with another huge problem, one that all researchers on school improvement know about but hardly anybody acts on with any intensity. I speak here of the well-known research finding that variations in student achievement are greater across classrooms within a school than across schools. Once you factor out the role of input qualities (that is, once you start to measure the value added by the school), the biggest factor at work is the individual teachers, and they differ from classroom to classroom within a school.

In a carefully controlled experiment in which teachers were randomly assigned classrooms, Nye, Konstantopoulos, and Hedges (2004) found that

> The differences among teachers [within a school] is substantial in comparison to the variance between schools. In reading, the between-teacher variance component is over twice as large as [the] between-school variance component at grade two and over 3 times as large at grade three. This suggests that naturally occurring teacher effects are larger than naturally occurring school effects. (p. 247)

I return shortly to the phrase "naturally occurring."

Put more starkly, students' learning and achievement differ greatly depending on whether a student gets an effective or an ineffective teacher. It is noteworthy that the range of effectiveness in low-SES schools is greater. In both high-SES and low-SES schools, between-teacher variance is greater than between-school variance, but in low-SES schools *the pattern is more pronounced*. As Nye and colleagues put it, "In low SES schools, it matters more *which* teacher a child receives than it does in high SES schools" (p. 254, emphasis in original).

Where does this lead? Let's merge three things: (1) class-to-class variations in teacher effectiveness within schools are large and most consequential; (2) these variations exist in naturally occurring ways, that is, they persist if you do nothing explicitly to alter them; and (3) all effective change strategies are socially based. As a consequence, we must focus on reducing bad variation (i.e., poor teaching) within schools (and, I say later, bad variation across like schools—apple-to-apple comparisons). Thus, the more you develop active professional learning communities within schools in which teachers observe one another's teaching, and work with school leadership to make ongoing improvements, the greater the consistency and quality of teaching across the whole school, at which point all students in the school benefit and keep on benefiting. And the more you do this, the more shared meaning and commitments, and related capacities, get generated. To say the least, this is easier said than done.

To start with intraschool variance, the goal has to be to find what motivates teachers to work on this problem. We are finding that this is going to be a lot harder than it sounds. One puzzle is to ask why so many teachers everywhere are disgruntled with their work, despite a high level of intrinsic commitment to it. We need, in other words, to change working conditions that get at and leverage intrinsic motivation to open classroom doors, initially within the school, in order to develop quality with greater consistency across classrooms within schools. At first glance, strategies based on developing professional learning communities look like the answer, and I do support their directional value. But a lot of the evidence indicates that PLCs (and other strategies) are not making their way with any substance and continuity inside the classroom. It may happen here and there, but not on any scale we need if we are to close the gap. We learned from Campbell (2005) how supremely difficult it is to change teacher norms of autonomy and loyalty. The Cross City Campaign for Urban School

Reform (2005) study, despite tens of millions of dollars and a lot of the right strategies, in the final analysis could not penetrate the classroom door.

Richard Elmore (2004a, 2004b) has been telling us for years that current strategies are not getting at the core of improving instructional practice in the classroom. Elmore laments:

> Educators equate professionalism with autonomy—getting to use their own judgment, to exercise discretion, to determine the conditions of their own work in classrooms and schools. In fact, professionalism outside of education is exactly the opposite of this definition. Professionals gain their social authority not by exercising autonomy, but by subscribing to an externally-validated body of knowledge, by agreeing to have their discretion limited by that knowledge, and by facing sanctions if they operate outside that body of knowledge. (2004a, p. 3)

If the threat of death does not motivate people who are ill, what on earth is going to motivate teachers to change? The answer has to be deep engagement with other colleagues and with mentors in exploring, refining, and improving their practice as well as setting up an environment in which this not only can happen but is encouraged, rewarded, and pressed to happen. This begs part of the question of how to do so, but let us finally admit that there is no other way. My conclusion is similar to Elmore's as he comments on some of the work he is doing with practitioners, helping them to get inside instructional practice.

> The theory of action behind [this process of examining practice] might be stated as follows: The development of systematic knowledge about, and related to, large-scale instructional improvement requires a change in the prevailing culture of administration and teaching in schools. Cultures do not change by mandate; they change by the specific displacement of existing norms, structures, and processes by others; the process of cultural change depends fundamentally on modeling the new values and behavior that you expect to displace the existing ones. (2004a, p. 11)

The only way we can accomplish the changes we need is through intense focus on improving classroom practice. We can do it by declaring that this is the focus: reduce bad variation by increasing consistency. Teachers and teacher leaders will have to take some risks here. It is one area that is both powerful and within the control of teachers: break down the autonomy of the classroom so that greater consistency of effective practice can be achieved. Really, compared with the status quo, there is little risk. In this more focused and intense work, teachers learn every day. They learn in context. There is nothing that better motivates people to make more investments of time, energy, and commitment than to grow better at something that has importance. Failure may be the initial motivator, but it is increased competence that leads us to do more and more.

We have suggested in *Breakthrough* (Fullan et al., 2006) a plan for systematically involving all schools and school systems in improving elementary school reform. It requires a full press toward intensive and focused improvement of all classrooms and schools in a given system. We think that this is achievable within our lifetime.

My initial focus as above was on within-school variation across classes, but the big solution is not just about intraschool improvement. We have found that collaboration across schools and districts—what we call lateral capacity building—pays enormous dividends in relation to new knowledge and wider commitments (Fullan, 2005, 2006). This network or cluster-based strategy can do double duty. The impact of school cluster networks can be used to reduce both intraschool classroom-to-classroom variations as well as school-to-school differences. We need to focus on reducing what I called "bad variation," whether it occurs within or between schools.

Socially based strategies such as collaboration and support, when combined with the other nine elements, become demandingly interactive. There is no stronger accountability than when it is reinforced daily with peers working on important problems in which internal and external transparency is evident.

Several of our guidelines reinforce the notion that purposeful action is the route to new breakthroughs. Socially based strategies mean that the emphasis is on doing rather than elaborate planning. This point is brought home powerfully in Doug Reeves's (2006) study. Reeves found that the size of the planning document is inversely related to the amount and quality of implementation!

In a large sample involving 280,000 students and 300 schools, schools were scored on 17 separate indicators related to adherence to the state or district formal requirements in the school improvement plans. The scores were then related to student achievement results: "The stunning finding is that the prettiness of the plan is inversely (or should we say perversely?) related to student achievement" (p. 64). Of those schools having high conformity with planning requirements, 25.6% of students scored proficient or higher on assessments, compared with 46.3% achievement for schools with low conformity to planning requirements.

This is not a message that says to abandon all planning (see Chapter 6). It means to reduce the distance between planning and action—formal planning documents are less important (indeed interfere with) implementation, execution, and monitoring. Put another way, the planning is built into the doing, feedback, and corrective action.

Reeves's finding was brought home in our own recent work in Ontario, where we are implementing a provincewide strategy to improve literacy and numeracy for all 72 districts and 4,000 elementary schools. We recently conducted case studies of eight districts that seemed to have sound strategies (along the lines in this book) and were getting results as measured by 3-year trends in student achievement (Campbell & Fullan, 2006). One of the cases is a francophone board just outside Ottawa—Conseil des Écoles Catholique de Langue Francaise du Centre-Est (CECLFCE). Prior to the initiation of our new capacity-building strategy, CECLFCE engaged in the practice of requiring school improvement plans that listed all activities that were to be held throughout the year, resulting in documents 50 pages thick or more—Reeves calls this the disease of "documentarianism." In the new era, the district emphasized a few key standards tied to action that would address student achievement. The written plans are now brief, less formal, and geared to action, monitoring, rapid feedback, and focused instructional improvement, including teachers learning from one another, and schools and the district working interactively. After years of bureaucratic requirements and stagnated student achievement scores, the CECLFCE is now on the move with increased student achievement in each of the past 3 years and more to come.

Assume That Lack of Capacity Is the Initial Problem and Then Work on It Continuously

Another guideline that is action based, and powerful, is capacity building. In a sense, all ten elements address capacity building, which I define as a policy, strategy, or action taken that increases the collective efficacy of a group to improve student learning through new knowledge, enhanced resources, and greater motivation on the part of people working individually and together.

The emphasis here is to rein in judgment at the early part of an improvement effort in favor of working on capacity building. Assume, in other words, that one reason the situation is not working is that people do not know how to improve it, or they do not believe it can be improved. At this stage, judgment is not a good motivator and is not perceived as fair (at later stages, judgment can be ramped up, so to speak, once it can be positioned as fair). The reason we want to spark the motivation of all or the majority of people is that this is what it will take for sustainable success—the wisdom and commitment of the crowd.

This emphasis on capacity building at the early stages is consistent with our knowledge about how people change. To secure new beliefs and higher expectations—critical to improvement—people first need new experiences that lead them to different beliefs. The review of research on social movements by Bate, Bevan, and Robert (2005) led them to conclude that "radical change often involves a collective, interrelational, and emergent process of learning and sense making" (p. 24). More explicitly, they concluded:

> Just as early studies in employee participation showed, workers did not have a high propensity to participate prior to the experience of participation; this came after, not before the experience. Put idiomatically, people cannot want "it" until they have tried it. The concrete experience of participating in a movement is crucial, meanings and value being formed *after the experience* not before it. (p. 31, emphasis added)

This is another reason why action is more important than developing elaborate planning documents.

All of this is consistent with Reeves (2006), our own work on change (behaviors change before beliefs), and Pfeffer and Sutton's findings (2000) on the barriers to closing the knowing–doing gap. Capacity building first, and judgment second—because this is what will motivate more people. Learning in context and learning every day are the keys. Capacity-building experiences develop skills, clarity (as you become more skilled, you become more specifically clear), and motivation. Since these are generated collectively, that is, shared by the group, they become potent new forces for breakthrough improvement.

Another reason capacity-building strategies work is that they give people concrete experiences that improvement is possible. People need proof that there is some reality to the higher expectations. Kanter (2004) says that pep talks or inspiring speeches are not convincing, or at least not for long: "That's why winning [new experiences that work]—or its closer approximation—is often necessary before people believe they can win" (p. 40). Positive experience is what is motivating.

Stay the Course Through Continuity of Good Direction by Leverage Leadership

In situations of poor performance, tightening the focus through greater control (but again, being low on judgment) is necessary at the beginning of the turnaround process. Often, however, there is little continuity for building on initial partial success in order to go deeper (Minthrop, 2004). Staying the course means that careful attention is paid to developing the leadership of others in the organization in the interests of continuity and deepening of good direction.

Leaders developing other leaders is at the heart of sustainability. This is Hargreaves and Fink's (2006) third principle, that "sustainable leadership spreads: It sustains as well as depends on the leadership of others" (p. 95). It is the last of my own eight principles of sustainability: "the long lever of leadership" (Fullan, 2005, p. 27). It is why I have concluded, for example, that the main mark of a principal at the end of his or her tenure is not just the impact on the bottom line of student achievement, but equally, how many good teachers the principal leaves behind who can go even further. You have to be around for a while to accomplish that, and the system must develop leadership succession policies with this goal in mind.

Build Internal Accountability Linked to External Accountability

Richard Elmore (2004b) defines internal accountability in terms of situations where individual responsibility, collective expectations, and accountability data within the school are aligned. The identical data look very different if the organization has the capacity for internal accountability. Data can be empowering or disabling; details, metrics, measurements, analyses, charts, tests, assessments, performance evaluations, report cards, and grades are the tools of accountability, but they are not neutral tools. They do not restore confidence by themselves. What matters is the culture that surrounds them. For losers, this is another sign that they are watched too closely, not trusted, and about to be punished. For winners, they are useful, even vital, means for understanding and improving performance. People embrace tools of accountability when they are in control—when the information empowers them and helps them succeed (Kanter, 2004).

External accountability does not work unless it is accompanied by development of internal accountability. This is why assessment for learning is such a powerful, high-yield strategy (Black, Harrison, Lee, Marshall, & William, 2003; Stiggins, 2005). It helps people clarify goals and where they are in relation to achieving them, and it gives them a tool for improvement because it links performance data with changes in instruction needed to increase achievement.

As educators become more assessment literate, they not only become more comfortable with specific data, they also seek and use assessment data. It is at this point that external accountability becomes more accepted, more transparently available, and more readily used for summative conclusions and judgments.

Establish Conditions for Evolution of Positive Pressure

Positive pressure is pressure that motivates. It is pressure that works both ways—government to schools and vice versa—and it is pressure that is seen as fair and reasonable. If some schools are performing poorly while facing highly challenging circumstances, governments are responsible (should be held accountable) for investing in greater capacity building. If schools receive more resources, they should feel the pressure to improve. Collaborative cultures lend support but also contain powerful peer pressure.

The evolution of positive pressure means taking all the excuses off the table. As we add resources, new capacities, and examples of other (similar) schools that are being more successful, and reduce the distractors (unnecessary paperwork, ineffective bureaucratic procedures, bad industrial relations with unions, and so on), being judgmental relative to a situation of persistent bad or mediocre performance eventually is justified.

The idea is for a system to evolve to where there is no legitimate reason left to be unsuccessful. Put another way, once you strip away all the possible legitimate excuses, most people should consider it fair and reasonable to ask whether it is the quality of leadership and the quality of teaching that are to blame in a given problematic situation. Once you establish conditions where the vast majority of people are motivated to improve things, the problems worth being judgmental about are more obvious. In the final analysis, positive pressure should be irresistible.

Build Public Confidence

You know that you are being successful when public confidence soars. Confidence is not granted by requesting it in advance of performance. It is a chicken-and-egg problem: We need support to perform better, and better performance garners further support. The social contract with society is, on the one hand, for education to do its utmost to reduce the gap of performance across its schools and subgroups as part of creating a more equal society; and on the other hand for society to invest more in education, tentatively and provisionally at first but willingly once progress is evident and continuous. Some of the public confidence I have in mind is local, a direct result of partnering with the community. Other endorsements are more societal, as when people generally value the public school system for its role in closing the educational gap as a crucial part of improving economic and health conditions for all.

Kanter (2004) calls the presence of external confidence "a network to provide resources": "Winning makes it easier to attract financial backers, loyal customers, enthusiastic fans, talented recruits, media attention, opinion leader support, and political goodwill. Continuing to win stimulates the network to grow in size, scope, and magnitude of investment" (p. 30). Or later: "The ultimate work of leaders lies in the connection between their groups and the wider network that provides support, loyalty, revenues, or capital. Leaders must prove to those in the wider circle that their investments are warranted" (p. 341).

Even more directly for us: "Public school leaders had to build credibility with elected officials, school boards, parents, neighborhood groups, and the press by showing that stakeholders' goals and needs would help shape plans for turning around low-performing schools" (p. 342). To accomplish this, leaders must use the ten elements of successful change discussed in this chapter to motivate and obtain the individual and collective involvement of everyone in the organization.

What this accomplishes is to create the conditions under which the vast majority of teachers will be motivated to invest in success. Such motivation is contagious because you literally get more support and pressure, both technically (knowledge) and emotionally. My colleague Ken Leithwood (2005) recently completed an excellent synthesis of research evidence on the theme of teacher working conditions that matter. The eight factors he identified that affect teachers' motivation and performance are entirely compatible with our discussion.

1. Individual sense of professional efficiency
2. Collective sense of professional efficacy
3. Organizational commitment
4. Job satisfaction
5. Stress and burnout
6. Morale
7. Engagement or disengagement from the school and the profession
8. Pedagogical content knowledge (p. 2)

The relationship between Leithwood's list and my ten elements is that he is reporting on research findings, while I am proposing strategies to *produce* the positive end of each of his factors.

One final and fundamental point. In our successful cases, we see a deep shift from "my" to "our."

- In the school, individual teachers stop thinking about "my classroom" and start thinking about "our school."
- In the districts, individual school leaders stop thinking about "my school" and start thinking about "our schools or districts."
- Across districts, individual district leaders stop thinking about "my district" and start thinking about "our districts, or state, or province."
- Across states or provinces, state leaders stop thinking about "my state" and start thinking about "our country."

This is "meaning writ large." And it is what the new meaning of change is all about. As we take up subsequent chapters, think about this larger sense of meaning and keep the ten elements of change in mind. Many a great idea gets lost in the dynamics of poor or inadequate change processes.

CHAPTER 4

Causes and Processes of Initiation

The pressures [for change] seem to subside with the act of adoption followed by the appearance of implementation.

—Berman and McLaughlin (1979, p. 1)

There is no shortage of recommendations about how the ills of education *should* be rectified. But the remedies remain pie in the sky as long as competing "shoulds" fight it out without an understanding of how to get started and how to keep going. This chapter and the next one contain a description of the educational change process and an explanation of why it works as it does.

The number and dynamics of factors that interact and affect the process of educational change are too overwhelming to compute in anything resembling a fully determined way. We do know more about the processes of change as a result of research of the past 40 years, which has shown that there are no hard-and-fast rules, but rather a set of suggestions or implications given the contingencies specific to local situations. In fact, Clark, Lotto, and Astuto (1984), Huberman and Miles (1984), and I (Fullan, 1999) suggest that the uniqueness of the individual setting is a critical factor—what works in one situation may or may not work in another. This is not to say that there are not guidelines, and we will get to them. Research findings on the change process should be used less as instruments of "application" and more as means of helping practitioners and planners "make sense" of planning, implementation strategies, and monitoring. It is also important to say that this is a possible task: "Schools, classrooms, and school systems can and do improve and the factors facilitating improvement are neither so exotic, unusual, or expensive that they are beyond the grasp of . . . ordinary schools" (Clark et al., 1984, p. 59).

There are two basic ways to look at educational reform. One is to examine and trace specific innovations to see how they fare, and to determine which factors are associated with success. Let us call this the *innovation-focused* approach. The second way is to turn the question on its head and ask how we develop the innovative capacity of organizations and systems to engage in continuous improvement. I shall refer to this as the *capacity-building focus*. These are not mutually exclusive approaches, as each can feed on the other. It is more a matter of which emphasis fits one's interest at a particular point in time. If you are concerned with a specific innovation, it helps to be able to design a strategy that takes into account each stage of development in its use. If you are trying to change a culture, such as establish a professional learning community, it is better to start with the institution.

THE CHANGE PROCESS

In this chapter and Chapter 5 we take the innovation focus. Most researchers now see three broad phases to the change process:

Phase I—variously labeled initiation, mobilization, or adoption—consists of the process that leads up to and includes a decision to adopt or proceed with a change.

Phase II—implementation or initial use (usually the first 2 or 3 years of use)—involves the first experiences of attempting to put an idea or reform into practice.

Phase III—called continuation, incorporation, routinization, or institutionalization—refers to whether the change gets built in as an ongoing part of the system or disappears by way of a decision to discard or through attrition (see Berman & McLaughlin, 1977; Huberman & Miles, 1984).

Figure 4.1 depicts the three phases in relation to outcomes, especially whether or not student learning is enhanced, and whether or not experiences with change increase subsequent capacity to deal with future changes.

FIGURE 4.1. A Simplified Overview of the Change Process

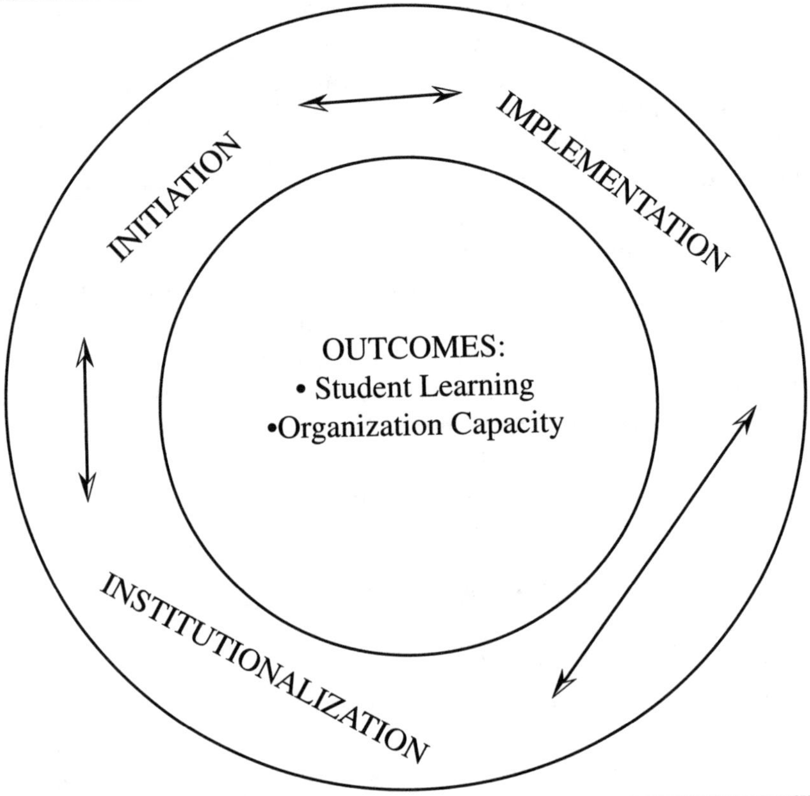

In simple terms, someone or some group, for whatever reasons, initiates or promotes a certain program or direction of change.
The direction of change, which may be more or less defined at the
early stages, moves to a phase of attempted use (implementation),
which can be more or less effective. Continuation, or institutionalization, is an extension of the implementation phase in that the
new program is sustained beyond the first year or two (or whatever time frame is chosen). Outcome, depending on the objectives,
can refer to several different types of results and can be thought
of generally as the degree of school improvement in relation to
given criteria. Results could include, for example, improved student learning and attitudes; new skills, attitudes, or satisfaction

on the part of teachers and other school personnel; or improved problem-solving capacity of the school as an organization.

Figure 4.1 presents only the general image of a much more detailed and snarled process. First, there are numerous factors operating at each phase. Second, as the two-way arrows imply, it is not a linear process but rather one in which events at one phase can feed back to alter decisions made at previous stages, which then proceed to work their way through in a continuous interactive way. For example, a decision at the initiation phase to use a specific program may be substantially modified during implementation, and so on.

The third set of variables, which are unspecified in Figure 4.1, concerns the scope of change and the question of who develops and initiates the change. The scope can range from large-scale externally developed innovations to locally produced ones. In either of these cases the teacher may or may not be centrally involved in development and/or decisions to proceed. Thus, the concept of "initiation" leaves open the question of who develops or initiates the change. The question is taken up at various places in the remainder of this chapter and in relevant chapters on particular roles.

The fourth complication in Figure 4.1 is that the total time perspective as well as subphases cannot be precisely demarcated. The initiation phase may be in the works for years, but even later, specific decision making and preimplementation planning activities can be lengthy. Implementation for most changes takes 2 or more years; only then can we consider that the change has really had a chance to become implemented. The line between implementation and continuation is somewhat hazy and arbitrary. Outcomes can be assessed in the relatively short run, but we would not expect many results until the change had had a chance to become implemented. In this sense, implementation is the *means* to achieving certain outcomes; evaluations have limited value and can be misleading if they provide information on outcomes only.

Fifth, and finally, given our concern with meaning, it cannot be assumed that people understand what they are getting into when a so-called "adoption" decision is made. This cuts both ways. If a school's teachers, for example, vote to adopt a particular innovation, let's say a comprehensive school reform model, they may not know what they don't know (Datnow, Hubbard, & Mehan, 2002; Murphy & Datnow, 2003). Similarly, if an administrator forges ahead with a given innovation in the face of ambivalence from staff, it may turn out that commitment gets generated during implementation. This is to say, then, that we need to keep an open mind about the process of change. In some ways the message of this book is that it matters less where the innovation comes from than it does what happens during the process of change. Our insights about the change process, discussed in the previous chapter, essentially endorse a ready-fire-aim mind-set. Ready is important. You have to work on key problems and establish basic conditions, but it is necessary to get to action (fire) sooner rather than later because that is where knowledge, skills, understandings, and commitments get sorted out (see Chapter 6 on planning).

The total time frame from initiation to institutionalization is lengthy; even moderately complex changes take from 2 to 4 years, while larger-scale efforts can take 5 to 10 years, with sustaining improvements still problematic. Greater use of the change knowledge embedded in policy and strategy will reduce the timeline for successful initiation and implementation. In any case, the single most important idea arising from Figure 4.1 is that *change is a process, not an event*—a lesson learned the hard way by those who put all their energies into developing an innovation or passing a piece of legislation without thinking through what would have to happen beyond that point.

So far we have been talking as if schools adopt one innovation at a time. This single innovation perspective can be useful for examining individual innovations, but the broader reality, of course, is that schools are in the business of contending simultaneously with *multiple innovations*, or innovation overload. Thus, when we identify factors affecting successful initiation and implementation, we should think of these factors operating across many innovations—and many levels of the system (classroom, school, district, state, nation). This multiplicity perspective inevitably leads one to look for solutions at the level of individual roles and groups, which I do in the chapters in Part II. This is so because it is only at the individual and small-group level that the inevitable demands of overload can be prioritized and integrated. At the same time, we should try to achieve greater policy alignment at the state level (see Chapter 12), but won't hold our breath waiting for this to occur.

What happens at one stage of the change process strongly affects subsequent stages, but new determinants also appear. Because the processes are so entangled, I will endeavor to identify a list of the main factors and to describe their influence at each stage. The ideas in this chapter and Chapter 5 will be used to help explain why the processes of initiation, implementation, and continuation function as they do. It also should be understood that all three phases should be considered at the outset. As one goes about the initiation of change, implementation planning must already be underway. The moment that initiating begins is the moment that the stage is being set for implementation and continuation.

FACTORS AFFECTING INITIATION

Initiation is the process leading up to and including the decision to proceed with implementation. It can take many different forms, ranging from a decision by a single authority to a broad-based mandate. At a general level, we might assume that specific educational changes are introduced because they are desirable according to certain educational values and meet a given need better than existing practices do. As we have seen, however, this is not the way it always or even usually happens.

There are countless variables potentially influencing whether a change program is started. Figure 4.2 depicts eight sources affecting initiation, which have been derived from recent literature. I make no claim that the list is exhaustive, only that there is evidence of support across many studies. The order is not important, although different combinations are. For example, community pressure combined with a problem-solving orientation will have quite different consequences than community pressure combined with a bureaucratic orientation. The main point is that innovations get initiated from many different sources and for different reasons. The matter of the need for change can be embedded in any one or several of the factors, depending on whose viewpoint one takes.

FIGURE 4.2. Factors Associated with Initiation

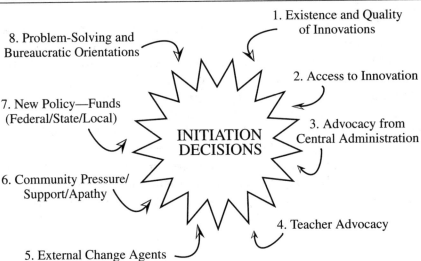

Existence and Quality of Innovations

Educational innovations exist in plentiful numbers. The question is what innovations are out there. It is well beyond the scope of this book to investigate the world of invention and development. Therefore, it will be impossible to draw systematic data-based conclusions about the content of available changes. The answer probably is that there are all kinds of innovations in existence, which could address a wide range of values, as we would expect in any pluralistic or heterogeneous society. And this number is rapidly and constantly expanding in an increasingly sophisticated technologically driven knowledge society.

Since 1983 the struggle between standardization and restructuring has produced changes that both limit (or focus, depending on your viewpoint) and liberate change possibilities. Relative to the former, for example, many states have begun to prescribe textbooks and link them to standardized state tests (McNeil, 2000;

Wise, 1988). Restructuring initiatives also have resulted in numerous local efforts as well as several high-profile national projects in the United States, including Success for All, the Coalition of Essential Schools School Development Program, and many more (see American Institutes of Research, 1999; Berends, Chun, et al., 2002).

Along with the question of what innovations are available is the issue of the quality of new programs. Program clarity and quality have been a major problem since the innovation boom of the 1960s. The situation has improved over the past decade and a half (i.e., there are better quality innovations "out there"), but it also has served notice with respect to how complicated decisions about innovation are in practice. A good example is the comprehensive school reform models mentioned earlier. I will leave the main conclusion about CSRs until Chapter 5 because it is ultimately an implementation and impact question. For now, let's just set the table.

The CSR models are intended to provide proven school-wide innovations that would be adopted by schools in order to improve student achievement, especially among more-disadvantaged and low-performing schools. New American Schools—a private, non-profit organization whose mission is to help schools and districts raise student achievement—has supported the development of the use of school reform designs. Since its inception, NAS has been involved in a development phase (1992–1993), a demonstration phase (1993–1995), and a scale-up phase (1995–2002). In addition, federal funding supported the use of reform models for school-wide improvement when Congress enacted the Comprehensive School Reform Demonstration (CSRD) program in 1997 and included it under Title 1. In the original legislation, 13 reform models were listed as recommended CSR designs, as well as the suggestion that schools could implement home-grown models. In the more recent No Child Left Behind legislation, reform models were not listed as a focus of the legislation, and more principles around issues of school-wide improvement were included. The decade-long experience (1991–2001) with whole-school reform models has been well evaluated by the Rand Corporation (Berends, Bodilly, & Kirby, 2002; Berends, Chun, et al., 2002) and by independent researchers such as Datnow and her colleagues (Datnow et al., 2002; Datnow & Kemper, 2003; Ross, Wang, Sanders, Wright, & Stringfield, 1999; Murphy & Datnow, 2003). We will draw on these studies when we examine implementation.

A second good example of well-designed programs comes from Hill and Crévola's (1999) description of standards-based reform in Victoria, Australia, focusing on literacy. They claim that improvement requires all of the critical elements of the school and of the school system working out what needs to change in order for them to operate effectively and in alignment. This model encompasses:

> Standards and targets
> Monitoring and assessment
> Classroom teaching programs
> Professional learning teams
> School and class organization
> Intervention and special assistance
> Home, school, and community partnerships
> Leadership and coordination

Over the past year we have taken Hill and Crévola's model and developed it into a full-blown model for getting "breakthrough" results in literacy (see Fullan, Hill, & Crévola, 2006). Numerous other examples of increased clarity and quality of instructional innovations can be identified, such as Good and Kaminski (2002) and Tomlinson (1998). The point here is not that well-designed reforms and similar programs provide the solution (see the concluding section of this chapter, on initiation dilemmas), but that the design and quality of innovations have improved dramatically over the past few years.

Access to Information

A second factor related to initiation is the selectivity that occurs as a result of differential access to information. The primacy of personal contact in the diffusion of innovations has been known for years (Katz, Lewin, & Hamilton, 1963), and its importance in education is concisely summarized by House (1974, chap. 1). District administrators and other central office personnel such as coordinators and consultants spend large amounts of time at conferences and workshops within ongoing professional networks of communication among their peers. Part and parcel of the development of innovations has been the proliferation of networks, partnerships, collaboratives, and other agencies that have transformed the infrastructure of opportunities to access and work interactively with others on common themes over a period of years. Without doubt, in recent years *availability* of innovative networks has grown by leaps and bounds, which is not to say that enough schools take advantage of them or that they implement programs well when they do.

Beyond schools, parents and communities, especially those whose members have limited formal education, are at a double disadvantage: They are unfamiliar with and not confident about technical matters, and they have almost no personal contact (or time and energy to develop contact) with even a small part of the educational universe. School boards have more direct responsibility in this realm but also are dependent on central administrators.

Finally, access to innovations, as is obvious but rarely emphasized, depends on an infrastructure of communication—ease of transportation, resources, and density of population and ideas in the geographical area. In this respect, urban and large school districts enjoy favorable conditions; rural and small school districts do not.

In sum, there is no doubt that the development of innovations will continue to grow dramatically in the world, and access will become more and more available. The remaining problem—the theme of this book—will be whether individuals and institutions have the capacity to operate effectively in this complex, messy system.

Advocacy from Central and/or School Administrators

Initiation of change rarely occurs without an advocate, and one of the most powerful is the chief district administrator, with his or her staff, especially in combination with school board support or mandate. In some cases, district leadership may not be interested in innovation, and little may happen. But when there is an interest, for whatever reason—mandate from a board, or a reform-minded or career-oriented administrator—it is the superintendent and central staff who combine access, internal authority, and resources necessary to seek out external funds for a particular change program and/or to obtain board support. Numerous studies have found this to be the case: the Rand Change Agent study (Berman & McLaughlin, 1977); Berman, McLaughlin, and associates' (1979) more intensive study of five school districts; Huberman and Miles's (1984) case studies of 12 districts; LaRocque and Coleman's (1989) study of district ethos in British Columbia; Elmore and Burney's (1999) study of District 2 in New York City; Supovitz's (2006) case study of Duval County, Florida; and our own work on district-wide reform (Fullan, Bertani, & Quinn, 2004; Sharratt & Fullan, 2006). All of these studies show that the chief district administrator and central district staff are an extremely important source of advocacy, support, and initiation of new programs.

For example, Huberman and Miles (1984) found that "central office administrators were at the locus of decision-making in 11 of the 12 cases" (p. 55). Hidden in these findings is the message that district administrators are often an important source of district-wide changes that favor groups that otherwise might be neglected. In Chapter 11 we also will see, in the case of districts, that the superintendent is crucial in maintaining a focus on which innovative directions to pursue (namely, those that are aligned and tuned to sustained instructional improvement for all schools in the system). At the same time, superintendents can be a source of overload if they take on too many disconnected innovations.

Meanwhile, at the school level, the principal has become increasingly important. The principal has always been the "gatekeeper" of change, often determining the fate of innovations coming from the outside or from teacher initiatives on the inside. With the advent of site-based management across the world, more and more onus for initiative has landed at the principal's doorstep. Principals are now expected to lead change, and thus they have become a critical source of initiation (Marzano, Waters, & McNulty, 2005).

Teacher Advocacy

While teachers as a group have less opportunity to come into contact with new ideas and less time and energy to follow through on those that they do become aware of, most teachers do innovate. In fact, the "innovation paradigm," which in effect traces the development and implementation of *formally* initiated innovations, is biased because it misses the thousands of small innovations that individual and small groups of teachers engage in every day. There is a strong body of evidence that indicates that teachers are often the preferred source of ideas for other teachers. On the other hand, the evidence is equally strong that opportunities for teachers to interact with one another are limited, and that when good ideas do get initiated by one or more teachers, the support of others is required if the ideas are to go anywhere.

When schools establish professional learning communities, teachers constantly search for new ways of making improvements. Rosenholtz (1989), as we saw, found this to be the case in her study involving 78 schools, as did Newmann and Wehlage (1995), McLaughlin and Talbert (2006), and many others. All these researchers, however, also conclude that the working conditions of teachers in the vast majority of schools are not conducive to sustained teacher innovation (Leithwood, 2005).

On a larger scale, national, state, and local teacher unions in some cases are becoming strong advocates of reform (see Consortium of Educational Change, 2000; Shanker, 1990). Indeed, a teacher union in Toronto is the initiator and sponsor of our *What's Worth Fighting For* trilogy (Fullan, 1997; Fullan & Hargreaves, 1992; Hargreaves & Fullan, 1998). While it is true that most teacher unions in the public's eye are known more for what reforms they are against, rather than what they favor, teacher unions can be powerful initiators when they do decide to lead reform.

These findings, taken together, indicate that many teachers are willing to adopt change at the individual classroom level and will do so under the right conditions (e.g., an innovation that is clear and practical, a supportive district administration and principal, opportunity to interact with other teachers, advocacy from the union, and outside resource help). There are several qualifiers:

Most teachers do not have adequate information, access, time, or energy; and the innovations they do adopt are often individualistic, on a small scale, and unlikely to spread to other teachers.

External Change Agents

Change agents or facilitators external to the district—that is, in regional, state, or national roles—play an important part in initiating change projects. Many roles at these levels are formally charged with the responsibility for stimulating and supporting change. The importance of these roles, especially at the initiation stage, has been documented over a number of years. What is new in the past decade is the enormous presence on a large scale of not-for-profit foundations and business partnerships. Much of the innovative money and opportunities for large-scale reform are made possible through foundations. Still, no matter how you dice it, strong leadership internal to the school or the district is a crucial variable. Without quality internal leadership, you end up not with limited innovation, but rather its opposite—too many fragmented, uncoordinated, flavor-of-the-month changes, something that Tom Hatch (2000) captured in his study "when multiple improvement initiatives collide."

Community Pressure/Support/Opposition/Apathy

Since communities vary and characteristics of school districts differ greatly, different combinations of factors will result in various initiation patterns—a perennial problem in understanding change processes. But when some of the main combinations are examined, we can make sense of the paradox that some communities support innovation, others block it, most are apathetic, and even more are all of those things at one time or another.

In general terms, and depending on the circumstances, communities can either (1) put pressure on district administrators (directly or through school boards) to "do something" about a problem, (2) oppose certain potential adoptions of which they become aware, or (3) do nothing (passive support or apathy). The meaning of these patterns is clarified by considering some evidence.

The most predictable initial pressure for change from the

community is likely to come as a result of population shifts. The Berman, McLaughlin, and associates (1979) study of five school districts demonstrates that major demographic changes (rapid growth in population or a change in composition that results in different social-class and cultural mixes) lead to the development of community efforts and demands for change. How the demands are handled depends very much on the problem-solving versus bureaucratic orientations to be discussed below. In other words, demands may or may not result in initiation, depending on a combination of factors. But the point is that communities can instigate educational change. (In one of the Berman and McLaughlin cases, for example, population growth led to community activism in a previously stagnant school system, the election of new board members, the hiring of an innovative superintendent, and the facilitation of change by other central staff, principals, teachers, and so forth.) And, as we shall see in Chapter 10, rapport between schools and communities is a powerful force for productive change.

Schaffarzick's study of 34 San Francisco Bay Area districts is also very revealing. He found that 62% of the curriculum decision cases in his sample did not involve lay participation (cited in Boyd, 1978, p. 613). Community apathy and indifference characterized these decisions. However, in the 19 cases that involved conflict and bargaining, the community groups nearly always prevailed. Concerning the selective role of communities, Daft and Becker (1978) found that highly educated ones correlated substantially with the adoption of innovations for college-bound students, but less-well-educated communities did *not* correlate with the greater likelihood of programs of benefit to high school terminating students. Bridge (1976) makes a similar point: "It is easier to organize parents, particularly lower class parents, to resist perceived threats than it is to organize them to achieve long term positive goals" (p. 370).

In putting these findings together, we can conclude that the role of the community in the initiation process is not straightforward, but it is understandable when we break it down into the following components:

1. Major demographic changes create turbulence in the environment, which may lead to initiation of change or irrecon-

cilable conflict, depending on the presence of other factors listed in Figure 4.2.

2. Most communities do not actively participate in change decisions about educational programs.
3. More highly educated communities seem to put general pressure on their schools to adopt high-quality, academic-oriented changes. They also can react strongly and effectively against proposed changes that they do not like.
4. Less-well-educated communities are not as likely to initiate change or put effective pressure on educators to initiate changes on their behalf. They are also less likely to oppose changes because of lack of knowledge, but once activated, they too can become effective.

New Policy and Funds

Increasingly, state and provincial governments are mandating new requirements, especially standards-based reforms. Indeed, the biggest change since the third edition of this book is the introduction of mandated reform by governments. We will examine these in more detail in terms of their consequences (strengths and weaknesses) in later chapters. Since we are talking here about "causes of adoption," we need only note that state and federal policymakers initiate many new social change programs that otherwise would never be formally adopted. Many major educational initiatives are generated through government policy making and legislation in areas in the greatest need of reform, such as special needs, desegregation, literacy and numeracy initiatives, teacher education, and the like. By and large, governments are becoming more insistent about the nature and accountability of educational reforms. If accompanied by sound strategies (i.e., actions based on solid change knowledge), they can have strong positive impact in relatively short order, as the case examples of England, and Ontario, Canada, show in Chapter 12.

Problem-Solving and Bureaucratic Orientations

The orientation that school districts take to external policy and funds is another story. Berman and McLaughlin (1977) discovered

3 decades ago that adoption decisions of school districts were characterized by either an opportunistic (bureaucratic) or a problem-solving orientation. Districts welcome external funds and/or policies either as an opportunity to obtain extra resources (which they use for other purposes and/or which represent a symbolic act of appearing to respond to a given need) or as a chance to solve particular local problems. Many schools and districts are, in the words of Bryk, Sebring, Kerbow, Rollow, and Easton (1998), "Christmas tree" organizations in which acquiring new projects is the name of the game.

We do not know the proportions of problem solvers versus bureaucrats in the school districts of North America. Pincus (1974) would have us believe that the properties of public school systems *qua* systems make them more bureaucratic than problem oriented. Pincus claims that compared with competitive firms

1. public schools are less motivated to adopt cost-reducing innovations unless the funds so saved become available for other purposes in the district;
2. they are less likely to adopt innovations that change the resource mix or the accustomed authority roles (e.g., that involve behavioral changes in role); and
3. they are more likely to adopt new instructional processes that do not significantly change structure, or to adopt new wrinkles in administrative management, because such innovations help to satisfy the demands of the public without exacting heavy costs. (pp. 117–118)

That is, in terms of the multidimensionality of implementation (see Chapter 2), schools are more likely to implement superficial changes in content, objectives, and structure than changes in culture, role behavior, and conceptions of teaching.

Three factors favorable to adoption are identified by Pincus (1974):

1. *bureaucratic safety,* as when innovations add resources without requiring behavioral change;
2. *response to external pressure* (in which "adoption" may ease the pressure); and
3. *approval of peer elites* (in the absence of clearly defined output cri-

teria, whatever is popular among leading professional peers is sometimes the determining criterion). (p. 120)

Thus, "schools tend voluntarily to adopt innovations which promote the schools' self-image" as "up-to-date . . . efficient . . . professional . . . responsive" (p. 122). Stated differently, it is relatively easy for schools to *adopt* complex, vague, inefficient, and costly (especially if someone else is paying) innovations as long as they do not have to *implement* them.

Bureaucratically speaking, then, the political and symbolic value of initiation of change for schools is often of greater significance than the educational merit and the time and cost necessary for implementation follow-through. However, the symbolic value is not unimportant. Such decisions may be necessary for political survival, may be needed first steps that set the preconditions for real change in practice, or may represent the only change possible in certain situations.

On the positive side, there are more examples recently of problem-solving initiatives at the school, district, and government levels, as we will witness in the relevant chapters. There are two trends that are putting pressure on systems to act differently. One is the standards-based reform strategies that are intensifying pressure and support with the goal of maximizing follow-through, that is, these strategies assume that adoption is only the beginning. The other is the capacity-building stances of local entities in which initiation begins at the grassroots level and reaches out to exploit state policies. In other words, the goal is to build capacities at the school and district levels so that schools and districts act in a problem-solving rather than a bureaucratic manner. The answer lies in combining top-down and bottom-up change forces, which now appears to be more possible (see the discussion of this dilemma in Chapter 12, p. 262).

THE DILEMMAS OF INITIATION

We have presented an amalgam of different factors that influence the initiation of change projects. The first message is that change is and always will be initiated from a variety of different sources and combination of sources. This presents constant opportunity for pursuing innovations or for the imposition of change, depending on the innovation and one's role in the process. As I said above, in many ways it matters less who initiates the change and more what the subsequent quality of the change process is.

There is no easy answer as to what represents successful initiation because, as with so many aspects of the change process, those contemplating change are faced with a series of dilemmas. Should we have a short or long time period for starting? Should we go for internal development or import external innovations? Should we work with volunteers or a more representative group? Should we go with large numbers or small numbers? Should we focus on instruction or on the organization, or on both? Should we try major change or start with minor change? Should we have lots of participation at the early stages or not?

The main leadership dilemma at the initiation stage is whether to seek majority agreement before proceeding versus being assertive at the beginning. The fact is that there is a great deal of inertia in social systems, requiring high energy to overcome. We know that top-down change doesn't work. But we also are finding out that bottom-up initiatives either fail to result in much or, when they do get off to a promising start, often fail to connect to the authority structure.

Even when there is a requirement of "buy in" by teachers, agreement can be superficial and uninformed. In Datnow and Stringfield's (2000) review of innovative programs, the authors observe:

> In several of our studies we found that educators adopted reform models without thinking through how the model would suit their school's goals, culture, teachers or students . . . even when opportunities to gather information were available, educators seldom made well-informed choices about reform designs.
>
> Policy and political decisions at state and district levels also often influenced schools' adoption of external reform designs, which also caused some local educators to adopt models quickly and without careful consideration of "fit." (p. 191)

Similarly, Hatch (2000) observes that adoption may be more likely to reflect how effective the campaigns for and against a proposed program have been rather than to demonstrate whether or not a school actually has learned enough about a program to make an informed choice or to embark on successful implementation.

And what about low-performing schools that fail to do anything or explicitly reject potentially effective innovations, so that no new initiatives are undertaken? Clearly they cannot be allowed to continue their inaction on the grounds that grassroots decisions are the only way to go (see Fullan, 2006).

Our temporary answer to these dilemmas is this: Local capacity is developed at the school level (see Chapters 7 and 8) to the point that schools actually do know how to go about sorting out and acting on required improvements. Some schools—a minority—currently are this good. Less than ideally, but necessary in cases of persistently low-performing or otherwise stuck schools, assertive leadership (including teacher leaders) is required. To put it one way, a principal or superintendent can get away with top-down or assertive leadership under two conditions: first, in situations where it turns out the idea is good; and second, when assertive initiation is combined with empowerment and choices as the process unfolds. The criterion here is *eventual* motivation to put energy into the reform direction—ownership, if you like. But note that ownership is something that develops over time if the ideas are good and if people have the capacity and opportunity to make informed judgments, which they may not be able to do early on.

Thus, the initiation of change does represent difficult dilemmas. The relationship between initiation and implementation is loosely coupled and interactive. The process of initiation can generate meaning or confusion, commitment or alienation, or simply ignorance on the part of participants and others affected by the change. Poor beginnings can be turned into successes depending on what is done during implementation. Promising startups can be squandered by what happens afterward.

At this point we know that initiation decisions occur all the time and come from a variety of sources. We have some inkling that, depending on the sources, the process followed, and the combination of contextual conditions in the situation, what happens after the initiation phase will be all over the map. We can now turn to the next critical phase in the process. Implementation is where the action is. The three key questions are: What is the relationship between the initiation process and subsequent implementation? What other factors emerge during implementation that determine which changes in practice actually occur? And what are the dynamics of continuation or discontinuation?

CHAPTER 5

Causes and Processes of Implementation and Continuation

Well, the hard work is done. We have the policy
passed; now all you have to do is implement it.
 —Outgoing deputy minister of education to colleague

Educational change is technically simple and socially complex. While the simplicity of the technical aspect is no doubt overstated, anyone who has been involved in a major change effort will intuitively grasp the meaning of and concur with the complexity of the social dimension. A large part of the problem of educational change may be less a question of dogmatic resistance and bad intentions (although there is certainly some of both) and more a question of the difficulties related to planning and coordinating a multilevel social process involving thousands of people.

As I described in Chapter 4, a great majority of policies and innovations over the past 35 years did not get implemented even where implementation was desired. Implementation consists of the process of putting into practice an idea, program, or set of activities and structures new to the people attempting or expected to change. The change may be externally imposed or voluntarily sought; explicitly defined in detail in advance or developed and adapted incrementally through use; designed to be used uniformly or deliberately planned so that users can make modifications according to their perceptions of the needs of the situation.

In this chapter I identify those factors that affect whether or not an initiated or decided-upon change happens in practice. The processes beyond adoption are more intricate, because they involve more people, and real change (as distinct from verbal or "on-paper" decisions) is at stake. Many attempts at policy and program change have concentrated on product development, legislation, and other formally expressed changes in a way that ignored the fact that what people did and did not do was the crucial variable. This neglect is understandable, for people are much more unpredictable and difficult to deal with than things. They are also essential for success.

The positive side is that the persistence of people-related problems in educational change has forged greater knowledge about what makes for success. If we constantly remind ourselves that educational change is a *learning experience for the adults involved* (teachers, administrators, parents, etc.) as well as for children, we will be going a long way in understanding the dynamics of the factors of change described in this chapter.

We must start by restating where implementation fits and why it is important. The simple implementation question is: What types of things would have to change if an innovation or a reform were to become fully implemented? As discussed in Chapter 2, several definable aspects of classroom or school life would be altered. Sticking with the classroom for the sake of simplicity, we suggested that changes would likely occur in (1) curriculum materials, (2) teaching practices, and (3) beliefs or understandings about the curriculum and learning practices. Implementation is critical for the simple reason that it is the *means* of accomplishing desired objectives. Recalling Charters and Jones's (1973) concern about the risk of appraising "nonevents," implementation may turn out to be nonexistent (i.e., no real change in the desired direction), superficial, partial, thorough, and so on. In a word, implementation is a variable, and if the change is a potentially good one, success (such as improved student learning or increased skills on the part of teachers) will depend on the degree and quality of change in actual practice.

It is not quite that simple, but the logic of the change process depicted earlier, in Figure 4.1, is essentially straightforward. However changes get initiated, they proceed (or not) to some form of implementation and continuation, resulting in some intended and/or unintended outcomes. In this chapter we are interested in the factors and processes that affect implementation and continuation. Our goal is to identify the critical factors that commonly influence change in practice and to obtain insights into how the implementation process works.

FACTORS AFFECTING IMPLEMENTATION

The idea of implementation and of the factors affecting actual use seems simple enough, but the concept has proven to be exceedingly elusive. Examples of successful improvement described in the research of the past 30 years seem to make common sense. More and more, the evidence points to a small number of key variables, although, as we shall see, the question of what to do remains exceedingly complex. Intrinsic dilemmas in the change process, coupled with the intractability of some factors, the uniqueness of individual settings, and variations in local capacity, make successful change a highly complex and subtle social process. Effective approaches to managing change call for combining and balancing factors that do not apparently go together—simultaneous simplicity–complexity, looseness–tightness, strong leadership–user participation, bottom-up/top-downness, fidelity–adaptivity, and evaluation–nonevaluation. More than anything else, effective strategies for improvement require an understanding of the process, a way of thinking that cannot be captured in any list of steps or phases to be followed (Fullan, 1985; see also the *Change Forces* series, Fullan, 1993, 1999, 2003).

We should keep in mind that we are interested in factors to the extent that they causally influence implementation (or more specifically, the extent to which teachers and students change their practices, beliefs, use of new materials, and corresponding learning outcomes) in the direction of some sought-after change. If any one or more factors are working against implementation, the process will be less effective. To put it positively, the more factors supporting implementation, the more change in practice will be accomplished. Finally, we should avoid thinking of sets of factors in isolation from one another. They form a *system of variables* that interact to determine success or failure. Educational change is a dynamic process involving interacting variables over time, regardless of whether the mode of analysis is factors or themes.

Figure 5.1 lists nine critical factors organized into three main categories relating to (1) the characteristics of the innovation or change project, (2) local roles, and (3) external factors. In describing the roles, I have tried to emphasize aspects that can be altered rather than those that are fixed or givens. The list is necessarily oversimplified. Each factor could be "unpacked" into several subvariables, as I do in later chapters. At this time the goal is to obtain an overview and feel for the main dynamics in the change process.

Factors Related to Characteristics of the Change

We start with four factors related to the characteristics of innovations themselves, namely, need, clarity, complexity, and quality.

FIGURE 5.1. Interactive Factors Affecting Implementation

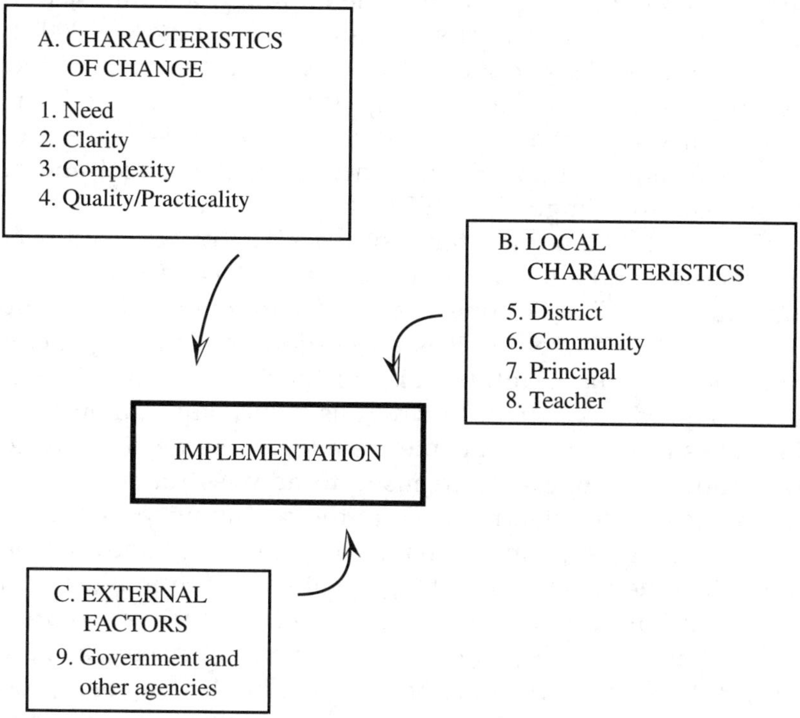

We saw in Chapter 4 that these issues cannot be resolved at the initiation stage. This lack of resolution carries over into implementation and becomes much more visible.

Need. As noted earlier, many innovations are attempted without a careful examination of whether or not they address what are perceived to be priority needs. Teachers, for example, frequently do not see the need for an advocated change. Several large-scale studies in the United States confirm the importance of relating need to decisions about innovations or change directions. In the Experimental Schools project, Rosenblum and Louis (1979) found that "the degree to which there was a formal recognition within the school system of unmet needs" (p. 12) was one of the four "readiness factors" associated with subsequent implementation. The Rand Change Agent study (Berman & McLaughlin, 1977) identified problem solving/orientation (i.e., identification of a need linked to selection of a program) as strongly related to successful implementation. The question of determining whether needs are agreed upon is not always straightforward. Datnow (2000) talks about one school's adoption of a New American School model: "In spite of the fact that the majority of teachers voted for the change, this was not a genuine vote, nor was it based on a process of critical inquiry into current practices at the school and what might need to change" (pp. 167–168).

Thus, while the importance of perceived or felt need is obvious, its role is not all that straightforward. There are at least three complications. First, schools are faced with overloaded improvement agendas. Therefore, it is a question not only of whether a given need is important, but also of how important it is relative to other needs. Needless to say, this prioritizing among sets of desirables is not easy, as people are reluctant to neglect any goals, even though it may be unrealistic to address them all. Second, precise needs are often not clear at the beginning, especially with complex changes. People often become clearer about their needs only when they start doing things, that is, during implementation itself. Third, need interacts with the other eight factors to produce different patterns. Depending on the pattern, need can become further clarified or obfuscated during the implementation process.

In summary, the "fit" between a new program and district

and/or school needs is essential, but it may not become entirely clear until implementation is underway (see Bodilly, 1998, and Bodilly & Berends, 1999, for evaluation of the New American Schools, which also emphasizes the need for fit). Huberman and Miles (1984) similarly remind us that by this early implementation stage, the people involved must perceive *both* that the needs being addressed are significant *and* that they are making at least some progress toward meeting them. Early rewards and some tangible success are critical incentives during implementation.

Clarity. Clarity (about goals and means) is a perennial problem in the change process. Even when there is agreement that some kind of change is needed, as when teachers want to improve some area of the curriculum or improve the school as a whole, the adopted change may not be at all clear about what teachers should do differently. Problems related to clarity appear in virtually every study of change, from the early implementation studies when Gross and associates (1971) found that the majority of teachers were unable to identify the essential features of the innovation they were using, to present studies of reform in which finding clarity among complexity remains a major problem (Fullan, 2003). And the more complex the reform the greater the problem of clarity. In short, lack of clarity—diffuse goals and unspecified means of implementation—represents a major problem at the implementation stage; teachers and others find that the change is simply not very clear as to what it means in practice.

There is little doubt that clarity is essential, but its meaning is subtle; too often we are left with *false clarity* instead. False clarity occurs when change is interpreted in an oversimplified way; that is, the proposed change has more to it than people perceive or realize. For example, an approved textbook easily may become *the* curriculum in the classroom yet fail to incorporate significant features of the policy or goals that it is supposed to address. Reliance on the textbook may distract attention from behaviors and educational beliefs critical to the achievement of desired outcomes. In Canada, new or revised provincial curriculum guidelines have been dismissed by some teachers on the grounds that "we are already doing that"; but this is another illustration of false clarity if the teachers' perceptions are based only on the more superficial goal and content aspects of the guidelines to the neglect of beliefs and teaching strategies. Similarly, many curriculum guidelines in Canada contain greater specificity of objectives and content than did previous guidelines, with the result that teachers and others welcome them as "finally providing direction." However, these guidelines may be used in a literal way without the realization that certain teaching strategies and underlying beliefs are essential to implementing the guidelines effectively. Worse still, teachers introducing reforms superficially may actually make matters worse, as Stigler and Hiebert (1999) found in their video analysis of grade 8 mathematics lessons in three countries.

On the other hand, I have cited evidence above that not everyone experiences the comfort of false clarity. Unclear and unspecified changes can cause great anxiety and frustration to those sincerely trying to implement them. Clarity, of course, cannot be delivered on a platter. Whether or not it is accomplished depends on the *process*. Nor is greater clarity an end in itself: Very simple and insignificant changes can be very clear, while more difficult and worthwhile ones may not be amenable to easy clarification.

Finally, another dilemma in the era of standardization is attempting to solve the clarity problem at the outset through prescribed solutions. Hargreaves (2003) rejects prescription as downright dangerous: having cult-like qualities; being applied mainly to districts serving poorer communities, with better-off communities being able to pursue richer and deeper learning goals while poor communities become mired in drabness. We also have written about the prescription trap, but offering that it is possible (and necessary) to become precise without being rigid (Fullan et al., 2006). The key is to work on clarity all through the implementation process.

Complexity. Complexity refers to the difficulty and extent of change required of the individuals responsible for implementation. The actual amount depends on the starting point for any given individual or group, but the main idea is that any change can be examined with regard to difficulty, skill required, and extent of alterations in beliefs, teaching strategies, and use of materials. Many changes, such as open education (Bussis et al., 1976), teaching mathematics for understanding (Stigler & Hiebert, 1999), breakthroughs in cognitive science (Bransford et al., 1999), effective schools (Sammons, 1999), parent involvement (Epstein et al., 2002), and so on, require a sophisticated array of activities, structures, diagnoses, teaching strategies, and philosophical understanding if effective implementation is to be achieved.

While complexity creates problems for implementation, it may result in greater change because more is being attempted. Berman and McLaughlin (1977) found that "ambitious projects were less successful in absolute terms of the percent of the project goals achieved, but they typically stimulated more teacher change than projects attempting less" (p. 88). Those changes that did occur were more thorough as a result of the extra effort that the project required or inspired. As Berman (1980) stated elsewhere, "little ventured, nothing gained." As noted in "The Return of Large Scale Reform" (Fullan, 2000), we are seeing even more complex and ambitious reforms, which require a greater understanding of "the big picture" as well as one's place in it. There is more to gain and correspondingly more to lose.

In summary, simple changes may be easier to carry out, but they may not make much of a difference. Complex changes promise to accomplish more, which is good news given the kinds of changes in progress these days, but they also demand more effort, and failure takes a greater toll.

Quality and Practicality of the Program. The last factor associated directly with the nature of change concerns the quality and practicality of the change project—whether it is a new curriculum, a new policy, or a restructured school. The history of the quality of attempted changes relative to the other three variables (need, clarity, complexity) is revealing. To say that the importance of the quality of the change is self-evident is to underestimate how initiation decisions are made (see Pfeffer & Sutton, 2006). Inadequate quality and even the simple unavailability of materials and other resources can result when adoption decisions are made on the grounds of political necessity, or even in relation to perceived need without time for development. Put differently, when adoption is more important than implementation, decisions frequently are made without the follow-up or preparation time necessary to generate adequate materials. Ambitious projects are nearly always politically driven. As a result, the time line between the initiation decision and startup is often too short to attend to matters of quality.

Part and parcel of the return of ambitious reform has been the realization that "large-scale" change requires greater attention to front-end quality. This attention to developing and continually refining "proven" innovations is what has driven Success for All (Slavin & Madden, 1998), New American Schools (Kearns & Harvey, 2000), and National Literacy and Numeracy (Barber, 2000; Earl et al., 2003). In many ways the big curriculum projects of the 1960s gave the role of curriculum materials a bad name. Since implementation was neglected, people concluded that curriculum materials were less important. We now draw a different conclusion.

> To achieve large scale reform you cannot depend on people's capacity to bring about substantial change in the short run, so you need to propel the process with high quality teaching and training materials (print, video, electronic). There is still the problem of superficial implementation when new materials are in use, and even new practices in evidence, without the deeper understanding required for substantial and sustained implementation. But you get farther, faster by producing quality materials and establishing a highly interactive infrastructure of pressure and support. Finally, the materials do not have to be treated as prescriptive. Many judgments can and should be made during implementation as long as they are based on evidence linking teacher practices with student performance. (Fullan, 2000, p. 23)

In short, it is possible, indeed necessary, to combine ambitious change and quality. I have maintained that it is what people develop in their minds and actions that counts. People do not learn or accomplish complex changes by being told or shown what to do. Deeper meaning and solid change must be born over time. Good change is hard work; yet engaging in a bad change or avoiding needed changes may be even harder on us. The goal, then, is to attempt substantial reform and do it by persistently working on multilevel meaning across the system over time.

Local Factors

This section analyzes the social conditions of change; the organization or setting in which people work; and the planned and unplanned events and activities that influence whether or not given change attempts will be productive. The local school system represents one major set of situational constraints or opportunities for effective change. The same program is often successful in one school system and a disaster in another. Some districts have a track record of continual innovative achievement; others seem to fail at whatever they attempt.

The individual school may be the unit of change, but frequently change is the result of system initiatives that live or die based on the strategies and supports offered by the larger organization. This is especially true of multilevel, complex system-oriented innovations where what is being changed is the organizational culture itself.

The School District. We have seen evidence that adoption decisions frequently are made without adequate follow-through, and that the difficulties (subjective realities) inherent in the process of change are not well understood. Most attempts at collective change in education seem to fail, and failure means frustration, wasted time, feelings of incompetence and lack of support, and disillusionment. Since introducing innovations is a way of life in most school systems, districts build up track records in managing change. Whatever the track record at a given point in time, it represents a significant precondition relative to the next new initiative. The importance of the district's history of innovation attempts can be stated in the form of a proposition: The more that teachers or others have had negative experiences with previous implementation attempts in the district or elsewhere, the more cynical or apathetic they will be about the next change presented, regardless of the merit of the new idea or program. Districts, provinces or states, and countries can develop an incapacity for change as well as a capacity for it.

Nothing is more gratifying psychologically than attempting a change that works and benefits students. Success can beget more success. If the subjective meaning of change is so central, it is worth stressing that people carry meanings from one experience to the next. This psychological history of change is a major determinant of how seriously people try to implement new programs. To predict and to understand individuals' and groups' responses to particular innovative programs, one must know their immediate past history.

The role of the district administration and central staff is the subject of Chapter 11, and we have some very clear new examples of what makes for district-wide success (Campbell & Fullan, 2006; Fullan et al., 2004; Sharratt & Fullan, 2006; Supovitz, 2006). To comment briefly here, individual teachers and single schools can bring about change without the support of central administrators, but district-wide change will not happen. Although it has always been said that the superintendent and the principal are critical to educational change, it is only recently that we are beginning to understand more specifically what that means in practice. All of the research cited in Chapter 11 shows that the support of central administrators is critical for change in district practice. It also shows that general support or endorsement of a new program by itself has very little influence on change in practice (e.g., verbal support without implementation follow-through). Teachers and others know enough now, if they didn't 20 years ago, not to take change seriously unless central administrators *demonstrate through actions* that they should.

All major studies show that the local implementation process at the district level is essential if substantial improvement is the goal. The chief executive officer and other key central administrators set the conditions for implementation to the extent that they show specific forms of support and active knowledge and understanding of the realities of attempting to put a change into practice. To state it most forcefully, district administrators affect the quality of implementation to the extent that they understand and help to manage the set of factors and the processes described in this chapter.

Board and Community Characteristics. It is very difficult to generalize about the role of communities and school boards vis-à-vis implementation. Smith and Keith (1971) and Gold and Miles (1981) tell the painful sagas of what happens when middle-class communities do not like the innovations they see in their schools. School boards can indirectly affect implementation by hiring or firing reform-oriented superintendents. Demographic changes often put increasing pressure on schools to adopt, if not implement, new policies. Major conflicts sometimes incapacitate districts in bringing about actual change; in a sense, certain adoption decisions have to be settled before energy can be turned to implementation. In situations where the school board and the district are *actively* working together, substantiated improvements can be achieved, compared with conflictful or uninvolved boards (LaRocque & Coleman, 1989). At the local school level, as we will see in Chapter 10, virtually all successful schools in the past decade have strong parent–school relationships that they have painstakingly developed (Coleman, 1998; Epstein et al., 2002). There is also an increasing number of incidents where school boards are taken over by the mayor or the state.

With respect to the role of school boards, Hess's (1999) depiction of "spinning wheels and policy churn" is still closer to the truth in many situations, although, as I have said, we have seen some examples of effective district-wide reform: All cases of success involve district/school board rapport and partnership (McAdams, 2006). All in all, the role of communities and school boards is quite variable, ranging from apathy to active involvement—with the latter varying from conflictual to cooperative modes, depending on the conditions.

The Principal. As we shift from the district to the school level, the meaning of the phrase "the school is the unit or center of change" will become evident. All major research on innovation and school effectiveness shows that the principal strongly influences the likelihood of change, but it also indicates that most principals do not play instructional or change leadership roles. Berman and McLaughlin (1977) found that "projects having the *active* support of the principal were the most likely to fare well" (p. 124, emphasis in original)—a finding replicated time and time again over the past 30 years. Principals' actions serve to legitimate whether a change is to be taken seriously (and not all changes are) and to support teachers both psychologically and with resources. Berman, McLaughlin, and associates (1979) note that one of the best indicators of active involvement is whether the principal attends workshop training sessions. If we recall the earlier dimensions of change (beliefs, teaching behavior, curriculum materials), we might speculate that unless the principal gains some understanding of these dimensions (not necessarily as an expert or an instructional leader), he or she will not be able to understand teachers' concerns—that is, will not be able to provide support for implementation. Such understanding requires interaction.

There is an abundance of other new evidence cited in Chapter 8 that describes how and why the principal is necessary for effective implementation. The principal is the person most likely to be in a position to shape the organizational conditions necessary for success, such as the development of shared goals, collaborative work structures and climates, and procedures for monitoring results. The new evidence reveals that effective principals help address "multiple innovations" by working on program coherence. We will see in Chapter 8 many of the specific actions that principals take to influence improvement—actions so well documented in the most recent research (Leithwood, Louis, Anderson, & Wahlstrom, 2004; Marzano, Waters, & McNulty, 2005).

The subjective world of principals is such that many of them suffer from the same problem in implementing a new role as facilitator of change as do teachers in implementing new teaching roles: What the principal should do *specifically* to manage change at the school level is a complex affair for which the principal often has little preparation. The psychological and sociological problems of change that confront the principal are at least as great as those that confront teachers. Without this sociological sympathy, many principals will feel exactly as teachers do: Other people simply do not seem to understand the problems they face.

The Role of Teachers. Both individual teacher characteristics and collective or collegial factors play roles in determining implementation. At the individual level, Huberman (1988) and others have found that a teacher's psychological state can make him or her more or less predisposed toward considering and acting on improvements. Some teachers, depending on their personality and influenced by their previous experiences and stage of career, are more self-actualized and have a greater sense of efficacy, which leads them to take action and persist in the effort required to bring about successful implementation.

One's psychological state can be a permanent or changeable trait, depending on the individual and on the conditions. Several researchers have found that some schools have a much higher proportion of change-oriented teachers than do others, as we will see in our analysis of professional learning communities in Chapters 7 and 8. Some of this is no doubt through selection, but it also seems to be the case that the culture or climate of the school can shape an individual's psychological state for better or for worse.

In the final analysis it is the actions of the individual that count. Since interaction with others influences what one does, relationships with other teachers is a critical variable. The theory of change that has been evolving in this book clearly points to the importance of peer relationships in the school. Change involves learning to do something new, and interaction is the primary basis for social learning. New meanings, new behaviors, new skills, and new beliefs depend significantly on whether teachers are working as isolated individuals or are exchanging ideas, support, and positive feelings about their work. The quality of working relationships among teachers is strongly related to implementation. Collegiality, open communication, trust, support and help, learning on the job, getting results, and job satisfaction and morale are closely interrelated. There is a vast difference between the "learning-impoverished" schools and the "learning-enriched" schools described by Rosenholtz (1989). Only 13 of the 78 schools in Rosenholtz's sample were classified as learning enriched, but they provide powerful models of work environments that stimulate continuous improvements.

Twenty-five years ago, Little (1981) made the best case for how teachers and principals work together in accomplishing meaningful reform.

> School improvement is most surely and thoroughly achieved when: Teachers engage in frequent, continuous and increasingly concrete and precise *talk* about teaching practice (as distinct from teacher characteristics and failings, the social lives of teachers, the foibles and failures of students and their families, and the unfortunate demands of society on the school). By such talk, teachers build up a shared language adequate to the com-

plexity of teaching, capable of distinguishing one practice and its virtue from another.

Teachers and administrators frequently *observe* each other teaching, and provide each other with useful (if potentially frightening) evaluations of their teaching. Only such observation and feedback can provide shared *referents* for the shared language of teaching, and both demand and provide the precision and concreteness, which makes the talk about teaching useful.

Teachers and administrators plan, design, research, evaluate and prepare teaching materials together. The most prescient observations remain academic ("just theory") without the machinery to act on them. By joint work on materials, teachers and administrators share the considerable burden of development required by long-term improvement, confirm their emerging understanding of their approach, and make rising standards for their work attainable by them and by their students. *Teachers and administrators teach each other* the practice of teaching. (pp. 12–13, emphasis in original)

Only two of the six schools in Little's study evidenced a very high percentage of these practices, but no more convincing picture of the conditions for developing *meaning* on the part of individual teachers and administrators could be portrayed than in the passage just quoted. Little's observations were prescient, as developing interactive communities of practice has turned out to be one of the leading strategies for reform. We see the modern manifestation of the power of teacher interaction in current attempts to proliferate professional learning communities. PLCs are becoming more prominent and more sharply defined, as we shall see in Chapters 7 and 8 (see also Dufour et al., 2006; Dufour, Eaker, & Dufour, 2005).

External Factors

The last set of factors that influence implementation places the school or school district in the context of the broader society. In Canada this means primarily the offices of the department or ministry of education of each province, faculties of education, and other regional institutions. In the United States the main authorities consist of state departments of education and federal agencies. Agencies such as regional R&D laboratories and centers, philanthropic foundations, universities, and other external partners also attempt to support educational implementation across the country, although I do not take up the roles of nongovernment agencies explicitly in this book.

What does the larger society think of its education system? Provincial/state and national priorities for education are set according to the political forces and lobbying of interest groups, government bureaucracies, and elected representatives. Legislation, new policies, and new program initiatives arise from public concerns that the education system is not doing an adequate job of teaching literacy and mathematics, developing career-relevant skills for the economic system, producing effective citizens, meeting the needs of at-risk children—children of poverty, recent immigrants, children with special needs—and so on. These "sources" of reform put pressure on local districts (sometimes to the point of force) and also provide various incentives for changing in the desired direction. New provincial guidelines are established as policy, new federal and state legislation is passed, new nationally sponsored projects are developed. Whether or not implementation occurs will depend on the congruence between the reforms and local needs, and how the changes are introduced and followed through.

Government agencies have been preoccupied with policy and program initiation, and until recently they have vastly underestimated the problems and processes of implementation. We have a classic case of two entirely different worlds—the policymakers on the one hand and the local practitioner on the other hand ("divergent worlds," as Cowden & Cohen, 1979, call them). To the extent that each side is ignorant of the *subjective* world of the other, reform will fail—and the extent is great. The quality of relationships across this gulf is crucial to supporting change efforts when there is agreement, and to reconciling problems when there is conflict among these groups: between provincial ministries and local school boards, administrators, and teachers; between state departments and local districts; and between federal project officers and local authorities.

The most straightforward way of stating the problem is to say that local school systems and external authority agencies have not learned how to establish a *processual* relationship with each other. The relationship is more in the form of episodic events than processes: submission of requests for money, intermittent progress reports on what is being done, external evaluations—paperwork, not people work. More recently, through greater accountability, standardization, and closer monitoring, departments of education have had some direct influence on accomplishing specific learning outcomes (see Chapter 12). Mostly, however, lack of role clarity, ambiguity about expectations, absence of regular interpersonal forums of communication, ambivalence between authority and support roles of external agencies, and solutions that are worse than the original problems combine to erode the likelihood of implementation.

The difficulties in the relationship between external and internal groups are central to the problem and process of meaning. Not only is meaning hard to come by when two different worlds have limited interaction, but misinterpretation, attribution of motives, feelings of being misunderstood, and disillusionment on both sides are almost guaranteed.

Government agencies have become increasingly aware of the importance and difficulty of implementation and are allocating resources to clarifying standards of practice, to requiring accountability-based assessments, to establishing implementation units, to assessing the quality of potential changes, to supporting professional development, to monitoring implementation of policies, and to addressing other factors discussed in this chapter.

In any case, with the increased focus on larger-scale reform, some government agencies are becoming more adept at combining "pressure and support" forces in order to stimulate and follow through in achieving greater implementation. But this is subtle because it requires integrating pressure and support in a seamless manner (Chapter 12).

FACTORS AFFECTING CONTINUATION

Implementation is the big hurdle at the level of practice, but the question of the continuation of initiated reforms should be considered in its own right. In a sense, continuation represents another adoption decision, which may be negative, and even if it is positive, may not get implemented. Berman and McLaughlin (1977) found that projects that were not implemented effectively were discontinued, as would be expected; but they also found that only a minority of those that were well implemented were continued beyond the period of federal funding. The reasons for lack of continuation were in the main the same ones that influenced implementation, except that their role became more sharply defined. Lack of interest or inability to fund "special projects" out of district funds and lack of money for professional development and staff support for both continuing and new teachers signaled the end of many implemented programs. Lack of interest and support at the central district office (e.g., on the part of those who had taken on the project for opportunistic reasons) was another reason for noncontinuation. Similarly, at the school level:

> The principal was the key to both implementation and continuation. After the end of the federal funding, the principal influenced continuation in direct ways. Often because of turnover in the original cadre of project leaders, projects would have decayed without active efforts by the principal to bring on new staff. It was extremely difficult for teachers to go on using project methods or materials without the principal's explicit support. (Berman & McLaughlin, 1977, p. 188)

Berman and McLaughlin identified a small number of cases in which continuation was sustained. In addition to the specific factors just cited (e.g., active leadership, professional development), the authors noted:

> District officials paid early attention to mobilizing broad-based support for the innovation. And after federal funding ended, mobilization efforts were increased to pave the way for the project's transition from its special status to its incorporation into key areas of district operations: the budget, personnel assignment, curriculum support activities, and the instruction program. In short, the groundwork and planning for sustaining a change agent project had the early, active, and continued attention of school district managers. (p. 20)

The problem of continuation is endemic to all new programs irrespective of whether they arise from external initiative or are internally developed. Huberman and Miles (1984) stress that continuation or institutionalization of innovations depends on whether or not the change (1) gets embedded or built into the structure (through policy, budget, timetable, etc.); (2) has, by the time of the institutionalization phase, generated a critical mass of administrators and teachers who are skilled in and committed to the change; and (3) has established procedures for continuing assistance (such as a trained cadre of assisters), especially relative to supporting new teachers and administrators.

Problems of continuation, even in the face of initial successful implementation, persist to this day. In their longitudinal set of studies, Datnow and Stringfield (2000) talk about the problem of "longevity of reform." In one study of eight schools that had implemented given reform models, only three "had clearly moved toward institutionalizing their reforms" (p. 196). In another study of one district, Datnow and Stringfield report:

> By the third year of our four-year study, only one of thirteen schools were still continuing to implement their chosen reform designs. Reforms expired in six schools. A significant challenge to the sustainability of reforms . . . was the instability of district leadership and the politics that accompanied it. In 1995–1996 [the] then superintendent actively, publicly promoted the use of externally developed reforms. During his tenure, the district created an Office of Instructional Leadership to support the designs' implementation. The following year, however, a new district administration eliminated this office, and district support for many of the restructuring schools decreased dramatically. (p. 198)

The entire set of research on whole school reform models reflects the problems of both implementation and continuation. The major study of the implementation of reform models over the first decade of implementation by Berends and associates (2002) identifies the main points.

- About half the sample sites were implementing at a level consistent with the designers of reform models.

- Within-school variance of implementation was greater than between-school variance, and increased over time.
- Rates of implementation of school reform models declined over time (i.e., over a 5–6-year period).
- School capacity to implement the models varied a great deal. Revealingly, principal leadership focusing on instruction and learning was more important for improving school performance than the models used. For example, in San Antonio there was no difference in student achievement in schools adopting reform models compared with those schools that did not adopt reform models. Principal leadership was linked to student performance in both types of schools.
- District context was a critical variable both in terms of the direct assistance and support provided for schools, and with respect to introducing other initiatives that clashed or were misaligned with reform designs.
- State context aggravated the district context problem by presenting high-stakes accountability requirements that conflicted with and/or diverted attention away from WSR model implementation.

In more detailed case studies, Datnow and her colleagues (2002) conducted a longitudinal study of 13 schools using whole-school reform models. At the end of 6 years only four of the 13 schools were still implementing the chosen reform designs (not to mention questions pertaining to quality of implementation and impact on student learning), leading the researchers to ask and answer the question: "Do reforms that are transplanted last? Most often the answer in this study was no" (p. 232).

One last caution: We talk about continuation as the third phase in a planned change process, but it should be clear that the process is not simply linear and that all phases must be thought about from the beginning and continually thereafter. For example, one of the most powerful factors known to undermine continuation is staff and administrative turnover. Very few programs plan for the orientation and inservice support for new members who arrive after the program is started. And arrive they do—chipping away, however unintentionally, at what is already a fragile process (or if used positively, they can help establish the critical mass to support new directions).

PERSPECTIVES ON THE CHANGE PROCESS

By way of conclusion, let us revisit the familiar problems of obtaining shared meaning on a large scale. The first is the tendency to oversimplify. Once you think you have a good idea, and you are facing urgent problems, there is a great vulnerability to legislating the solution. These ready-made remedies make matters worse, as they narrow the curriculum and in effect try to control the uncontrollable. There are no shortcuts to achieving shared meaning, including providing it on a platter.

Second, even if we identify the right set of factors, there is a devil of a time getting them in place in new situations. This is the pathways problem. To know what success looks like, and even to know how it works in one situation, is not the same thing as getting it in place in another situation. Success is about one-quarter having the right ideas and three-quarters establishing effective processes that sort out and develop the right solution suited to the context in question.

Third, implementation and continuation are not just technical problems. Even the best technical ideas, in the absence of passion and commitment, do not go very far. Oakes and associates (1999) are very clear about this point. Schools that had multiyear projects, good technical support, and commitment were not successful over time. Oakes and associates found that "unless [teachers] were bound together by a moral commitment to growth, empathy, and shared responsibility, [they] were as likely to replicate the prevailing school culture as to change it" (p. 825).

In short, the broad implications of the implementation and continuation process have several interrelated components. The first is that the crux of change involves the development of meaning in relation to a new idea, program, reform, or set of activities. Meaning has both cognitive (knowledge) and affective (moral) dimensions. Both must be cultivated and connected. And it is *individuals working in interaction with others* who have to develop new meaning, and these individuals and groups are insignificant parts of a gigantic, loosely organized, complex, messy social system that contains myriad different subjective worlds.

The causes of change also become more easily identifiable and understood once we possess an underlying conception of what constitutes change as a process over time. The factors of implementation and continuation reinforce or undercut each other as an interrelated system. Single-factor theories of change are doomed to failure. Arguments that product quality is more important than teacher attitude, or that external factors are more important than internal ones, or that teachers are more central than administrators, are pointless. Effective implementation depends on the *combination* of all the factors and themes described in this chapter. The characteristics of the change, the makeup of the local district, the character of individual schools and teachers, and the existence and form of external relationships interact to produce conditions for change or nonchange. It takes a fortunate combination of the right factors—a critical mass—to support and guide the process of relearning, which respects the maintenance needs of individuals and groups and at the same time facilitates, stimulates, and prods people to change through a process of incremental and decremental fits and starts on the way to institutionalizing (or, if appropriate, rejecting) the change in question.

So, now we know why implementation and continuation are so difficult. Datnow and Stringfield (2000) summarize:

> Our research has documented that reform adoption, implementation, and sustainability, and school change more generally, are not processes that result from individuals or institutions acting in isolation from one another. Rather, they are the result of the interrelations between and across groups in different contexts, at various points in time. In this way, forces at the state and district levels, at the design team level, and at the school and classroom levels shape the ways in which reforms fail or succeed. (p. 199)

If the theory of change emerging at this point leads us to conclude that we need better implementation plans and planners, we are embarking on the infinite regress that characterizes the pursuit of a theory of "changing." To bring about more effective change, we need to be able to explain not only what causes it but how to influence those causes. To implement and sustain programs successfully, we need better implementation plans; to get better implementation plans, we need to know how to change our planning and follow-through process; to know how to change our planning process, we need to know how to produce better planners and implementers, and on and on. Is it any wonder that the planning, doing, and coping with educational change is the "science of muddling through" (Lindblom, 1959)? But it is a *science*. All of which is another way of saying that Chapter 6 is ready to begin.

Planning, Doing, and Coping with Change

Few, if any, strategies can be purely deliberative, and few can be purely emergent. One suggests no learning, the other, no control.

—Mintzberg (1994, p. 25)

For the growing number of people who have attempted to bring about educational change, "intractability" is becoming a household word. Being ungovernable, however, is not the same as being impervious to influence. And the inability to change *all* situations we would ideally like to reform does not lead to the conclusion that *no* situation can be changed.

The short scoop on the role of planning is to design strategies that zero in on capacity building with a focus on results, have a bias for action, and refine and strengthen the strategy through close interaction with the field using evidence-based decisions as you go. I pursue this theme in three sections: "Why Planning Fails," "Success Is Possible," and "Planning and Coping."

WHY PLANNING FAILS

We trained hard but it seemed every time we were beginning to form up into teams we were reorganized. I was to learn later in life that we tend to meet any situation by reorganizing, and what a wonderful method it can be for creating the illusion of progress while producing confusion, inefficiency, and demoralization.

—Gaius Petronius, A.D. 66, cited in Gaynor (1977, p. 28)

Understanding why most attempts at educational reform fail goes far beyond the identification of specific technical problems such as lack of good materials, ineffective professional development, or minimal administrative support. In more fundamental terms, educational change fails partly because of the assumptions of planners and partly because solving substantial problems is an inherently complex business. These two issues are explored in the next two subsections.

Faulty Assumptions and Ways of Thinking About Change

There are three interrelated reasons why most planning fails. It fails to take into account local context and culture; it is dangerously seductive and incomplete; and, paradoxically, too much emphasis is placed on the planning relative to the action part. In a word, the assumptions of policymakers are frequently *hyperrational* (Pfeffer & Sutton, 2000, 2006; Wise, 1977, 1988).

One of the initial sources of the problem is the commitment of reformers to see a particular desired change implemented. Commitment to *what should be changed* often varies inversely with knowledge about *how to work through a process of change*. In fact, strong commitment to a particular change may be a barrier to setting up an effective process of change, and in any case they are two quite distinct aspects of social change. The adage, "Where there's a will there's a way," is not always an apt one for the planning of educational change. There is an abundance of wills, but they are *in* the way rather than pointing the way. As we have seen, a certain amount of vision is required to provide the clarity and energy for promoting specific changes, but vision by itself may get in the way if it results in impatience, failure to listen, and so on. Stated in a more balanced way, promoters of change need to be committed to and skilled in the *change process* as well as in the change itself.

Lighthall's (1973) incisive critique of Smith and Keith's (1971) famous case study of the failure of a new open-concept elementary school provides strong support for the hypothesis that leadership commitment to a particular version of a change is negatively related to the ability to implement it. Lighthall states, as I do throughout this book, that educational change is a process of coming to grips with the *multiple* realities of people, who are the main participants in implementing change. The leader who presupposes what the change should be and acts in ways that preclude others' realities is bound to fail. Lighthall describes Superintendent Spanman's first speech to the Kensington school faculty.

> Spanman's visit to Kensington School was to make a presentation to the 21-member faculty. It was not for the purpose of discussing with them their joint problems of creating a whole new kind of education. His purpose was to express to the faculty parts of his reality; it was not to exchange his for theirs. Inasmuch as it was the faculty who were to carry the educational goals and images of his reality into action—that is, to make much of his reality their realities, too—and inasmuch as no person responds to realities other than his own, Spanman's selection of a one-way form of communication was self-defeating. In order for his reality to become part of theirs he would have to have made part of theirs his. (p. 263)

Innovators who are unable to alter their realities of change through exchange with would-be implementers can be as authoritarian as the staunchest defenders of the status quo. This is not to say that innovators should not have deep convictions about the need for reform or should be prepared to abandon their ideas at the first sign of opposition. Rather, for reasons that should be very clear from Chapters 2 through 5, innovators need to be open to the realities of others: sometimes because the ideas of others will lead to alterations for the better in the direction of change, and sometimes because the others' realities will expose the problems of implementation that must be addressed and at the very least will indicate where one should start.

Lighthall (1973) documented how the superintendent and principal at Kensington continually imposed only their own realities and how their stance led in a relatively short time to disastrous results. Lighthall observed:

> The tendency is widespread for problem-solvers to try to jump from their private plans to public implementation of these plans without going through the [number of realities] necessary to fashion them in accordance with problems felt by the adult hu-

mans whose energy and intelligence are needed to implement the plans. (p. 282)

Sarason (1971) states it another way: "An understandable but unfortunate way of thinking confuses the power (in a legal or organizational chart sense) to effect change with the process of change" (p. 29). In short, one of the basic reasons why planning fails is that planners or decision makers of change are unaware of the situations faced by potential implementers. They introduce changes without providing a means to identify and confront the situational constraints and without attempting to understand the values, ideas, and experiences of those who are essential for implementing any changes.

But what is wrong with having a strong belief that a certain aspect of schooling should be changed? Is it not appropriately rational to know that a given change is necessary, and to make it policy, if one is in a position to do so? Aside from the fact that many new programs do not arise from sound considerations, there are other more serious problems. The first problem is that there are many competing versions of what should be done, with each set of proponents equally convinced that its version is the right one. Forceful argument and even the power to make decisions do not at all address questions related to the process of implementation. The fallacy of rationalism is the assumption that the social world can be altered by seemingly logical argument. The problem, as George Bernard Shaw observed, is that "reformers have the idea that change can be achieved by brute sanity."

Wise (1977) also describes several examples of excessive rationalization, as when educational outcomes are thoroughly prescribed (e.g., in competency-based education) without any feasible plan of how to achieve them. Wise characterizes the behavior of some policymakers as wishful thinking.

> When policy makers require by law that schools achieve a goal which in the past they have not achieved, they may be engaged in wishful thinking. Here policy makers behave as though their desires concerning what a school system should accomplish, will in fact, be accomplished if the policy makers simply decree it. (p. 45)

Wise goes on to argue that even if rational theories of education were better developed—with goals clearly stated, means of implementation set out, and evaluation procedures stated—they would not have much of an impact, because schools, like other social organizations, do not operate in a rational vacuum. Some may say that they should, but Wise's point is that they do not, and wishing them to do so shows a misunderstanding of the existing culture of the school.

The second missing element is the failure of reformers to go to the trouble of treating local context and culture as vital. Micklethwait and Wooldridge (1996) remind us that policymakers often impose ideas without taking into account local context and are vulnerable to adopting quick fixes. Senge and associates (1999) make a similar point: "The fundamental flaw in most innovators' strategies is that they focus on their innovations, on what they are trying to do—rather than on understanding how the larger culture, structures, and norms will react to their efforts" (p. 26).

In *What's Worth Fighting for Out There*, Hargreaves and I (1998) argued that we need to take a very different planning approach to so-called resisters because (1) they may have some good ideas, and (2) you ignore them at your peril if they stay around for implementation. There are, in other words, good technical and political reasons for taking resisters more seriously. In some cases, resistance may be a source of learning. Resisters may be right. They may have "good sense" in seeing through the change as faddish, misdirected, and unworkable (Gitlin & Margonis, 1995). Thus, resistance to change can be instructive. As Maurer (1996) observes:

> Often those who resist have something important to tell us. We can be influenced by them. People resist for what they view as good reasons. They may see alternatives we never dreamed of. They may understand problems about the minutiae of implementation that we never see from our lofty perch atop Mount Olympus. (p. 49)

In a similar vein, according to Heifetz (1994), a counterintuitive rule of thumb is required in order to reject "one's emotional impulse to squash those in the community who raise disturbing questions. Consequently, an authority should protect those whom he [or she] wants to silence. Annoyance is often a signal of opportunity" (p. 271). It is a mistake for principals to support only like-minded innovators. As Elmore (1995) puts it: "Small groups of self-selected reformers apparently seldom influence their peers" (p. 20). They just create an even greater gap between themselves and others that eventually becomes impossible to bridge. This is not to say that resistance should carry the day, but rather that we need more powerful and sensitive strategies to help instigate the learning and commitment that are necessary for actual implementation and sustained impact.

Another serious flaw concerns the seductive nature of planning when one is aching for a clear solution to urgent problems. Our first guideline for action for principals (and all leaders) is "steer clear of false certainty" (Hargreaves & Fullan, 1998, p. 105). In times of great uncertainty there is an understandable (but dangerous) need to want to know what to do.

Stacey (1996a), the "complexity theorist," explains why.

> We respond to the fact that situations are uncertain and conflictual with a rigid injunction that people be more certain and more consensual. . . . This denial of uncertainty itself allows us to sustain the fantasy of someone up there being in control and, perhaps, of things turning out for the best if we simply do what we are told, and so it protects us for a while from anxiety. However, because that defensive response involves dependency and a flight from reality, it hardly ever works. (pp. 7–8)

Management, leadership, and change gurus can bring about especially seductive kinds of dependency. Their charismatic authority promises people a way out of the chaos that they feel. Gurus cultivate dependent disciples rather than independent thinkers. In his study of the guru phenomenon, psychiatrist Anthony Storr (1997) notes that this is because gurus need the reassurance and sense of certainty that having disciples gives them so they can cope with and put aside their own inner doubts. What disciples get out of the relationship is the comfort of someone else taking responsibility for their decisions. Storr eloquently warns us that "the charisma of certainty is a snare which entraps the child who is latent in us all." Disciples of modern gurus, he concludes, are "looking for what they want in the wrong place" (p. 223). I think this is also what Peter Drucker was getting at when he allegedly said, "People refer to gurus because they don't know how to spell charlatan."

False certainty also occurs when you think you have a good idea, but it turns out that it is incomplete. In Hill and Celio's (1998) words, reform theories often have "zones of wishful thinking"; that is, for the reform to be successful, certain things have to happen "that the reform needs, but cannot cause" (p. 2). In further work, Hill, Campbell, and Harvey (2000) analyze seven competing reform proposals: standards-based, teacher development, new school designs, decentralization and site-based management, charter schools, school contracting, and vouchers—all of which represent incomplete and wishful-thinking theories of reform.

In addition to the problem of multiple, disconnected innovations, Hill, Campbell, and Harvey conclude:

> We learned that there is a plausible case for each of the proposals: each addresses a real problem and would probably cause real changes in public education if fully implemented. But we also found that none of the proposals was sufficient because none could deliver all of the changes its proponents intended unless other changes which the proposal itself could not deliver, occurred at the same time. For example, reforms based on teacher training do not create incentives to overcome some teachers' reluctance to put in the time and effort to improve their knowledge and skills. In a similar vein, reforms such as vouchers do not in themselves guarantee that there will be a plentiful supply of high-quality independent school providers or that enough teachers and principals to run such schools exist. (p. 23)

Finally, planning fails paradoxically because too much emphasis is placed on planning and plans. Pfeffer and Sutton (2000, 2006) provide the definitive analysis of the too-much-planning problem. In *The Knowing–Doing Gap* (2000) they identified five main barriers to action in their research on businesses, which are equally applicable to reform in school systems:

1. *When talk and planning substitute for action.* The researchers found a tendency in companies to treat talking about something, gathering data, and writing plans as equivalent to

doing something. If you believe in "ready-fire-aim," this is the equivalent of "ready-ready-ready." In this sense the size of the planning or strategy document is inversely related to the amount and quality of action.

2. *When memory substitutes for new action.* People in unthinking organizations keep on doing what has always been done without reflecting on why they are doing it. They thus do not question existing practices, and they are poor at reacting to external changes. Decisions are made on implicit, untested, and inaccurate models of behavior and performance.

3. *When fear prevents acting on knowledge.* Fear-based approaches to management presume that unless people are under pressure and fearful for their futures, they won't work diligently. Pfeffer and Sutton found two negative consequences in organizations that were governed by fear: (1) it drove employees to focus only on the short term, often causing problems for the long term; and (2) it created a focus on individual survival, not the collective good. Punishing people for making mistakes leads to coverup, safe short-term choices, and playing it safe.

4. *When measurement obstructs good judgment.* A preoccupation with measurement results in systems of monitoring that (a) are too complex with too many separate measures, (b) are highly subjective in implementation, and (c) often miss important elements of performance. No matter what the intention, complex measurement and monitoring systems can result in overload and confusion. Either people's behavior is unaffected, or they become overwhelmed and demoralized, or the wrong behavior is encouraged.

5. *When internal competition turns friends into enemies.* Who is the enemy? People inside the firm or external competitors? If internal competition is the management philosophy, it (a) fosters disloyalty to peers and the firm as a whole, (b) undermines teamwork, and (c) inhibits knowledge sharing and the spread of best practices.

Pfeffer and Sutton (2006) examine these problems more deeply in their new book on "evidence-based management." They identify three basic harmful tendencies: casual benchmarking in which organizations borrow superficial aspects of best practices—the product—rather than coming to grips with the underlying philosophy; doing what (seems to have) worked in the past; and following deeply held yet unexamined ideologies. It seems obvious to say, but one of the key high-yield capacities that has emerged in the past 5 years is the ability to use data to guide decisions, compounded by the fact that there is a surfeit of information bombarding us (see also Fullan et al., 2006). What is difficult to master, say Pfeffer and Sutton, is *wisdom*—"the ability to act with knowledge while doubting what you know" (p. 174).

Doug Reeves (2006) in education also has fingered detached planning as worse than doing nothing at all: "Exquisitely formatted planning documents are worse than a waste of time. They are in fact inversely related to student achievement" (p. ix). Echoing the themes across the chapters in this book, Reeves says that what works for both equity and excellence "are monitoring, evaluation, values, beliefs, and implementation—not one more stack of beautifully bound documents" (p. ix).

Complex Problems

Solving complex problems on a continuous basis is enormously difficult because of the sheer number of factors at play. It is further complicated because the *sine qua non* of successful reform is whether *relationships improve*; in fact, we have to learn how to develop relationships with those we might not understand and might not like, and vice versa (Fullan, 2001).

Chaos or complexity theorists put it best.

> Most textbooks focus heavily on techniques and procedures for long-term planning, on the need for visions and missions, on the importance and the means of securing strongly shared cultures, on the equation of success with consensus, consistency, uniformity and order. [However, in complex environments] the real management task is that of coping with and even using unpredictability, clashing counter-cultures, disensus, contention, conflict, and inconsistency. In short, the task that justifies the existence of all managers has to do with instability, irregularity, difference and disorder. (Stacey, 1996b, pp. xix–xx)

Stating the case more fully (and dauntingly), Stacey (1996b) argues:

> A complexity theory of organization is built on the following propositions:
> - All organizations are webs of nonlinear feedback loops connected to other people and organizations (its environments) by webs of nonlinear feedback loops.
> - Such nonlinear feedback systems are capable of operating in states of stable and unstable equilibrium, or in the borders between these states, that is far-from-equilibrium, in bounded instability at the edge of chaos.
> - All organizations are paradoxes. They are powerfully pulled towards stability by the forces of integration, maintenance controls, human desires for security and certainty, and adaptation to the environment on the one hand. They are also powerfully pulled to the opposite extreme of unstable equilibrium by the forces of division and decentralization, human desires for excitement and innovation, and isolation from the environment.
> - If the organization gives in to the pull to stability it fails because it becomes ossified and cannot change easily. If it gives in to the pull to instability it disintegrates. Success lies in sustaining an organization in the borders between stability and instability. This is a state of chaos, a difficult-to-maintain dissipative structure.
> - The dynamics of the successful organization are therefore those of irregular cycles and discontinuous trends falling within qualitative patterns. Fuzzy but recognizable categories taking the form of archetypes and templates.
> - Because of its own internal dynamics, a successful organization faces completely unknowable specific futures.
> - Agents within the system cannot be in control of its long-term future, nor can they install specific frameworks to make it successful, nor can they apply step-by-step analytical reasoning or planning or ideological controls to long-term development. Agents within the system can only do these things in relation to the short term.
> - Long-term development is a spontaneously self-organizing process from which new strategic directions may emerge. Spontaneous self-organization is political interaction and learning in groups. Managers have to use reasoning by analogy.
> - In this way managers create and discover their environments and the long-term futures of the organizations. (p. 349)

The positive side or, if you like, the "solution" involves developing learning organizations. In their field book, Senge and colleagues (2000) argue that fiat or command can never solve complex problems; only a learning orientation can.

> This means involving everyone in the system in expressing their aspiration, building their awareness, and developing their capabilities together. In a school that's learning, people who traditionally may have been suspicious of one another—parents and teachers, educators and local business people, administrators and union members, people inside and outside the school walls, students and adults—recognize their common stake in the future of the school system and the things they can learn from one another. (p. 5)

Complex indeed! Anything else is tinkering.

SUCCESS IS POSSIBLE

Recognizing the limitations of planning is not the same thing as concluding that effective change is unattainable. But in order to determine if planned educational change is possible, it would not be sufficient to locate situations where change seemed to be working. We would need to find examples where a setting had been *deliberately transformed* from a previous state to a new one that represented clear improvement. We need to know about the causes and dynamics of how change occurs.

Over the past decade we and others have been using complexity theory and related action-orientated strategies to achieve successful change on an increasingly large scale (Barber & Fullan, 2005; Fullan, 2006; Fullan et al., 2006). There have been a number of clear examples of how school districts and schools improved the quality of education through a process of deliberate change. The good news is that we have well-documented cases at the school level (see Chapters 7 and 8), at the district level (Chapter 11), and recently at the state level (Chapter 12). The bad news is twofold. First, the successful examples are still in the minority in the sense that only a small proportion of schools, districts, and states have been successful in their attempts. The second worry is more disturbing. There is reason to believe that hard-won successes over a period of 5 to 10 years cannot be sustained under current conditions; furthermore, it appears that the accomplishments are real, but not deep. In other words, even the successful cases cannot be expected to last or to be deep. Sustainability remains problematic, although we are getting a better handle on the problem (Fullan, 2005; Hargreaves & Fink, 2006).

Be that as it may, successful change is possible in the real world, even under difficult conditions. And many of the reasons for the achievements can be pinpointed. There are classrooms, schools, communities, districts, and states that have altered the conditions for change in more favorable, workable directions. Not every situation is alterable, especially at certain periods of time; but it is a good bet that major improvements can be accomplished in many more settings than is happening at present.

PLANNING AND COPING

We have come to the most difficult problem of all. What can we actually do to plan for and cope with educational change? This section contains an overview of the assumptions, elements, and guidelines for action. Additional specific implications for particular roles and agencies (e.g., teacher, principal, superintendent, and federal or state/provincial agencies) are left for the appropriate chapters in Parts II and III. First, I introduce the topic by indicating some of the basic issues and by noting that advice will have to vary according to the different situations in which we find ourselves. Second, I provide some advice for those who find that they are forced to respond to and cope with change introduced by others. Third, the bulk of the section is addressed to the question of how to plan and implement change more effectively.

In general, there are four logical types of change situations we could face as individuals. These are depicted in Figure 6.1. There are many different specific roles even within a single cell that cannot be delineated here, but people generally find themselves in one of the four situations depending on whether they are initiating/promoting a change or are on the receiving end, and whether

FIGURE 6.1. Change Situations According to Authority Position
        and Relation to the Change Effort

		Authority position	
		YES	NO
Relation to change effort	Initiator or promoter	I Planner (e.g., policymaker)	II Planner (e.g., developer)
	Recipient or responder	III Coper (e.g., principal)	IV Coper (e.g., teacher)

or not they are in authority positions. I start with coping, or being on the receiving end of change (cells III and IV), because this is the most prevalent situation.

Coping with Change

Those in situations of having to respond to a particular change should assume neither that it is beneficial nor that it is useless; that much is clear from the previous analysis. The major initial stance should involve *critical assessment*, that is, determining whether the change is desirable in relation to certain goals and whether it is "implementable"—in brief, whether it is worth the effort, because it *will* be an effort if it is at all worthwhile. Several criteria would be applied: Does the change address an unmet need? Is it a priority in relation to other unmet needs? Is it informed by some desirable sense of vision? Are there adequate (not to say optimal) resources committed to support implementation (such as technical assistance and leadership support)? If the conditions are reasonably favorable, knowledge of the change process outlined in previous chapters could be used to advantage—for example, pushing for technical assistance, opportunities for interaction among teachers, and so on. If the conditions are not favorable or cannot be made to be favorable, the best coping strategy consists of knowing enough about the process of change so that we can understand why it doesn't work, and therefore not blame ourselves; we also can gain solace by realizing that most other people are in the same situation of nonimplementation. In sum, the problem is one of developing enough meaning vis-à-vis the change so that we are in a position to implement it effectively or reject it, as the case may be.

Those who are confronted with unwanted change and are in authority positions (cell III) will have to develop different coping mechanisms from those in nonauthority positions (cell IV). For the reader who thinks that resisting change represents irresponsible obstinacy, it is worth repeating that nonimplementable programs and reforms probably do more harm than good when they are attempted. The most responsible action may be to reject innovations that are bound to fail and to work earnestly at those that have a chance to succeed. Besides, in some situations resistance may be the only way to maintain sanity and avoid complete cynicism. In the search for meaning in a particular imposed change situation, we may conclude that there is no meaning, or that the problem being addressed is only one (and not the most important or strategic) of many problems that should be confronted. The basic guideline is to work on coherence by selecting and connecting innovations, thereby reducing disjointed overload while increasing focus (see Chapter 8 for how principals can do this, and Chapter 11 for how district administrators can do it).

We should feel especially sorry for those in authority positions (middle management in district offices, principals, intermediate government personnel in provincial and state regional offices) who are responsible for leading or seeing to implementation, but do not want or understand the change—either because it has not been sufficiently developed (and is literally not understandable) or because they themselves have not been involved in deciding on the change or have not received adequate orientation or training. The psychiatrist Ronald Laing captures this situation in what he refers to as a "knot."

> There is something I don't know
> that I am supposed to know.

I don't know what it is I don't know,
and yet am supposed to know,
And I feel I look stupid
if I seem both not to know it
and not know *what* it is *I* don't know.
Therefore, I pretend I know it.
This is nerve-wracking since I don't
know what I must pretend to know.
Therefore, I pretend I know everything.
—R. D. Laing, *Knots* (1970)

This is a ridiculous stance, to be sure, as painful as it is unsuccessful. It can, of course, be successful in the sense of maintaining the status quo. Depending on one's capacity for self-deception, it can be more or less painful as well. In any case, teachers know when a change is being introduced or supported by someone who does not believe in it or understand it. Yet this is the position in which many intermediate managers find themselves, or allow themselves to be. Those in authority have a need for meaning, too, if for no other reason than that the change will be unsuccessful if they cannot convey their meaning to others.

Planning and Implementing Change

The implications for those interested in planning and implementing educational change (cells I and II) are very important, because we would all be better off if changes were introduced more effectively. It is useful to consider these implications according to two interrelated sets of issues: What *assumptions* about change should we note? How can we plan and implement change more effectively?

The advice about effective planning and implementation is consistent. It all amounts to focus, persistence, implementation, monitoring, corrective action, and humility in the face of change. Reeves's (2006) leadership for learning framework embodies these elements. As does my own "capacity building with a focus on results" set of strategies, which have been applied at the district (Campbell & Fullan, 2006; Sharratt & Fullan, 2006) and system levels (Fullan, 2006).

Pfeffer and Sutton (2006, chap. 9) reinforce these ideas with their own nine implementation principles for profiting from evidence-based management.

1. Treat your organization as an unfinished prototype.
2. No brag, just facts.
3. Master the obvious and the mundane.
4. See yourself and your organization as outsiders do.
5. Power, prestige, and performance make you stubborn, stupid, and resistant to valid evidence.
6. Evidence-based management is not just for senior executives (it must permeate all levels of the organization).
7. Like everything else, you still need to sell it.
8. If all else fails, slow the spread of bad practices.
9. The best diagnostic question: What happens when people fail?

Relative to the ninth principle, Pfeffer and Sutton state that "if you look at how the most effective systems in the world are managed, a hallmark is that when something goes wrong, people face the hard facts, learn what happened and why, and keep using those facts to keep on getting better" (p. 232).

Planning and implementation are about one's theory of action, or the assumptions one makes about how to go about effective change. The same tool or instrument can be a great success in one situation, and a failure in another, not for the obvious reason that contexts differ, but because of the underlying philosophy or thinking about change held by those leading. These assumptions are powerful and frequently subconscious sources of actions. When we begin to understand what change is as people experience it, we begin also to see clearly that assumptions made by planners of change are extremely important determinants of whether the realities of implementation get confronted or ignored. The analysis of change carried out so far leads me to identify ten "do" and "don't" assumptions as basic to a successful approach to educational change.

1. Do not assume that your version of what the change should be is the one that should or could be implemented. On the contrary, assume that one of the main purposes of

the process of implementation is to *exchange your reality* of what should be with the realities of implementers and others concerned, through interaction with them. Stated another way, assume that successful implementation consists of some transformation or continual development of initial ideas. Have good ideas, be inspirational, but engage others in their realities.

2. Assume that any significant innovation, if it is to result in change, requires individual implementers to work out their own meaning. Significant change involves a certain amount of ambiguity, ambivalence, and uncertainty for the individual about the meaning of the change. Thus, effective implementation is a *process of clarification*. It is also important not to spend too much time in the early stages on needs assessment, planning, and problem definition activities—school staff have limited time. Clarification is likely to come in large part through reflective practice.

3. Assume that conflict and disagreement are not only inevitable but fundamental to successful change. Since all groups of people possess multiple realities, any collective change attempt will necessarily involve conflict. Assumptions 2 and 3 combine to suggest that all successful efforts of significance, no matter how well planned, will experience an implementation dip in the early stages. Smooth implementation is often a sign that not much is really changing.

4. Assume that people need pressure to change (even in directions that they desire), but it will be effective only under conditions that allow them to react, to form their own position, to interact with other implementers, to obtain assistance, to develop new capacities, and so on. It is all right and helpful to express what you value in the form of standards of practice and expectations of accountability, but only if coupled with capacity-building and problem-solving opportunities.

5. Assume that effective change takes time. It is a process of "development in use." Unrealistic or undefined time lines fail to recognize that implementation occurs developmentally. Significant change in the form of implementing specific innovations can be expected to take 2 or 3 years;

bringing about institutional reforms can take 5 or 10 years. At the same time, work on changing the infrastructure (policies, incentives, and capacity of agencies at all levels) so that valued gains can be sustained and built upon. Don't expect change overnight but do press for significant results in the foreseeable future (within one election period, as I frequently put it).

6. Do not assume that the reason for lack of implementation is outright rejection of the values embodied in the change, or hard-core resistance to all change. Assume that there are a number of possible reasons: value rejection, inadequate resources to support implementation, poor capacity, insufficient time elapsed, and the possibility that resisters have some good points to make.

7. Do not expect all or even most people or groups to change. Progress occurs when we take steps (e.g., by following the assumptions listed here) that *increase* the number of people affected. Our reach should exceed our grasp, but not by such a margin that we fall flat on our face. Instead of being discouraged by all that remains to be done, be encouraged by what has been accomplished by way of improvement resulting from your actions.

8. Assume that you will need a *plan* that is based on the above assumptions and that addresses the factors known to affect implementation. Evolutionary planning and problem-coping models based on knowledge of the change process are essential. Remember Pfeffer and Sutton's (2006) definition of wisdom: "the ability to act with knowledge while doubting what you know" (p. 174).

9. Assume that no amount of knowledge will ever make totally clear what action should be taken. Action decisions are a combination of valid knowledge, political considerations, on-the-spot decisions, and intuition. Better knowledge of the change process will improve the mix of resources on which we draw, but it will never and should never represent the sole basis for decision.

10. Assume that changing the culture of institutions is the real agenda, not implementing single innovations. Put another way, when implementing particular innovations, we

should always pay attention to whether each institution and the relationships among institutions and individuals are developing or not. Capacity for selective change as a sustainable resource is what success is all about.

In other words, do not be seduced into looking for the silver bullet. Given the urgency of problems, there is great vulnerability to off-the-shelf solutions. But most external solutions have failed. The idea is to be a critical consumer of external ideas, while working from a base of understanding and altering local context. There is no complete answer "out there."

We conclude, then, as Mintzberg, Ahlstrand, and Lampei (1998) have, that "strategy formation is complex space."

Strategy formation is judgmental designing, intuitive reasoning, and emergent learning; it is about transformation as well as perpetuation; it must involve individual cognition and social interaction, cooperation as well as conflict; it has to include analyzing before and programming after as well as negotiating during; and all of this must be in response to what can be a demanding environment. Just try to leave any of this out and watch what happens! (pp. 372–373)

It is time now to fill some of this complex space with people. The chapters in Part II portray the social realities and possibilities of those most directly involved and affected by educational reform.

EDUCATIONAL CHANGE AT THE LOCAL LEVEL

CHAPTER 7

The Teacher

*Low morale, depressed, feeling unfairly blamed for the
ills of society? You must be a teacher.*
— Times Education Supplement (1997, p. 1)

Educational change depends on what teachers do and think—it's
as simple and as complex as that. It would all be so easy if we
could legislate changes in thinking. Classrooms and schools become effective when (1) quality people are recruited to teaching,
and (2) the workplace is organized to energize teachers and reward accomplishments. The two are intimately related. Profes-
sionally rewarding workplace conditions attract and retain good
people. Using sustained improvement as the criterion, this chapter
progresses from the negative—the situation for most teachers—to
glimpses of the positive. Progress has been made, but teaching
remains an underdeveloped profession.

The conditions of teaching, with pockets of exceptions, appear
to have deteriorated over the past 2 decades. Reversing this trend,
as I argue in this chapter, must be at the heart of any serious
reform effort. Teacher stress and alienation are at an all-time high,
judging from the increase in work-related illness, and from the
numbers of teachers leaving or wanting to leave the profession.
The range of educational goals and expectations for schools and
the transfer of family and societal problems to the school, coupled
with the imposition of multiple, disconnected reform initiatives,
present intolerable conditions for sustained educational development and satisfying work experiences.

I start in this chapter with a sketch of where most teachers
are. From there I move to the phenomenon of the introduction of
change—in nine out of ten cases a gross mismatch, as far as the
world of the teacher is concerned. But change is a double-edged

sword, and in one out of ten cases we will see what makes for
success. We also will see the promise, and the problems of establishing on a large scale professional learning communities as a
solution. Finally, I take up the matter of professionalism at the
crossroads, for teaching is at a critical juncture in its evolution as
a profession.

WHERE TEACHERS ARE

Starting where teachers are means starting with multifaceted diversity, overload, and limits to reform, because this is the situation
for most teachers. As we shall see, there are notable exceptions to
this modal pattern, which represent hints of what could be. For
most teachers, however, daily demands crowd out serious sustained improvements.

It is clearly not possible to describe in a few pages the school
lives of 3 million teachers in diverse settings across North America,
let alone across the world. The following, written by a teacher,
provides a composite picture that, despite the flamboyance of the
language, captures the experience of many high school teachers:

> Teachers routinely have to teach over 140 students daily. On
> top of that, we have lunch duty, bus duty, hall duty, home
> room duty. We go to parents' meetings, teachers' meetings, in-
> service meetings, curriculum meetings, department meetings,
> county-wide teachers' meetings, school board meetings, and
> state teachers' conferences. We staff the ticket booths and con-
> cession stands at football and basketball games. We supervise
> the production of school plays, annuals, newspapers, dances,
> sports events, debates, chess tournaments, graduation ceremo-
> nies. We go on senior trips. We go on field trips to capital build-
> ings, prisons, nature centers, zoos, courtroom trials. We choke
> down macaroni and cheese and USDA peanut butter at lunch
> (and have to pay for it). We search lockers during bomb threats.
> We supervise fire drills and tornado alerts. We write hall passes,
> notes to the principal, the assistant principal, parents and our-
> selves. We counsel. We wake up every morning to the reali-
> zation that the majority of our students would far rather be
> someplace else. On top of that everyone's yelling at us—state

legislatures, parents, and SAT scores. To add injury to insult, colleges and universities are getting all huffed up and grumpy and indignant over the increasingly poor preparation of the students we're sending them. Well, just who do they think taught us how to teach? How much support and prestige do they accord their own schools of education? (Wigginton, 1986, p. 191)

The situation of elementary school teachers is different, but no more attractive. Most urban teachers in North America, for example, increasingly face ethnic and language diversity, children with special needs, one-parent families, and a bewildering array of social and academic expectations for the classroom. After reviewing the goals of education—mastery of basic skills, intellectual development, career education, interpersonal understandings, citizenship participation, enculturation, moral and ethical character development, emotional and physical well-being, creativity and aesthetic self-expression, and self-realization—Goodlad (1984, chap. 2) concludes *we want it all*.

Teachers all over the world are feeling beleaguered. Teachers in England express their reactions to impending high-stakes inspection of their school, and to the detailed paper accountability that it demands.

Whatever criticism they make, it's going to feel, however stupid it is, that the last 20 years have been for nothing. It's not about what progress schools have made in the last 15 years. It's "Schools fail." "Head [principal] to be removed." "Hit team going in." It doesn't matter what you look at. It's about failure in schools.

I don't want to lose my optimism. People always say that I am optimistic but I am beginning to lose it. I don't want to be negative, for I enjoy some parts, but I'm worrying about the level of support for others I can sustain [as a teacher leader] as I see them suffering more and more. We seem to have become [whiners] but that is not really who we are. (Jeffrey & Wood, 1997, p. 330)

The widespread introduction in the past 5 years of "turnaround" policies and requirements for failing schools has exacerbated the plight of teachers without furnishing the conditions for more fundamental, sustained reform in those situations. The naming of failed schools and the fishbowl atmosphere of turnaround schools, along with external assistance, have produced much agony and some temporary improvement, but have failed to create lasting solutions for the students and teachers in failing schools (Fullan, 2006; Minthrop, 2004).

The circumstances of teaching, including the added pressure of accountability, ask a lot of teachers in terms of daily maintenance and expectations for student success for all, and give back little in the time needed for planning, constructive discussion, thinking, and just plain rewards and time for composure. The central tendency of these conditions, as I will describe in this section, is decidedly negative in its consequences. (As readers will know, this observation does not mean we should do away with pressure, but rather calls for finding the right blend of "positive pressure"— pressure that motivates; see Chapters 3 and 12).

Let us start 3 decades ago with one of the most respected and widely quoted studies of what teachers do and think—Lortie's classic study *School Teacher* (1975). After reviewing Lortie's conclusions, I will ask, What, if anything, has changed over the years? Lortie based his study on 94 interviews with a stratified sample of elementary and secondary school teachers in the greater Boston area (called the Five Town sample), questionnaires to almost 6,000 teachers in Dade County, Florida, and various national and local research studies by others. His findings can best be summarized as follows:

1. Teacher training (see also Chapter 13) does not equip teachers for the realities of the classroom. Nor could it be expected to do so in light of the abruptness of the transition. In September, the young teacher (who typically was a student in June) assumes the same responsibility as the 25-year teacher veteran. For both the beginning and experienced teacher, issues of classroom control and discipline are one of the major preoccupations. Lortie claims that for most teachers there is always a tension between the task-oriented controlling aspect of a teacher's role and the relational reaching-the-student aspect.

2. The cellular organization of schools means that teachers

struggle with their problems and anxieties privately, spending most of their time physically apart from their colleagues.

3. Partly because of the physical isolation and partly because of norms of not sharing, observing, and discussing one another's work, teachers do not develop a common technical culture. The picture is not one of "colleagues who see themselves as sharing a viable, generalized body of knowledge and practice" (Lortie, 1975, p. 79). In many ways student learning is seen as determined either by factors outside teachers' control (such as family background) or by unpredictable and mysterious influences. According to Lortie, the lack of a technical culture, an analytic orientation, and a serious sharing and reflection among teachers creates ambiguity and ad hocness: "The teacher's craft is marked by the absence of concrete models for emulation, unclear lines of influence, multiple and controversial criteria, ambiguity about assessment timing, and instability in the product" (p. 136). A teacher is either a good teacher or a bad one; a teacher has either a good day or a bad one. It all depends.

4. When teachers do get help, the most effective source tends to be fellow teachers, and second, administrators and specialists. Such help is not frequent and is used on a highly selective basis. For example, teachers normally do not relate objectives to principles of instruction and learning outcomes of students. Rather, "they describe the 'tricks of the trade' they picked up—not broader conceptions that underlie classroom practice" (p. 77). As to the frequency of contact, 45% of the Five Town teachers reported "no contact" with other teachers in doing their work, 31% reported "some contact," and 24% reported "much contact" (p. 193). There is some indication that teachers desire more contact with fellow teachers—54% said that a good colleague is someone who is willing to share (p. 194). Again, this refers more to "tricks of the trade" than to underlying principles of teaching and to the relationship of teaching to learning.

5. Effectiveness of teaching is gauged by informal, general observation of students—50% of the teachers in Dade County

responded in this vein. The next most frequent choice related to the results of tests—a very distant 13.5%. In short, teachers rely heavily on their own informal observations.

6. The greatest rewards mentioned by teachers were what Lortie labels "psychic rewards": "the times I reached a student or group of students and they have learned" (p. 104). Over 5,000 (86%) of the 5,900 teachers in Dade County mentioned this source of gratification. The next most frequent response—respect from others—was selected by 2,100, or 36% of the sample.

7. Lortie also found that "striking success with one student" here and one student there was the predominant source of pride (as distinct from raising test scores of the whole group) (p. 121). For secondary school teachers, the success stories often did not become visible until one or more years after graduation, when a former student returned to thank a teacher. In comparing single successes with group results, it is revealing that 64% of the Five Town teachers mentioned the former category, and only 29% mentioned the latter, as a major source of satisfaction.

8. One of the predominant feelings that characterize the psychological state of teachers and teaching is *uncertainty*—teachers are not sure whether they have made any difference at all. Intangibility, complexity, and remoteness of learning outcomes, along with other influences (family, peer, and societal) on students, make the teacher's assessment of his or her impact on students endemically uncertain (Lortie, 1975, chap. 6). Of the Five Town teachers, 64% said that they encountered problems in assessing their work; two thirds of them said the problems were serious (p. 142).

9. Of particular relevance to innovation, when Lortie asked teachers how they would choose to spend additional work time, if they received a gift of 10 hours a week, 91% of the almost 6,000 teachers in Dade County selected classroom-related activities (more preparation, more teaching with groups of students, more counseling). "It is also interesting," writes Lortie, "that 91 percent of the first choices are *individualistic*; they are all tasks which teachers normally

perform alone" (p. 164, emphasis added). Second, the lack of time and the feeling of not having finished one's work are a perennial problem experienced by teachers. Unwanted or unproductive interruptions, Lortie observes, "must be particularly galling" (p. 177). Among the Five Town teachers, Lortie found that 62 of the 98 reasons for complaints given by teachers "dealt with time erosion or the disruption of work flow" (p. 178). One can see immediately how unwanted innovations can be another source of annoyance.

So, what has changed over the past 30 years? Not much! For example, a decade later Goodlad (1984) and his colleagues studied a national sample in the United States of 1,350 teachers and their classrooms. His conclusions about the modal patterns of classroom life are not inspiring.

- The dominant pattern of classroom organization is a group to which the teacher most frequently relates as a whole.
- Each student essentially works and achieves alone within a group setting.
- The teacher is virtually autonomous with respect to classroom decisions—selecting materials, determining class organization, choosing instructional procedures.
- Most of the time the teacher is engaged in either frontal teaching, monitoring students' seatwork, or conducting quizzes. Relatively rarely are students actively engaged in learning directly from one another or initiating processes of interaction with teachers.
- There is a paucity of praise and correction of students' performance, as well as of teacher guidance in how to do better next time.
- Students generally engage in a rather narrow range of classroom activities—listening to the teacher, writing answers to questions, and taking tests and quizzes.
- Large percentages of the students surveyed appeared to be passively content with classroom life.
- Even in the early elementary years there was strong evidence of students not having time to finish their lessons or not understanding what the teacher wanted them to do.
- The teacher has little influence or involvement in schoolwide and other extra-classroom matters. (pp. 123–124, 186)

Goodlad proceeds to analyze the conditions under which teachers work. The theme of autonomous isolation stands out. Although teachers functioned independently, "their autonomy seemed to be exercised in a context more of isolation than of rich professional dialogue" (p. 186). Inside schools, "teacher-to-teacher links for mutual assistance or collaborative school improvement were weak or nonexistent" (p. 186). A large majority said that they never observed another teacher teaching, although 75% at all levels of schooling stated that they would like to observe other teachers at work (we shall return to the potential of this latter finding later in this chapter). Teachers also reported that they were not involved in addressing school-wide problems. Outside the school, aside from casual contacts at inservice workshops and meetings, Goodlad found that "there was little to suggest active, ongoing exchanges of ideas and practices across schools, between groups of teachers, or between individuals even in the same schools" (p. 187).

A few years later, Rosenholtz's (1989) study of 78 schools in Tennessee corroborated many of Goodlad's observations. The majority of schools (65 of the 78) were classified by Rosenholtz as relatively "stuck" or "learning impoverished" for both teachers and students. She described these schools as showing little or no attention to school-wide goals. These schools also were characterized by isolation among teachers, limited teacher learning on the job, teacher uncertainty about what and how to teach, and low commitment to the job and the school. This constellation of factors functioned in these schools as a vicious negative cycle to suppress teacher and student desire for achievement. Rosenholtz says "stuck schools" are characterized by

> little attachment to anything or anybody. Teachers seemed more concerned with their own identity than a sense of shared community. Teachers learned about the nature of their work randomly, not deliberately, tending to follow their individual instincts. Without shared governance, particularly in managing student conduct, the absolute number of students who claimed teachers' attention seemed greater . . . teachers talked of frustration, failure, tedium and managed to transfer those attributes to the students about whom they complained. (p. 208)

Rosenholtz explains that isolation and uncertainty are associated with settings where teachers are able to learn little from their colleagues and therefore are not in a strong position to experiment and improve.

Fast forward another decade from Goodlad and we find Hargreaves (1994) talking about "the intensification of teachers' work," in which demands have increased relentlessly.

- Intensification leads to reduced time for relaxation during the working day...
- Intensification leads to lack of time to retool one's skills and keep up with one's field
- Intensification creates chronic and persistent overload...
- Intensification leads to reductions in the *quality* of service, as corners are cut to save on time. (pp. 118–119, emphasis in original)

More recently, in a study of teachers in four countries (Australia, New Zealand, the United Kingdom, and the United States), Scott, Stone, and Dinham (2000) found that teachers still point to the psychic rewards of "seeing children progress" and "making a difference in young people's lives," but they also found a prominent negative theme across the four countries, which the authors labeled "the erosion of the profession" (p. 4). This domain included decrease in status and recognition of the profession; outside interference in and deprofessionalization of teaching, pace, and nature of educational change; and increased workload. In the teachers' words:

Teaching isn't like it used to be and the money isn't worth the abuse we cop day in and day out (Australia).

Classroom teachers are bombarded with paperwork. We spend so much time on useless paperwork that planning, evaluating and teaching time are seriously impacted (U.S.).

Teachers feel like puppets—other people pull our strings. There is little vision left in the teaching profession—it's been weeded out over the last 10 years (U.K.). (p. 8)

But wait, you say, what about the increasing presence of professional learning communities? Surely they represent the kind of direction espoused in this book. The answer is yes, but only *potentially*, because they are proving to be difficult to establish with any depth and spread.

ENTER CHANGE

Of course, change has already entered, and the question is, How can we deal with it and turn it to our and others' advantage? Aside from being inevitable, change is needed. It is necessary because high proportions of students are alienated, performing poorly, or dropping out. Students' lives in school are far less than they should be.

But here we are talking about teachers. In a direct sense, change is needed because many teachers are frustrated, bored, and burned out. Lortie's teachers were not exactly thriving on psychic rewards, primarily because they did not have access to new ideas and had few opportunities for growth. As Sarason (1971) observes, "If teaching becomes neither terribly interesting nor exciting to many teachers, can one expect them to make learning exciting to students?" (pp. 166–167).

In an indirect sense, teachers need to increase their capacity for dealing with change because if they don't, they are going to continue to be victimized by the relentless intrusion of external change forces.

Examining Teacher Interaction

Teacher isolation and its opposite—collegiality—provide the best starting point for considering what works for the teacher. It may be recalled from Chapter 5 that at the teacher level, the degree of change was strongly related to the extent to which teachers *interact* with one another and to others providing technical help and peer support and pressure. Within the school, collegiality among teachers, as measured by the frequency of communication, mutual support, help, and so forth, was a strong indicator of implementation success. Virtually every research study on the topic has found this to be the case. And it does make eminent sense in terms of the theory of change espoused in this book. Significant educational change consists of changes in beliefs, teaching style, and materials, which can come about *only* through a process of personal development in a social context. As Werner (1980) observes in explaining the failure of social studies curriculum in Alberta:

> Ideally, implementation as a minimum includes shared understanding among participants concerning the implied presuppositions, values and assumptions which underlie a program, for if participants understand these, then they have a basis for rejecting, accepting or modifying a program in terms of their own school, community and class situations. To state the aim another way, implementation is an ongoing construction of a shared reality among group members through their interaction with one another within the program. (pp. 62–63)

There is no getting around the *primacy of personal contact*. Teachers need to participate in skill-training workshops, but they also need to have one-to-one and group opportunities to receive and give help and more simply to *converse* about the meaning of change. Under these conditions teachers learn how to use an innovation as well as to judge its desirability on more information-based grounds; they are in a better position to know whether they should accept, modify, or reject the change. This is the case with regard to both externally developed ideas and innovations decided upon or developed by other teachers. Purposeful interaction is essential for continuous improvement.

Fortunately, over the past decade, research has provided a much more specific picture of how purposeful interaction operates within successful schools. The key term is "professional learning community," or what we refer to as "collaborative work cultures" (Fullan & Hargreaves, 1992). The most recent work on PLCs is especially strong, at least on paper (see Dufour et al., 2006; Dufour, Eaker, & Dufour, 2005; Stoll et al., 2006).

I start with Rosenholtz's (1989) description of the collaborative work culture of the 13 "moving" or "learning-enriched" work environments in her study. Figure 7.1 contains an adapted summary of the main school-based elements associated with the successful schools in Rosenholtz's research. There are other factors influencing the six themes, the interactions among which are mul-

FIGURE 7.1. Learning-Enriched Schools

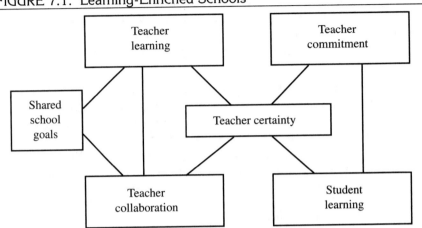

tifaceted, but the composite picture of how successful collaborative schools work is clear and convincing.

As Rosenholtz observes, teacher uncertainty (or low sense of
efficacy) and threats to self-esteem are recurring themes in teaching (Ashton & Webb, 1986). In learning-enriched schools, compared with learning-impoverished schools, Rosenholtz found that
teachers and principals collaborated in goal-setting activities (or
vision building) that "accentuated those instructional objectives
toward which teachers should aim their improvement efforts" (p.
6), and that shared goals served to focus efforts and mobilize resources in agreed-upon directions. Principals and teacher leaders
actively fostered collegial involvement: "Collective commitment
to student learning in collaborative settings directs the definition
of leadership toward those colleagues who instruct as well as inspire awakening all sorts of teaching possibilities in others" (p.
68). In effective schools, collaboration is linked with norms and
opportunities for continuous improvement and career-long learning: "It is assumed that improvement in teaching is a collective
rather than individual enterprise, and that analysis, evaluation,
and experimentation in concert with colleagues are conditions under which teachers improve" (p. 73). As a result, teachers are more
likely to trust, value, and legitimize sharing expertise, seeking ad-

vice, and giving help both inside and outside of the school. They are more likely to become better and better teachers on the job: "All of this means that it is far easier to learn to teach, and to learn to teach better, in some schools than in others" (p. 104).

Becoming better teachers means greater confidence and certainty in deciding on instructional issues and in handling problems. Rosenholtz (1989) found that

> Where teachers request from and offer technical assistance to each other, and where school staff enforces consistent standards for student behavior, teachers tend to complain less about students and parents. Further, where teachers collaborate, where they keep parents involved and informed about their children's progress, where teachers and principals work together to consistently enforce standards for student behavior, and where teachers celebrate their achievements through positive feedback from students, parents, principals, colleagues, and their own sense, they collectively tend to believe in a technical culture and their instructional practice. (p. 137)

Teacher certainty and teacher commitment feed on each other, as Rosenholtz found, increasing teachers' motivation to do even better. All of these factors served to channel energy toward student achievement. Teachers in the learning-enriched schools were less likely to conform to new state or district policies that they judged ill-conceived or as directing energies from classroom priorities, and more likely to assess innovations in terms of their actual impact on students.

Newmann and his colleagues (Kruse, Louis, & Bryk, 1995; Newmann & Wehlage, 1995) have gone ever further in tracing the link between professional learning community, teacher learning, and student performance. In essence, their argument about the internal workings of successful schools is that professional communities make the difference because, in their words:

- Teachers pursue a clear purpose for all students' learning.
- Teachers engage in collaborative activity to achieve the purpose.
- Teachers take collaborative responsibility for student learning.

[And]

- Schoolwide teacher professional community affected the level of classroom authentic pedagogy, which in turn affected student performance.
- Schoolwide teacher professional community affected the level of social support for student learning, which in turn affected student performance. (Newmann & Wehlage, 1995, pp. 30, 32)

What happens in these schools is that teachers as a group and as subgroups examine together how well students are doing, relate this to how they are teaching, and then make improvements. We have called this the need for teachers to become "assessment literate" (Hargreaves & Fullan, 1998; see also Black et al., 2003; Stiggins, 2005). Assessment literacy involves

1. The capacity to examine student performance data and results, and to make critical sense of them.
2. The capacity to act on this understanding by developing classroom and school improvement plans in order to make the kinds of changes needed to increase performance.
3. The capacity of teachers to be effective players in the accountability arena by being proactive and open about school performance data, and by being able to hold their own in the contentious debate about the uses and misuses of achievement data in an era of high-stakes testing.

Our full-blown model for being continuously assessment literate is contained in Fullan, Hill, and Crévola (2006), but for now let us continue down the path of research (and eventually development) on collaborative schools. Bryk and colleagues (1998) traced the evolution of reform in the Chicago school system. After 10 years of monitoring the results and beginning to see success in more and more elementary schools, Bryk and colleagues drew the following conclusion:

In schools making systemic changes, structures are established which create opportunities for such interactions to occur. As teachers develop a broader say in school decision making, they may also begin to experiment with new roles, including working collaboratively. This restructuring of teachers' work signifies a broadening professional community where teachers feel more comfortable exchanging ideas, and where a collective sense of responsibility for student development is likely to emerge. These characteristics of systemic restructuring contrast with conventional school practice where teachers work more autonomously, and there may be little meaningful professional exchange among co-workers. (p. 128)

Bryk and Schneider's (2002) work in Chicago on "trust in schools" continued and deepened the theme of the consequences of collaboration or its opposite. Using longitudinal data, they identified "trust" as a crucial variable. They defined trust as consisting of four components: respect, competence, personal regard for others, and integrity. They traced how trust played itself out in the key relations of principal–teachers, teachers–teachers, teachers–students, and school professionals–parents. Because they had data across years, Bryk and Schneider were able to assess the impact of high and low trust. What they found was

Schools reporting strong positive trust levels in 1994 were three times more likely to be categorized as improving in reading and mathematics than those with very weak trust reports . . . all schools with weak trust reports in both 1994 and 1997 had virtually no chance of showing improvement in either reading or mathematics. (p. 111)

Bryk and Schneider show that relational trust facilitates teachers' efforts to be innovative in the classroom and to reach out to parents, fosters problem solving, undergirds a system of group accountability, and creates a moral resource for improvement due to the "development of strong personal attachments to the organization and beliefs in its mission" (p. 117).

Virtually identical findings come from James, Connolly, Dunning, and Elliot's (2006) in-depth study of 12 "very effective primary schools" in Wales, United Kingdom. They found that highly effective schools dealing successfully with disadvantaged students had, to use their words, a central characteristic and six key supporting elements. They describe the central characteristic as "a productive, strong, and highly inclusive culture that focuses on ensuring effective and enriched teaching for pupils and improving and further enriching teaching for learning for all pupils" (pp.

78–79). The six supporting characteristics are: leadership depth and intensity; the mindset of being empowered, proactive, and optimistic; a teaching team modus operandi; the engagement of pupils and their parents; a very efficient and effective organization and management; and mutual support, validation, and valuing between the school and the community. The overall effect was a highly motivating and energized collaborative culture in which people were passionate about their work together and deeply focused on making and continuing to make changes that would get results. Of particular significance in James and colleagues' study, is how "system leadership" flourished in the 12 schools—leadership at the school, community, district, and larger levels. Engaging the entire system is at the heart of fundamental reform (Fullan, 2005, 2006).

We are getting a common message here, but the balance point is that these strong, productive cultures are difficult to develop and maintain, and remain in the minority. Let us continue to pursue this line of discussion. McLaughlin and Talbert (2001) conducted a study of the role of professional learning communities in 16 high schools in California and Michigan. What they found was confirmatory and revealing as they got inside complex high schools more specifically than have other researchers. They suggest that there are three patterns of teaching practice.

1. Enacting traditions of practice (in which traditional subject-based teaching occurs, and only traditional students succeed)
2. Lowering expectations and standards (in which teachers water down subjects in the face of low-motivated students, which has limited success)
3. Innovating to engage learners (in which subjects and teaching are considered dynamic in order to involve all students, which leads to greater learning by all)

In lowering expectations, for example, teachers tend to locate the problem in the student, as in the following comment from a math teacher:

Oh man, you just sit here and you think how can anybody be that stupid . . . how can they be this damn stupid. The kid is where the problem is today. There is nothing wrong with the curriculum. If I could just get people that wanted to learn, then I could teach and everything would be wonderful. (McLaughlin & Talbert, 2001, p. 13)

By contrast, innovating to engage students involves:

teachers [who] move beyond or outside established frames for instruction to find or develop content and classroom strategies that will enable students to master core subject concepts. . . .
An English teacher uses writing groups; a math teacher creates groups of three ["no more than that," he advises], a science teacher has all but abandoned texts to connect students through lab-based group projects. (pp. 17, 20)

Dovetailing with the theme of this chapter, McLaughlin and Talbert found that "a collaborative community of practice in which teachers share instructional resources and reflections in practice appears essential to their persistence and success in innovating classroom practice" (p. 22). In other words, teachers who were successful with all students, especially those traditionally turned off by school, were constantly figuring out and sharing what works (much like Stigler and Hiebert's [1999] Japanese teachers). More to the point here, these teachers "taught in schools and departments with a strong *professional community* engaged in making innovations that support student and teacher learning and success" (p. 34, emphasis in original).

Overall, McLaughlin and Talbert found that most high school departments lacked a culture of sharing and jointly developing practice. But they found some exceptions, such as differences between departments *within* the same school. For example, "Oak Valley's English department has the strongest technical culture of any department in our sample while the same school's social studies department ranks among the weakest" (p. 47). A veteran English teacher at Oak Valley comments:

It's everyday practice that teachers are handing [out] sample lessons they've done, or an assignment that they've tried, and [discussed] when it worked [or] how they would do it differently. Or a new teacher joins the staff and instantly they are paired up with a couple of buddies . . . and file drawers and computer disks and everything are just made readily available. (p. 50)

In contrast, teachers in the Social Studies department speak of "my materials" but never mention their colleagues as resources. Most revealing is that teachers talk about students with radically different assumptions about learning. English teachers' comments are uniformly positive: "We have excellent students, cooperative, and there's good rapport with the teachers." A Social Studies teacher in turn says, "The kids—there's no quest for knowledge. Not all, but that's in general it's not important to them. They just don't want to learn." Note that these teachers are talking about the *same* students!

McLaughlin and Talbert sum up Oak Valley's two departments.

> In the Social Studies department, autonomy means isolation and reinforces the norms of individualism and conservatism. In the English department, professional autonomy and strong community are mutually reinforcing, rather than oppositional. Here collegial support and interaction enable individual teachers to reconsider and revise their classroom practice confidently because department norms are mutually negotiated and understood. (p. 55)

McLaughlin and Talbert show what a dramatic difference these experiences have for the motivation and career commitments of teachers.

> When teachers from the Oak Valley English and Social Studies departments told us how they feel about their job, it was hard to believe that they teach in the same school. Oak Valley English teachers of all pedagogical persuasions express pride in their department and pleasure in their workplace: "Not a day goes by that someone doesn't say how wonderful it is to work here," said one. In contrast, social studies teachers, weary of grappling alone with classroom tensions, verbalize bitterness and professional disinvestment. Several plan to leave the school or the profession. (pp. 83–84)

McLaughlin and Talbert proceed with similar analyses that we need not report in detail here. For example, they compare two math departments in different schools, one with a well-developed professional community, the other steeped in isolationism. Across all 16 schools, they found only three school-wide learning communities.

In short, weak departments contain teachers who disengage from their jobs, while strong departments evidence teachers who see themselves as lifelong learners. It is not just any kind of professional learning community that counts. Collaboration is powerful, which means it can be powerfully bad as well as powerfully good. Little (1990) warned us about this problem more than 15 years ago.

> The content of teachers' values and beliefs cannot be taken for granted in the study or pursuit of teachers' collegial norms of interaction and interpretation. Under some circumstances, greater contact among teachers can be expected to advance the prospects for students' success; in others, to promote increased teacher-to-teacher contact may be to intensify norms unfavorable to children. (p. 524)

And

> Bluntly put, do we have in teachers' collaborative work the creative development of well-informed choices, or the mutual reinforcement of poorly informed habit? Does teachers' time together advance the understanding and imagination they bring to their work, or do teachers merely confirm one another in present practice? What subject philosophy and subject pedagogy do teachers reflect as they work together, how explicit and accessible is their knowledge to one another? Are there collaborations that in fact erode teachers' moral commitments and intellectual merit? (p. 525)

In a wonderfully insightful summary diagram, McLaughlin and Talbert make the same point (see Figure 7.2). Weak professional communities are bad, no matter how you cut it. Strong teacher communities can be effective or not depending on whether they collaborate to make breakthroughs in learning or whether

FIGURE 7.2. Communities of Practice and the Work of
     High School Teachers

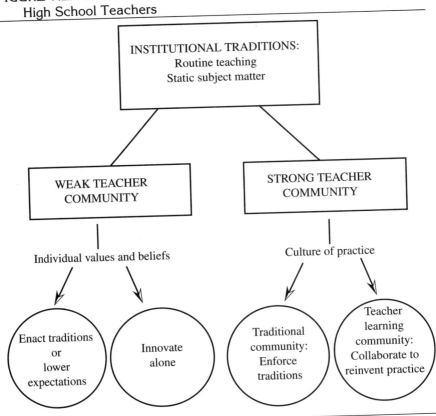

Source: McLaughlin & Talbert, 2001

they reinforce methods that do not get results. In other words,
when teachers collaborate to reinforce one another's bad or ineffective practices, they end up making matters worse.

Developing Professional Learning Communities

We are now in a position to zero in on professional learning communities. On the research side, Kruse and her colleagues (1995)
made the case most succinctly. They note that there are five critical elements that underpin effective PLCs: reflective dialogue, de-

privatization of practice, collective focus on student learning, collaboration, and shared norms and values. Then they identify two major sets of conditions. One is "structural"—in particular, time to meet and talk, physical proximity, interdependent teaching roles, communication structures, and teacher empowerment and school autonomy. The other condition is what Kruse and her colleagues call "social and human resources" (or what we refer to as culture) and includes openness to improvement, trust and respect, cognitive and skill base, supportive leadership, and socialization (of current and incoming staff). They claim, as I do, that the structural conditions are easier to address than the cultural ones. They conclude by observing: "Professional community within schools has been a minor theme in many educational reform efforts since the 1960s. Perhaps it is time that it became a major rallying cry among reformers, rather than a secondary whisper" (p. 6).

Well, it has become a rallying cry for many and certainly has spread in popularity, especially in the past 5 years. It also has served to bring to the fore two conflicting forces: We now know what PLCs should look like (and do look like in the minority of cases); at the same time, we are finding out how very difficult they are going to be to establish on a wide scale. Before turning to the details, let me furnish my own three reasons why PLCs are running into difficulty. These three reasons conspire to prevent progress. First, policymakers do not believe in, do not invest in, or otherwise fail to focus on their development. Indeed, a case could be made that certain policies in vogue, such as narrow accountability schemes, create conditions that inhibit collaboration (see Hargreaves, 1994). Second, when it gets right down to it, many teachers silently play the privatization card, that is, they find privatization a lot less risky than opening the doors of the classroom, even or especially to colleagues. Third, and an amalgam of the previous two, the large-scale development of PLCs is hard—very hard because we are talking about changing culture, one that has endured for at least a century.

When you look at actual cases, the promise and pitfalls of PLCs become evident. I consider two here (McLaughlin & Talbert, 2006; Supovitz, 2006), along with some promising practical resources for developing PLCs on the ground (Dufour et al., 2006; Dufour, Eaker, & Dufour, 2005; Stoll et al., 2006).

Drawing on several of their studies of schools pursuing PLCs, McLaughlin and Talbert (2006) find that these cultures serve to develop three interrelated functions: "they build and manage knowledge; they create shared language and standards for practice and student outcomes; and they sustain aspects of their school culture vital to continued, consistent norms and instructional practice" (p. 5). While providing clear detailed examples of teacher learning communities in action that produce learning results for students, McLaughlin and Talbert ultimately lament, "Why are teacher learning communities rare?" (p. 113). Their answer is similar to mine (developing such communities represents a complex cultural change that is hard to do and is not appealing to policymakers who want a quick fix), although I don't think they give enough attention to teacher resistance to deprivatizing the classroom.

Supovitz's (2006) fine case study of Duval County school district in Florida, which we take up in Chapter 11, supplies another close look at the perils of PLCs even when they are strongly and explicitly promoted over time. Duval County's "Framework for Implementation" consisted of five elements in concert: high performance management through standards, safe schools, use of data, learning communities, and accountability. With 5 years of sustained and focused effort, student achievement did increase moderately in many of Duval's 150 schools, but it was not at all clear what the learning communities strategy actually meant in practice. At one point Supovitz finds teacher autonomy as a phenomenon "quite astounding" (p. 123). It is not a blame statement aimed at teachers when he observes:

> The terrain on which teachers act autonomously is as wide open as the Mohave Desert. There are currently no boundaries that allow leaders to distinguish between legitimate and illegitimate forms of teacher autonomy. In such an environment, it seems that all expressions of autonomy are legitimate because no clear distinctions can be made. (p. 123)

Despite learning communities being an explicit strategy in the district, and despite many structural mechanisms for enacting strategies for sharing practices and using data for improvement, after 5 years Supovitz found that "the possibilities created by professional learning communities—rigorous inquiry into the problems and challenges of instructional practice and the support of that practice—seemed only to be occurring in pockets of the district" (p. 174).

When it comes to PLCs, the strong and clear statements of worth seem to be more normative (what should happen) than real, except in the minority of cases. Fortunately the press for PLCs and the resources to aid and abet them are becoming increasingly explicit. The work by Dufour and colleagues (2006) is especially powerful. Having led the development of PLCs in both elementary and secondary schools, and now being associated with pockets of successful examples across all levels, they essentially "take all the excuses off the table" for policymakers and practitioners alike. Their guide to action for creating PLCs starts with the definition of the core elements of PLCs now familiar to us. Dufour and colleagues define PLCs as consisting of six interrelated elements: a focus on learning, a collaborative culture with a focus on learning for all, collective inquiry into best practice, an action orientation (learning by doing), a commitment to continuous improvement, and a focus on results. In addition to showing how these six elements work in their own right and interdependently, Dufour and colleagues furnish a rubric that is aimed at assessing one's culture in terms of 12 dimensions (more detailed than the six) according to four stages: preinitiation, initiation, developing, and sustaining. Most important of all, they go deeply into the realities of developing collaborative cultures. They reveal that conflict is inevitable and show how to confront it constructively. Above all, their handbook draws two conclusions—developing and maintaining PLCs is damn hard work, and there are no excuses for not getting on with it.

Another very helpful set of resources arises from a research study of PLCs in England by Stoll and her associates (2006). Starting with an investigation of professional learning communities, Stoll and her team identified a now-familiar list of characteristics: shared values, collective responsibility for learning, collaboration focused on learning, group as well as individual learning, reflective professional inquiry, openness/networks/partnerships, inclusive membership, and mutual trust/respect/support. Based on their findings, they have produced 13 small booklets (typically 10 pages or less) as source materials, ranging from "creating and sustaining an effective professional learning community" to "deciding where you are as professional learning community" to "assessing the impact of your professional learning community."

One final set of cautions. First, I have used the shorthand term PLCs. Do not be misled by this. I am not talking about implementing an innovation or program called "Professional Learning Community." In our own work we don't use the term very much, preferring to go straight to capacity building and collaborative cultures within and across the three levels of school and community, district, and state. So make no mistake about it, transforming the *culture* of schools and the systems within which they operate is the main point. It is not an innovation to be implemented, but rather a new culture to be developed.

Second, in the spread of PLCs, we have found that the term travels a lot faster than the concept, a finding common to all innovations. The concept is deep and requires careful and persistent attention in thorough learning by reflective doing and problem solving.

Third, it is a grave mistake to think of PLCs as only an intra-school phenomenon. PLCs should not, ironically, become isolated collaborative cultures. I know of more than one superintendent who has lamented that he or she has one or more PLCs but they don't talk to each other across schools. As we will see in Chapter 11, all schools in the district need to develop in concert. As districts foster collaborative cultures, cross-school learning, or what we call lateral capacity building, is crucial. In large-scale reform, *isolated PLCs are verboten*. In fact, we use lateral capacity building as a strategy to foster PLCs on a wider scale. Both intra- and inter-school learning are required for system transformation.

PROFESSIONALISM AT THE CROSSROADS

Teaching needs to become a highly intellectual as well as a highly caring profession. Because it takes place under intense social and political circumstances, it is also a profession that demands great emotional intelligence. The question is, can the profession become that good? We have just answered this question by pointing to how even the most impressive, well-funded strategies have failed to make much difference in classrooms on any scale. We stressed in our recent book, *Breakthrough*, that the starting point for working toward a solution is the sobering realization that it cannot be done *unless each and every teacher is learning every day* (Fullan et al., 2006). Personal learning in a collective enterprise is the *sine qua non* of large-scale success. How important is it that *all* teachers are learning all the time? We need only reflect on the frightening findings based on research tracing the impact of individual teachers on student success: "Students who had good teachers three years in a row showed a significant increase in their percentile rankings on state examination—regardless of socioeconomic factors" (Education Commission of the States, 2000, p. 5).

Imagine having poor teachers 3 years in row! The teaching profession is at a crossroads because schools by and large are not places where teachers learn collectively every day. Professional learning "in context" is the only learning that ultimately counts for changing classrooms. This is not a slogan, but is the essence of the *new meaning* of educational change that will work for all. Elmore (2004) got it right: "Improvement is more a function of *learning to do the right things* in the settings where you work" (p. 73, emphasis in original). He concludes, as I have discussed previously:

> The problem [is that] there is almost no opportunity for teachers to engage in continuous and sustained learning about their practice *in the settings in which they actually work*, observing and being observed by their colleagues in their own classrooms and classrooms of other teachers in other schools confronting similar problems. (p. 73, emphasis added)

In short, in addition to attracting and training better teachers and leaders, we must change the very cultures within which they work. And this has proven to be an intractable problem to do on any scale. My proof for this conclusion is that we knew specifically and clearly a quarter of a century ago how powerful collaborative or collegial cultures were and how they functioned (Little, 1981). Twenty-five years is a long time to sit on knowledge that serves the very moral core of school improvement.

As this whole book claims, this is not just an individual problem. It is a system problem. It includes teachers, individually and collectively, but if there is any changing to be done, *everyone is implicated*. We have recently furnished a set of ideas and techniques for school communities to generate their own *Learning Places* (Fullan & St. Germain, 2006). The infrastructure surrounding teachers is also critical and at this point not all that helpful in building powerful changes in context. Subsequent chapters take up aspects of this wider infrastructure one by one. I start with the most immediate source of help or hindrance—the school principal.

CHAPTER 8

The Principal

Effective principals attack incoherence.
—Bryk, Sebring, Kerbow, Rollow, and Easton
(1998, p. 287)

Forget about the principal as head of the school for a moment and think of her or him as someone just as buffeted as the teacher is by wanted or unwanted and often incomprehensible changes—and, what is more, *expected to lead these very changes.* Change is only one of the forces competing for the principal's attention, and usually not the most compelling one. And when it is compelling, as is the case recently, it is difficult to focus and sustain the work needed for reform to be effective. Yet some principals are actively engaged as initiators or facilitators of continuous improvements in their schools. The principal is in the middle of the relationship between teachers and external ideas and people. As in most human triangles, there are constant conflicts and dilemmas. How the principal approaches (or avoids) these issues determines to a large extent whether these relationships constitute a Bermuda triangle of innovations.

An understanding of what reality is *from the point of view of people within the role* is an essential starting point for constructing a practical theory of the meaning and results of change attempts. This phenomenology is social science's contribution to addressing the frequent lament, "No one understands me." In the field of educational change, everyone feels misunderstood. One of the most revealing and frustrating indicators of the difficulties in educational change is the participants' frequent experience of having their intentions not only misunderstood but interpreted exactly opposite of what they meant. Principals should have no problem claiming their fair share of frustration, since the role of the principal has become dramatically more complex and overloaded over the past decade. On the optimistic side, very recent research has identified some specific change-related behaviors of principals who deal effectively with educational change. It is time to go beyond the empty phrase, "The principal is the gatekeeper of change."

While research on school improvement is now into its fourth decade, systematic research on what the principal actually does and its relationship to stability and change is quite recent. Some of the earlier implementation research identified the role of the principal as central to promoting or inhibiting change, but it did not examine the principal's role in any depth or perspective. By the 1990s, research had accumulated that put principals front and center in leading improvement at the school and community levels. Today, no serious change effort would fail to emphasize the key role of the principal. Most provide both professional development and altered job descriptions highlighting the role of the principal in leading change on the ground. The irony is that as the change expectations heighten, the *principalship* itself has become overloaded in a way that makes it impossible to fulfill the promise of widespread, sustained reform.

I start with a description of where principals are. I then turn to the part of their role that interests us the most—what principals do and don't do in relation to change. In the last section of the chapter, I talk about the complexity of leadership and offer some guidelines for how principals might lead change more effectively. I also should acknowledge at the outset that effective principals share—in fact, develop—leadership among teachers. So we are really talking about assistant principals, department heads, grade-level coordinators, and teacher leaders of all types in the school.

WHERE PRINCIPALS ARE

"Pressure drives heads to drink" (2000) blares a headline in the *Times Education Supplement* in England. The article reports that among the principals and deputy principals in the district of Warwickshire (a district with 250 schools), 40% had visited the doctor with stress-related problems in the past year, and 30% were taking medication. Warwickshire was selected, says the article, because it was considered to be a well-run district—a good employer!

With the move toward the self-management of schools, the principal appears to have the worst of both worlds. The old world is still around, with expectations that the principal will run a smooth school and to be responsive to all; simultaneously, the new world rains down on schools with disconnected demands, expecting that at the end of the day the school constantly should be showing better test results and ideally becoming a learning organization.

In *What's Worth Fighting for in the Principalship?* (Fullan, 1997), I reported on a study of 137 principals and vice principals in Toronto. The growing overload experienced by principals was evident over 20 years ago: 90% reported an increase over the previous 5 years in the demands made on their time, including new program demands, the number of board priorities and directives, and the number of directives from the Ministry of Education. Time demands were listed as having increased in dealing with parent and community groups (92% said there was an increase), trustee requests (91%), administration activities (88%), staff involvement and student services (81%), social services (81%), and board initiatives (69%).

Principals and vice principals also were asked about their perceptions of effectiveness: 61% reported a *decrease in principal effectiveness*, with only 13% saying it was about the same, and 26% reporting an increase. The same percentage, 61%, reported decreases in "the effectiveness of assistance from immediate superiors and from administration." Further, 84% reported a decrease in the authority of the principal; 72%, a decrease in trust in leadership of the principal; and 76%, a decrease in principal involvement in decision making at the system level. To the question, "Do you think the principal can effectively fulfill all the responsibilities assigned to him/her?" 91% responded "no" (Fullan, 1997, p. 2).

The discouragement felt by principals in attempting to cover all the bases is aptly described in the following three responses from interviews conducted by Duke (1988) with principals who were considering quitting:

The conflict for me comes from going home every night acutely aware of what didn't get done and feeling after six years that I ought to have a better batting average than I have.

If you leave the principalship, think of all the "heart-work" you're going to miss. I fear I'm addicted to it and to the pace of the principalship—those 2,000 interactions a day. I get fidgety in meetings because they're too slow, and I'm not out there interacting with people.

The principalship is the kind of job where you're expected to be all things to all people. Early on, if you're successful, you have gotten feedback that you are able to be all things to all people. And then you feel an obligation to continue to do that which in your own mind you're not capable of doing. And that causes some guilt. (p. 309)

Duke was intrigued by the "dropout rate" of principals after encountering an article stating that 22% of Vermont administrators employed in the fall of 1984 had left the state's school systems by the fall of 1985. In interviewing principals about why they considered quitting, he found that sources of dissatisfaction included policy and administration, lack of achievement, sacrifices in personal life, lack of growth opportunities, lack of recognition and too little responsibility, relations with subordinates, and lack of support from superiors. They expressed a number of concerns about the job itself: the challenge of doing all the things that principals are expected to do, the mundane or boring nature of much of the work, the debilitating array of personal interactions, the politics of dealing with various constituencies, and the tendency for managerial concerns to supersede leadership functions. Duke suggested that the reasons principals were considering quitting were related to fatigue, awareness of personal limitations, and awareness of the limitation of career choices. Principals experienced reality shock, "the shock-like reactions of new workers when they find themselves in a work situation for which they have spent several years preparing and for which they thought they were going to be prepared, and then suddenly find that they are not." Duke concludes:

A number of frustrations expressed by these principals derived from the contexts in which they worked. Their comments send a clear message to those who supervised them: principals need autonomy *and* support. The need for autonomy may require supervisors to treat each principal differently; the need for support may require supervisors to be sensitive to each principal's view of what he or she finds meaningful or trivial about the work. (p. 312, emphasis in original)

There is no question that the demands on the principalship have become even more intensified over the past 10 years, 5 years, 1 year. More and more principals in almost every Western country are retiring early; more and more potential teacher leaders are concluding that it is simply not worth it to take on the leadership of schools.

Wanted: A miracle worker who can do more with less, pacify rival groups, endure chronic second-guessing, tolerate low levels of support, process large volumes of paper and work double shifts (75 nights a year). He or she will have carte blanche to innovate, but cannot spend much money, replace any personnel, or upset any constituency. (Evans, 1995, p. 5)

Is this an impossible job? A job that is simply not worth the aggravation and toll it takes? Even students notice, such as this secondary student: "I don't think being a head is a good job. You have to work too hard. Some days [the head] looks knackered— sorry, very tired" (Day, Harris, Hadfield, Toley, & Beresford, 2000, p. 126).

At the present time, the principalship is not worth it, and therein lies the solution. If effective principals energize teachers in complex times, what is going to energize principals? We are now beginning to see more clearly examples of school principals who are successful. These insights can help existing principals become more effective; even more, they provide a basis for establishing a system of recruiting, nurturing, and supporting and holding accountable school leaders (see Chapter 14).

THE PRINCIPAL AND CHANGE

Until recently the principal was often neglected in the formulation of strategies for reform. As research mounted about the significant

impact of the principal, for better or for worse, on reform outcomes, policymakers began to incorporate the role of school leaders in leading change initiatives. This has not proven easy to do,
and in fact has helped to illuminate the fundamental difficulties
of changing school cultures. Let us trace the evolution of this interesting phenomenon over the past decade, and especially the
past 5 years. I know of no improving school that doesn't have a
principal who is good at leading improvement. "Almost every
single study of school effectiveness has shown both primary and
secondary leadership to be a key factor," says Sammons (1999) in
her major review.

The first half of my argument—to consolidate the case for
how and why the principal is crucial for success—is presented in
this section. In the following section I take up the second half of
the analysis to show the problems encountered when you take
these findings seriously and attempt to incorporate them into
change strategies. There are several quality studies of school leadership across different countries that provide consistent and clear,
not to say easy, messages (Bryk & Schneider, 2002; Bryk et al.,
1998; Day et al., 2000; James et al., 2006; Leithwood et al., 2004,
2005; Marzano et al., 2005; McLaughlin & Talbert, 2001, 2006;
Newmann, King, & Youngs, 2000).

Bryk and his colleagues (1998) have been tracing the evolution
of reform in Chicago schools since 1988. In schools that evidenced
improvement over time (about one third of 473 elementary schools):

> Principals worked together with a supportive base of parents,
> teachers, and community members to mobilize initiative. Their
> efforts broadly focused along two major dimensions: first,
> reaching out to parents and community to strengthen the ties
> between local school professionals and the clientele they are to
> serve; and second, working to expand the professional capaci-
> ties of individual teachers, to promote the formation of a coher-
> ent professional community, and to direct resources toward en-
> hancing the quality of instruction. (p. 270)

These successful principals had (1) an "inclusive, facilitative
orientation"; (2) an "institutional focus on student learning"; (3)
"efficient management"; and (4) "combined pressure and sup-

port." They had a strategic orientation, using school improvement plans and instructional focus to "attack incoherence."

> In schools that are improving, teachers are more likely to say that, once a program has begun, there is follow-up to make sure it is working and there is real continuity from one program to another. In our earlier research, we dubbed schools with high levels of incoherence "Christmas tree schools." Such schools were well-known showcases because of the variety of programs they boasted. Frequently, however, these programs were uncoordinated and perhaps even philosophically inconsistent. (Bender, Sebring, & Bryk, 2000, pp. 441–442)

In continued work in Chicago, Bryk and Schneider (2002) found that principals are crucial for shaping "trust in schools," which has dramatic influences, both direct and indirect, on the effectiveness of the school, as noted in Chapter 7. They refer to "the *centrality* of principal leadership" in developing and sustaining relational trust, which establishes the conditions for success (p. 137, emphasis added). They conclude that "only when participants demonstrate their commitment to engage in such work [focused on improvement] and see others doing the same can a genuine professional community grounded in relational trust emerge. [In this respect] principals must take the lead" (p. 139).

Other studies of schools improving are variations on these same themes. In Chapter 7, we saw the effects of strong and weak professional communities in the high schools studied by McLaughlin and Talbert. Leadership (or lack of it) at the department and/or school level accounted for a large part of these differences.

> These very different worlds reveal how much department leadership and expectations shape teacher community. The English department chair actively maintained open department boundaries so that teachers would bring back knowledge resources from districts and out of district professional activities to the community. English faculty attended state and national meetings, published regularly in professional journals, and used professional development days to visit classrooms in other schools. The chair gave priority for time to share each other's writing, discuss new projects, and just talk. English department leadership extended and reinforced expectations and opportunities

for teacher learning provided by the district and by the school, developing a rich repertoire of resources for the community to learn.

None of this applied down the hall in the social studies department, where leadership enforced the norms of privatism and conservatism that Dan Lortie found central to school teaching. For example, the Social Studies chair saw department meetings as an irritating ritual rather than an opportunity: "I don't hold meetings once a week; I don't even necessarily have them once a month." Supports or incentives for learning were few in the social studies department. This department chair marginalized the weakest teachers in the department, rather than enabling or encouraging their professional growth. (McLaughlin & Talbert, 2001, pp. 107–108)

Recall from Chapter 7 that only 3 of 16 high schools demonstrated school-wide professional communities. In these comparisons McLaughlin and Talbert talk about "the pivotal role of principal leadership."

The utter absence of principal leadership within Valley High School is a strong frame for the weak teacher community we found across departments in the school; conversely, strong leadership in Greenfield, Prospect and Ibsen has been central to engendering and sustaining these school-wide teacher learning communities. Principals with low scores [on leadership, as perceived by teachers] generally are seen as managers who provide little support or direction for teaching and learning in the school. Principals receiving high ratings are actively involved in the sorts of activities that nurture and sustain strong teacher community. (p. 110)

In their more recent and systematic review of professional learning communities, McLaughlin and Talbert (2006) again tout the principal as central to success. They show that principals are in a strategic position to promote or inhibit the development of a teacher learning community in their schools. They found that effective principals "leverage teacher commitment and support for collaboration," "broker and develop learning resources for teacher communities," and "support transitions between stages of community development" (p. 56). In so doing principals also spread and develop leaders across the school, thereby creating a critical mass of distributive leadership as a resource for the present and the future.

Day and his colleagues (2000) in England wrote a book on the leadership roles in 12 schools, all of which "had consistently raised student achievement levels—in this sense they were 'improving schools'—and all the headteachers were recognized as being instrumental in this and in the overall success of the schools" (p. 1). We observe a now-familiar refrain.

> The vision and practices of these heads were organized around a number of core personal values concerning the modeling and promotion of respect [for individuals], fairness and equality, caring for the well-being and whole development of students and staff, integrity and honesty. (p. 39)

These school leaders were "relationship centered," focused on "professional standards," "outwards looking in" (seeking ideas and connections across the country), and "monitoring school performance." Day and associates conclude:

> Within the study, there was also ample evidence that people were trusted to work as powerful professionals, within clear collegial value frameworks, which were common to all. There was a strong emphasis upon teamwork and participation in decision-making (though heads reserved the right to be autocratic). Goals were clear and agreed, communications were good and everyone had high expectations of themselves and others. Those collegial cultures were maintained, however, within contexts of organization and individual accountability set by external policy demands and internal aspirations. These created ongoing tensions and dilemmas, which had to be managed and mediated as part of the establishment and maintenance of effective leadership cultures. (p. 162)

Additional confirmation and clarity are furnished by Newmann and his colleagues (2000), who used the more comprehensive concept of "school capacity," which in turn affects instructional quality and student assessment in the school as a whole. School capacity consists of the collective effectiveness of the whole staff working together to improve student learning for all. Five interrelated components of school capacity were identified:

1. Teachers' knowledge, skills, and dispositions
2. Professional community
3. Program coherence
4. Technical resources
5. Principal leadership

First, professional development related to the knowledge, skills, and dispositions of teachers as individual staff members is a necessary but insufficient element. Obviously this is important and can make a difference in individual classrooms, but unless connected to collective learning, it fails to influence the culture of the school. Hence the second factor, which is that there also must be organization development because social or relationship resources are key to school improvement. Thus, schools must combine individual development with the development of *school-wide professional communities*. Individual and collective development need to be twinned if they are to result in increased school capacity.

However, individual development combined with professional communities is still not sufficient, unless it is channeled in a way that combats the fragmentation of multiple innovations by working on *program coherence*, "the extent to which the school's programs for student and staff learning are coordinated, focused on clear learning goals, and sustained over a period of time" (Newmann et al., 2000, p. 5). Program coherence is organizational focus and integration. Fourth, instructional improvement requires additional *resources* (materials, equipment, space, time, and access to expertise). Finally, school capacity cannot be developed in the absence of quality leadership. Put differently, *the role of the principal is to cause the previous four factors to get better and better in concert*. Elmore (2000) agrees.

> The job of administrative leaders is primarily about enhancing the skills and knowledge of people in the organization, creating a common culture of expectations around the use of those skills and knowledge, holding the various pieces of the organization together in a productive relationship with each other, and hold-

ing individuals accountable for their contributions to the collective result. (p. 15)

James and colleagues (2006), whose study we reviewed in Chapter 7, supplies an even more compelling and deeply nuanced account of the role of school heads in 12 "very effective primary schools" in Wales. Without exception, say James and colleagues, "they all recognized and articulated the importance of enabling the pupils to learn and of continually improving teaching in the school" (p. 89). These school heads also developed leadership in others, had a modesty about themselves, grasped the big picture, and fostered partnerships with governing bodies, the local authority, and networks beyond the school. The role of leadership, suggest James and colleagues, concerns "those behaviours that enabled others to take up their role in relation to the institution's main and defined task" (p. 97).

My colleague Ken Leithwood has been studying and developing school leadership for 4 decades. Leithwood, Bauer, and Riedlinger's (2006) current research in New Orleans is an excellent example of testing the limits of the principalship (if there was ever a litmus test for the role of principal under trying conditions, it has to be New Orleans—pre- and/or post-Katrina). Principals were part of a fellows program that supported and cultivated their leadership over time. Leithwood and his colleagues drew 10 lessons from their multiyear study of these principals:

1. Dramatic individual change is possible.
2. One good experience can jump-start a continuous learning ethos.
3. Ongoing support is needed if leaders are to influence student learning.
4. Training should encompass the team as well as the individual principal.
5. Direct, practical help in data-driven decision making is especially critical in the current policy environment.
6. Practice what you preach.
7. A little bit of money goes a long way.
8. For a long-term impact, build a community of leaders.
9. Use the community of leaders to retain successful leaders.

10. Use inspiring leadership models to recruit new leaders.

Leithwood and colleagues stress that a key factor was the availability of opportunities "to continuously discuss and examine programs and practices, to incorporate feedback from fellows, to nurture the network among fellows and otherwise act as steward of the mission" (p. 23).

As part of a major multiyear initiative being conducted under the auspices of the Wallace Foundation, Leithwood and his team (2004) recently analyzed existing research studies in order to determine what we know about "how leadership influences student learning." Not only did they review the research field, they also included a "review of reviews," thus consolidating a massive amount of research on the topic. This comprehensive review found that successful leaders engaged in three sets of core practices.

1. Setting directions (shared vision and group goals, high performance expectations)
2. Developing people (individual support, intellectual/emotional stimulation, modeling)
3. Redesigning the organization (collaborative cultures and structures, building productive relations with parents and the community)

Leithwood's group concluded that school leadership accounts for one quarter of the variation on student achievement explained by school-level variables (school-level variables themselves are but a smaller set of other factors such as family background).

In another thorough review, Marzano, Waters, and McNulty (2005) drew similar conclusions. In *School Leadership That Works*, they examined 69 studies involving 2,802 schools and approximately 1.4 million students and 14,000 teachers. They also found a .25 correlation between the leadership behavior of the principal and student achievement. They identified 21 specific behaviors that influence student learning, most of them indirectly (but nonetheless explicitly), through shaping the culture and relationships of people within the school and between the school and the outside.

It should be clear, then, that school improvement is an organizational phenomenon, and therefore the principal, as leader, is the key. With all this confirmation from the research literature and with many current attempts to situate the principal as change leader, one would think that it would be a slam dunk to make progress. Well it is not, and here is where progress means digging deeper into the problem and its solution.

THE COMPLEXITY OF LEADERSHIP

Let us first examine three cases where the role of the principal was featured as a core part of the change strategy. First recall the case studies of Chicago, Milwaukee, and Seattle conducted by the Cross City Campaign for Urban School Reform (2005). Money galore and a lot of the seemingly "right" components were incorporated into a district-wide multiyear strategy: a focus on literacy and math, a concentration on assessment for learning data, plenty of professional development, and an emphasis on principals as instructional leaders, with significant accompanying professional development. The end result was limited impact on the classroom. Although they were positioned to play a key role, "principals had multiple responsibilities that often worked at cross purposes with their role of instructional leaders" (p. 9).

With even more prominence, the principalship was central to the delivery of the high-profile, highly supported literacy and math reform in the San Diego City Schools District in the 1997–2002 period (Hubbard, Mehan, & Stein, 2006). The theory of action envisioned principals as "the most critical resource in the professional guidance and instructional direction of school." Called on to be "leaders of instruction," principals were to spend more time in classrooms, engaging teachers in conversations about instruction, and to spend less time on administrative, logistical and financial matters" (p. 75). Principals also received considerable targeted support, including close working with relationships with instructional leaders (a former area superintendent role refashioned to support school improvement). All principals in the district engaged in walk-throughs with their instructional leader, monthly principal conferences where instruction was the only topic, mentorship, support groups, and visits to other schools to observe exemplary practice. In other words, the strategy called for highly detailed and explicit roles for principals as instructional change agents on an ongoing basis. Yet, enormous difficulties were encountered in linking school leadership to instructional improvement across classrooms. I will turn to explanations in a moment, but first one more case.

Supovitz's (2006) case study of Duval County in Florida is equally instructive. Again this is a case of district-wide, 5-year (at this point) reform with a relentless focus on instruction. And once more, principals are recognized as key players, "integral to the spread of instructional reform" (p. 85). Considerable emphasis and support were provided for the professional development of principals for their new role. And again it did not pan out as envisioned.

What is going on here? Finally, policymakers and district leaders take the research findings on the role of principals seriously, and still hit a wall. In my view, there are three fundamental explanations. First, maybe districts have the strategy wrong. They are expecting principals to carry out roles that are centrally (district) determined. In this case principals are in the unenviable role of trying to figure out somebody else's strategy. Second, maybe the role as instructional leader is far more daunting than people imagined. Thus, the capacity to be this good requires understanding and skills beyond the preparation and inservice development experiences of most principals. Third, the new expectations have been added on to the traditional ones without any consideration of whether the new role in its entirety is feasible under the current working conditions faced by principals.

I favor all three explanations in combination. The net effect is that the principalship is being placed in an impossible position. In short, the changes required to transform cultures are far deeper than we understood; principals do not have the capacity to carry out the new roles; and principals are burdened by too many role responsibilities that inhibit developing and practicing the new competencies—add-ons without anything being taken away. Hard change, low capacity, plenty of distractions—a recipe for frustration. In sum, the principal is key, but we haven't yet figured out how to position the role to fulfill the promise.

Chapter 7 and this one, in combination, present a powerful

message for school reform. Remember the study that found that students who got three good teachers in 3 successive years did much better? Well, students in schools led by principals who foster strong professional communities are much more likely to encounter three good teachers in a row, whether it be on the same day or over the years. The problem is that such schools are in the minority. Definitely unfinished business on the change agenda.

CHAPTER 9

The Student

> *Why in a democratic society, should an individual's first real contact with a formal institution be so profoundly antidemocratic?*
> —Bowles and Gintis (1976, pp. 250–251)

In the field of educational innovation it is surprising how many times a teacher will finally shout out of desperation, "But what about the students?" Innovations and their inherent conflicts often become ends in themselves, and students get thoroughly lost in the shuffle. When adults do think of students, they think of them as the potential beneficiaries of change. They think of achievement results, skills, attitudes, and jobs. *They rarely think of students as participants in a process of change and organizational life.* While research in the 1980s began to look at students as active participants in their own education, and it has become clearer what should be done, too little actually has happened to enhance the role of students as members of the school as an organization.

In this chapter, I continue to pursue the main theme of the book. Educational change, above all, is a people-related phenomenon for each and every individual. Students, even little ones, are people, too. Unless they have some meaningful (to them) role in the enterprise, most educational change, indeed most education, will fail. I ask the reader not to think of students as running the school, but to entertain the following question: What would happen if we treated the student as someone whose opinion mattered in the introduction and implementation of reform in schools? If meaning matters to the success of teachers and principals, it doesn't take much imagination to realize that meaning is central to student success. *Engagement* is the key word. All successful education ends up engaging the hearts and minds of students. It was one thing to try to do this when only 50% of the student population went on to continuing education; it is an entirely more complex matter when we attempting to involve 95% or more of students in meaningful learning.

Little progress has been made since the first edition of this book in 1982 in treating the student as a serious member of the school. While cognitive scientists and sociologists have made the case for the more fundamental role of students in their learning, the latter remains only an unfulfilled potential. To be clear about the argument at the outset, cognitive scientists claim that, traditionally, teaching has "focused too narrowly on the memorization of information, giving short shrift to critical thinking, conceptual understanding, and in-depth knowledge of subject matter" (National Research Council, 1999, p. 25). Teaching and learning for deep understanding (so that learners can critically apply what they know to comprehending and addressing new problems and situations) has now become the goal of this new and radical pedagogy (Bransford et al., 1999; Gardner, 1999).

At the same time, but operating entirely independently, sociologists have long argued that schools reproduce a hierarchical status quo in a way that actually increases the gap between those who are well off in the first place and those who are disadvantaged. This inequitable circumstance, they say, is deeply embedded in the structures and cultures of society, and manifested in turn in school systems (Oakes et al., 1999).

The new common ground for both cognitive scientists and sociologists concerns *motivation and relationships*, that is, it is only when schooling operates in a way that connects students relationally in a relevant, engaging, and worthwhile experience, that substantial learning will occur. That only a small proportion of students are so engaged is a measure of the seriousness of the problem.

To state the matter differently, the more that accountability systems become focused only on cognitive achievement, the greater the gap will become between those students who are doing well and those who are not. This is so because the main problem with disengaged students is that they lack a meaningful personal connection with teachers and others in the school; in other words, they lack the motivational capacity to become engaged in learning. Incidentally, this is why emotional development for children must go hand-in-hand with cognitive development. Emotionally developed students have the individual and social skills that enable them to become motivationally engaged with other learners, which in turn is a route to greater cognitive achievement (see Gordon, 2005). Of course, emotional intelligence is a desired goal in its own right because it produces better citizens who can function well in a complex, stressful world (Goleman, 1995, 1998).

In short, we must combine the ideas of cognitive scientists, who are working on the problem of how to engage all learners, with the insights of sociologists, who show how power relations in the school must be altered if we are to make substantial progress on this agenda. When these two forces become integrated into the culture of professional learning communities, educators in these types of schools function in effect as "moral change agents," or in Oakes and associates' (1999) phrase, educators with "a passion for the public good." But where are students in this equation? I will discuss two facets of student engagement in the context of *reconstituting classroom culture* and *reconstituting school culture*.

WHERE STUDENTS ARE

Research on the experiences of students has been limited and dispersed across many fields. Access to and furthering of this work has just been aided tremendously by the impressive *International Handbook of Student Experience in Elementary and Secondary Schools* put together by my colleague Dennis Thiessen (in press). Containing 28 chapters and over 1,300 pages, this handbook pretty much brings together what we know at this stage. It shows the dearth of attention in any substantial way to student engagement, but also the promise that there is a strand in this research that brings the student to life. Thiessen starts with the conclusion by Erickson and Shultz (1992), who focused on student experiences and the curriculum. In this research, students "are shown as *doing* in the classroom rather than as *thinking, intending,* and *caring*" (p. 480, emphasis in original). Erickson and Schultz conclude:

In sum, virtually no research has been done that places student experience at the center of attention. We do not see student interests and their known and unknown fears. We do not see the mutual interest of students and teachers or see what the student or the teacher thinks or cares about during the course of that mutual interest. If the student is visible at all in a research study she is usually viewed from the perspective of adult educator's interests and ways of seeing, that is, as failing, succeeding, motivated, mastering, unmotivated, responding, or having a misconception. Rarely is the perspective of the student herself explored. Much further research needs to be done to uncover the kinds of variations in student experience that may obtain within and across subject matters and within and across grade levels. Indeed, we have suggested here that the evolution of student experience with curriculum should be studied across the entire student career in school. We know relatively little about the social and cognitive ecology of student experience of curriculum. How does this vary with the social backgrounds of students and teachers, and by types of schools in which they learn and teach? Presently we do not understand how intellect, will, culture, and politics meet at the intersection of curriculum materials, classroom arrangements, pedagogical approaches, and students, within whose subjective experience learning presumably takes place (pp. 467–468).

From 1970 to 1977, I was involved in a research project focusing on the role of students in Ontario schools (see Fullan & Eastabrook, 1973; Fullan, Eastabrook, & Biss, 1977). My colleagues and I started with a survey of students in 46 Ontario schools representing a range of large-city, medium-sized-city, suburban, and rural settings. Information was gathered from a random sample of students in grades 5 through 13 (Ontario high schools went up to grade 13 at the time). The information was collected directly by us in classrooms using a questionnaire. The original sample was 3,972, from which we obtained 3,593 returns, or a 90% response rate. Questions included both fixed-choice formats and open-ended questions that asked for comments. We categorized the responses according to three levels: elementary school (grades 5–6, or 5–8 in some schools), junior high (grades 7–9), and high school (grades 9–13, or 10–13 in some schools). The following summarizes our main findings:

1. A minority of students thought that teachers understood their point of view, and the proportion decreased with educational level—41%, 33%, and 25% from elementary, junior high, and high school, respectively.
2. Less than one fifth of the students reported that teachers asked for their opinions and ideas in deciding what or how to teach (19%, 16%, 13%), a finding that we consistently replicated in subsequent work in a large number of classrooms in other schools.
3. Principals and vice principals were not seen as listening to or being influenced by students.
4. Substantial percentages of students (29%, 26%, 50%), including one out of every two high school students, reported that "most of my classes or lessons are boring."

Written comments on open-ended questions elaborated the meaning of the fixed-format responses. About 1,000 students (of the total of almost 3,600) wrote comments about their school. Of these, about 30% reflected such positive attitudes as:

- Teachers are friendly. (elementary)
- This school is great. (junior high)
- I think the school I go to is good the way it is now. It doesn't need any changes. (junior high)
- I like my school because it has modern techniques, teaching methods, and facilities. It is a clean and up-to-date school. I think they should keep the school just the way it is. (high school)

The other 70% of the comments were indicative of what we labeled generally "the alienation theme":

- I think schools should make students feel comfortable, and not tense. (high school)
- I feel that teachers don't really care about what happens to students as long as they get paid. (elementary)
- I know that school is important to me and that I need it to get anywhere in life. But I'm beginning to realize that this reason is not good enough. I don't enjoy school at this

point. It is the last place I want to be. If I wasn't so shy I imagine I could express these feelings to a teacher, but I've never spoken to one, not even about extra help. (high school)

- I'm only in school so I can go to university so as to make more money than if I quit school now. I do not particularly like school, in fact sometimes I hate it, but I don't particularly want to be poor. (high school)

Our questions on principals and vice principals stimulated many comments from junior high and senior high students, along the following lines:

- I have never spoken to the principal, and I don't even know who the vice principal is.
- It's hard to say anything about the principal. He's always hiding.
- We never see him, and I think the only kids he knows is the head boy and the head girl. He seems like a nice man, but who really knows, when he is always in his office.

Finally, we asked students an open-ended question about what they thought of the questionnaire and the project. This opened a floodgate. Over one third of the students wrote responses, nearly all of which indicated that students were interested in the topics and had something to say. Typical of these 1,200 responses were the following:

- I think this project is very interesting in many ways. It asks many questions that I have never been asked before. (elementary)
- I think it's great the grown-ups want our opinion. I feel that they treat us like babies. (elementary)
- It brought me to thinking about things I had never thought much about, and is giving you at the institution, knowledge of what we students think about the school. (junior high)
- No comment. Only that this may help the teachers or planning board realize what lousy classes and subjects we are taking. (high school)

- I think this is an excellent project. It gives the man at the bottom of the ladder a chance to unleash his feelings and say something about this damn school. (high school)

Over the years, not much has changed for most students, other than the fact that life has become more complicated. Based on his nationwide study, Goodlad (1984) states that "learning appears to be enhanced when students understand what is expected of them, get recognition for their work, learn quickly about their errors, and receive guidance in improving their performance" (p. 111). Yet, he found that "over half of the upper elementary students reported that many students did not know what they were supposed to do in class" (p. 112). At least 20% of high school students did not understand teachers' directions and comments. Striking at the core of the theme in this book, Goodlad observes:

> Somewhere, I suspect, down in the elementary school, probably in the fifth and sixth grades, a subtle shift occurs. The curriculum—subjects, topics, textbooks, workbooks, and the rest—comes between the teacher and student. Young humans come to be viewed only as students, valued primarily for their academic aptitude and industry rather than as individual persons preoccupied with the physical, social, and personal needs unique to their circumstances and stage in life. (p. 80)

As students moved through the grades, Goodlad and his colleagues found that "there was increasingly less use of teacher praise and support for learning, less corrective guidance, a narrowing range and variety of pedagogical techniques, and declining participation by students in determining the daily conduct of their education" (p. 125). We see, says Goodlad, "a decline from lower to upper grades in teachers' support of students as persons and learners" (p. 126).

Sarason (1982) similarly claims that students at the elementary level are not party to how classroom patterns are established. He conducted an informal observational study to see how the rules of the classroom were formed (what he calls the "constitution of the classroom") and what assumptions about students were implicit in the process. In Sarason's words, "The results were quite clear." The rules invariably were determined by the teacher, and teachers never solicited the opinions and feelings of students in developing rules. Sarason suggests several assumptions underlying the observed behavior.

1. Teacher knows best;
2. Children cannot participate constructively in the development of rules;
3. Children are not interested in such a discussion;
4. Rules are for children, and not for the teacher (rules state what children can and cannot do, but not what a teacher could or could not do), and so on. (pp. 175–176)

Sarason observed that teachers rarely, if ever, discussed their own thinking about planning and learning. Issues never came up pertaining to teachers' assumptions and theories of learning and thinking, whether children were interested in these matters, and whether they were able to talk about them. Rather, the task of the student was to get the right answer and know the facts. Sarason comments that teachers "unwittingly [created] those conditions that they would personally find boring" (p. 182).

The central issue, however, is contained in the following passage:

> The point I wish to emphasize is that it appears that children know relatively little about how a teacher thinks about the classroom, that is, what he takes into account, the alternatives he thinks about, the things that puzzle him about children and about learning, what he does when he is not sure of what he should do, how he feels when he does something wrong. (p. 185)

I referred earlier to students' lives becoming more complex. Dryden (1995) spent a year observing in classrooms in a high school in Ontario and concluded that "so much is going on in each kid's life, every story is so complicated" (p. 84). Students often are disengaged from their own learning, and it is enormously difficult for teachers to enter their world. Many teachers, reports Dryden, end up, metaphorically speaking, teaching "to the front row," reaching 10 or fewer students in a class of 30. Noddings (2005) captures this frustration in the student–teacher relationship.

The single greatest complaint of students in school is, "They don't care." . . . They feel alienated from their schoolwork, separated from adults who try to teach them, and adrift in a world perceived as baffling and hostile. At the same time, most teachers work very hard and express deep concern for their students. In an important sense, teachers do care, but they are unable to make the connections that would complete caring relationships with their students. (p. 2)

A starting point, then, is to understand the fundamental reasons and consequences of student disengagement in learning. In one of the very few studies that asked students what they thought, Rudduck, Chaplain, and Wallace (1996) provide a comprehensive summary of the consequences of disengagement as perceived by students.

1. *Perceptions of themselves*—disengaged pupils:
   - have lower self-concepts and self-esteem than engaged peers;
   - have characteristics that tend to make it difficult to achieve academically; these include: "giving up easily at school work" . . . ;
   - are more likely to be fed up with school on a regular basis.

2. *Perception of school work*—disengaged pupils:
   - find homework difficult, given they are often struggling in class;
   - dislike subjects with a high proportion of writing (e.g., English);
   - dislike subjects where they do not understand (esp. modern languages);
   - have increased anxiety about their ability, as they near exams.

3. *Relationship with peers*—disengaged pupils:
   - are more likely to have been involved in bullying incidents;
   - feel under pressure from their immediate friends if they exhibit achievement behavior;
   - are perceived by many of their engaged peers as a hindrance and annoyance to their own classroom work.

4. *Relationship with teachers*—disengaged pupils:
   - perceive teachers as generally unfair to pupils, but particularly unfair to them;
   - believe teachers express negative behaviors toward them both verbally and non-verbally;

- would like a teacher they could trust to talk things through with;
- consider teachers to be largely responsible for their failure at school.

5. *Perceptions of the future*—disengaged pupils:
   - show high levels of anxiety about their future chances in the working world;
   - despite negative messages from the school want to persist and have some examination success;
   - see a direct relationship between examination success and getting a job;
   - are more likely to plan to get a job at 15. (p. 111)

Sadly, high percentages of students are disengaged, and the proportion increases as the student gets older. In short, when it comes to change, new approaches are needed that attract all students to become engaged with their own learning and that of their peers. This applies both to students who appear to be doing well and especially to those disconnected to begin with.

THE STUDENT AND CHANGE

I already have foreshadowed the two interrelated changes that must occur in the cultures of classrooms and schools if *all students* are to find education engaging and meaningful. And there is a strand of research and innovative practice over the past decade that Thiessen (in press) labels: "How students are actively involved in shaping their own learning opportunities and in the improvement of what happens in classrooms and schools." The two themes, as I have said, involve changing the way teaching occurs in the classroom, and changing the way students participate in shaping the culture of the school.

Reconstituting Classroom Culture

First let me reiterate that, when it comes to how they and others are being treated, students do notice! Especially affected are what McLaughlin and Talbert (2001) call "nontraditional students" (those who do not come from advantaged backgrounds—these days, the majority of students). Even traditional students don't reach deep understanding if we use more advanced indicators of learning (e.g., applying knowledge to solve problems in novel situations), but they do get good grades and like the clarity of knowing what is expected.

However, McLaughlin and Talbert (2001) note that nontraditional students struggle in these "teacher-directed, sometimes impersonal classrooms."

> For example, a high-achieving Latina at Valley described her experience with the math teacher who feels all of his students are "the problem."
>
> Ooh I dread that class. I didn't do well. At the end I got a B, but it wasn't what I was hoping for . . . it was a hard class, because he didn't really explain the material. It was like he taught college also at the same time that he teaches high school. So it's sort of like, he brought those techniques to high school. And he'd move around really quick, and you couldn't follow him. And it was just really difficult. (p. 27)

By changing this situation, teachers make a difference: "Teachers who understand their non-traditional students are of a voice in saying that changes in classroom practices are essential not only to meet the needs of contemporary students, but also to support teachers' sense of efficacy." Said one teacher: "Teachers have been used to lecturing and teaching the lesson . . . and they aren't getting satisfaction from kids' achievement now, because they aren't achieving. We need to grow and change and evolve too" (pp. 28–29). Teachers who were successful with all students, need we remind ourselves, "taught in schools and departments with a strong professional community engaged in making innovations that support student and teacher learning and success" (p. 34).

Still sticking with the classroom, new pedagogical breakthroughs are having great positive impact via new developments in "assessment for learning." Assessment for learning engages students in their own learning by using direct and immediate data on learning performance to alter learning keyed to the needs and interests of the individual. One of the leading figures in this field in the United States, Richard Stiggins (2005), has characterized these developments as essential for serving the new 95% versus traditional teaching, which served at best half that percentage.

And assessment for learning does change the place of students and consequently the role of teachers in the learning equation. The work of Paul Black and his colleagues (2003) in England makes this crystal clear. Assessment for learning, Black reminds us, is "any assessment for which the first priority is to serve the purpose of promoting students' learning" (p. 2). Black and his group worked with 36 teachers of English and mathematics in six secondary schools in England. The goal was to improve four areas of classroom learning: questioning, feedback through marking classroom assignments, peer and self-assessment by students, and the formative use of summative tests (i.e., external accountability tests). As Black and colleagues found: "It is very difficult for students to achieve a learning goal unless they understand that goal and can assess what they need to do to reach it. So self-assessment is essential to learning. In practice peer assessment turns out to be an important complement and may even be a prior requirement for self-assessment" (pp. 49–50). One student put it as follows: "After a student marked my investigation, I can now acknowledge my mistakes easier. I hope that it is not just me who learnt from the investigation but the student who marked it did also. Next time I will have to make my explanations clearer, as they said 'it is hard to understand.' . . . I will now explain my equation so it is clear" (p. 66). The overall effect on the teacher—learner nexus is considerable.

> As the teachers came to listen more attentively to the students' responses they began to appreciate more fully that learning was not a process of passive reception of knowledge but one which the learners were active in creating their own understanding. . . . The teachers gradually developed learning environments that focused on improvement and this was achieved through evolving and supporting collaborative learning within their classrooms. (p. 59)

As the project unfolded, many teachers moved away from the perception of their students as having fixed levels of ability. Teachers began to realize (i.e., experience) that it is the students who have to do the learning. Something teachers already knew became more explicit and more amenable to corrective action, namely, that teachers cannot do the learning for students. One teacher expressed his learning this way.

> It became obvious that one way to make *significant, sustainable* change was to get the students doing more of the thinking. I then began to search for ways to make the learning process more transparent to the students. Indeed, I now spend my time looking for ways to get students to take responsibility for their learning at the same time making the learning more collaborative. (pp. 94–95, emphasis added)

These pedagogical changes make a difference in the engagement of students and, as Black and colleagues found, have a positive impact on both enjoyment of learning and achievement on external tests: "If [these practices] were replicated across the whole school they would raise the performance of a school at the 25th percentile of achievement nationally to the upper half" (p. 29). I know I sound like a broken CD, but the reason we have to make these changes is that we now are serving, for the first time, 95%+ of a student population that is larger, more diverse, and more complex than ever before. This means that the classroom culture has to change, and if that is to occur, we have to go wider. Thus, we need closer to 100% of the classrooms engaged, and for this we need to mobilize the entire professional community, a point strongly made in Chapters 7 and 8.

Reconstituting School Culture

The good news is that there is a pedagogical movement underway toward the kinds of learning experiences portrayed by Bransford, Black, and others. The bad news is that it has not moved very far. The next phase, I would claim, requires inviting students into the equation as proactive participants. But so far I have been talking about teachers, figuring out what they have to do differently in order to reach more students in the classroom—a dramatic change in the culture of the classroom, to be sure. But what if we invited students to go even farther? What if student voice mattered? Rudduck and associates (1996) make this very suggestion.

> Those bent on improvement in schools might usefully start by inviting pupils to talk about what makes learning difficult for them, about what diminishes their motivation and engagement, and what makes some give up and others settle for a "minimum risk, minimum effort" position—even though they know that doing well matters. (p. 31)

Rudduck and associates also make the point that "behind the mask of nonchalance that some pupils wear to hide their anxiety about the future is a concern to succeed and some realization of the consequences of not making the grade" (p. 3). Further:

> The pupils interviewed had quite a sophisticated understanding of those aspects of the school system which obstructed their learning and those aspects that were supportive . . . [they] all had their own concerns about school, even those who were achieving well across the curriculum. Their comments showed that they had ideas about how schools should be, that they were prepared to explain their views, and that teachers could learn from consultation with them. (p. 85)

Rudduck (in press) has continued this work. As she observes, "Over the last 20+ years, schools have changed less in their regimes and patterns of relationships than young people have changed" (p. 1036). Even those interested in student voice may not take the risk to go far enough, seeing "students primarily as sources of interesting and usable data, but less likely to have goals that are expressed in terms of community" (p. 1041). Students soon tire of invitations that "(a) express a view on matters they do not think are important; (b) are framed in the language they find restrictive, alienating, or patronizing; and (c) seldom result in action or dialogue that affects the quality of their lives" (p. 1069).

Rudduck acknowledges the challenges involved in taking student voice seriously, including the personal risks involved in innovation, the problem of finding time in a crowded curriculum, the debate about performance and what is valued, and many others. Yet she says when students do get involved through skilled facilitation, they have been effective in addressing problems and issues basic to school improvement. Rudduck (in press) conducted a survey of teachers concerning their consulting pupils project.

In the survey, 84% of the teachers said that consultation was having a positive impact on students' self-esteem; 80% thought that consultation was helping students develop a more positive attitude to schools and learning; and 75% thought it was helping students develop more positive attitudes to teachers.

Fielding (2001) pushes the argument even further in his "students as radical agents of change" study. As with all of the sources I use in this book, Fielding's study is not about armchair advocacy. All the sources are based on action, thereby promoting evidence-based debate (Pfeffer & Sutton, 2006). Fielding and his team worked in Sharnbrook Upper School in Bedfordshire, England, with three cohorts of students on a "students as researchers project." Students and teacher leaders "were trained in research and evidence gathering techniques, as well as establishing a shared understanding of the values, dispositions, and commitments which would make partnership between students and staff both real and demanding" (p. 125). Over the three cohorts, students and teachers investigated a series of topics: student voice, student experience of practice teachers, the school's assessment system, careers in education, the quality of school meals, the life skills program, and a 3-year research project with Chile using student researchers as the key agents in the development of pedagogies and curriculum materials dedicated to the development of education in and for democracy. Several of the projects "had substantial and immediate impact" on the school (p. 126).

Another program that has been treating students seriously is the Manitoba School Improvement Program (MSIP) (Earl & Lee, 1999; Pekrul & Levin, in press). For 15 years this program has been supporting grassroots teachers to change how they work with students and fellow teachers. Students who once seemed sullen and unreachable often became the most ardent advocates for positive change once the right connection had been made. One student spoke about how "what seemed to be an impossible path to walk in life, has been altered," thanks to teachers who had worked with her. "But what I am most thankful for is that all of you have exposed me to an atmosphere of hope and strength" (Earl & Lee, 1999, p. 33).

Around 1998 MSIP entered a second phase that is based primarily on developing strategies and mechanisms for high school students to participate in helping to shape new directions for student engagement and learning. As it has evolved, MSIP has moved closer and closer to student voice in a large number of Manitoba high schools (50 of the 200 high schools in Manitoba have had projects with MSIP, not all of them on student voice). Pekrul and Levin (in press) conclude that "combining collaborative and authentic tasks that build skills and confidence, and widening the arena of student influence, student voice processes give students a credible voice in and allow them to have an impact on the institution that plays a major role in their lives" (p. 1272). Various research projects and discussion have been launched that explore students' lives in school, including central learning questions such as "what is the purpose of learning"; "what are the conditions that facilitate learning"; and "what are the processes to facilitate and support learning" (p. 1285). Time and again students are found to have valuable and realistic ideas, and of course become more aware of these learning issues as they examine them. Pekrul and Levin identify the lessons learned in the past decade of this work.

- Motivated, engaged students are central to lasting school improvement.
- MSIP schools that have been most open to and supportive of student voice have consistently found—sometimes to their surprise—that students can be tremendous allies in their work, including having a powerful effect on parental and community support for change.
- Student voice is not just about supporting school improvement but has educational benefits in its own right . . . students have found the experience valuable to their learning as well as developing confidence and leadership skills.
- Although student voice has many positive aspects it is not nearly as widespread one might wish.
- Student voice only happens when there is commitment and support from the school . . . students need support to help them develop their voices effectively.
- Because students tend to have short time horizons, they need to see action following from their participation. (pp. 1294–1297)

As I said earlier in this chapter, elementary school students also have insights and ideas. Primary students even have clear views about their principals, especially if these principals are visible leaders, as Day and associates (2000) found: "There was a recognition [on the part of students] that all students, in exchange for a safe and caring environment, were expected to work hard, and that hard work would be rewarded" (p. 123).

Children, in other words, are vastly underutilized resources. A dramatic example is contained in Senge and associates' (2000) field book on education in an chapter entitled "Children as Leaders," which describes the efforts of the Children's Peace Movement in Colombia, organized by young people ages 6 through 18. Against horrendous odds, they are trying to raise questions about improving what is a daily lethal environment.

> More than 850,000 Colombian children have been forced out of their homes by violence during the past dozen years. Sixty percent of those displaced children dropped out of a school. At least 2000 children under the age of 15 are enlisted or in paramilitary groups, some as young as eight years old. More than 4000 children were murdered in 1996 alone, with the number continuing to rise each year; and impunity is widespread. (p. 546)

The Children's Peace Movement responds, perhaps initially raising more questions than providing answers:

> The level on which most children "understood" this complex situation is different from that of adults. They think less about political and economic concerns and more about justice and fairness. Perhaps as a result, their definition of peacemaking is very broad—it includes any activity that improves the quality of life in a community affected by violence. (p. 549)

This is obviously an extreme situation, but it illustrates the point. Society is complex. Children's characteristics and needs are diverse. Not only must they be part of the solution, but in many cases they turn out to have better ideas. The wisdom of the crowd strikes again! (Surowiecki, 2004).

In their call for a radical breakthrough in education, Wilson and Barsky (2006) say, "We cannot overemphasize the need to vastly expand the role of children in the adult work of school, and to ensure that this work (a) is instructive for each child's education, and (b) drastically reduces the daily pressures on teachers, school administrators, and other paid workers in the school" (p. 10).

Integral to the argument in this chapter is that treating students as *people* comes very close to "living" the academic, personal, and social educational goals that are stated in most official policy documents. But more than that, involving students in constructing their own meaning and learning is fundamentally essential pedagogically—they learn more and are motivated to go even further.

In the same way that professional learning communities establish powerful pressure and support learning conditions for motivating disengaged teachers, working through the difficulties of connecting with disaffected students is the route to both cognitive and affective attainment with students. This reminds us that this work must tackle both faces of student engagement: the culture of the classroom in terms of day-to-day learning, and the culture of the school and community. A second reminder: Student engagement strategies must reach all students, those doing okay but bored by the irrelevance of school, and those who are disadvantaged and find schools increasingly alienating as they move through the grades. The irony is that the majority of teachers want to do well by their students; and the majority of students know that success in school is beneficial. Meaning must be accomplished at every level of the system, but if it is not done at the level of the student, *for the vast majority of students,* all is lost.

CHAPTER 10

The Parent and the Community

Whose school is it, anyway?

—Gold and Miles (1981)

In *What's Worth Fighting for Out There*, Hargreaves and I (1998) argued that the "out there" is now "in here." We observed that the boundaries of the school are now more permeable and more transparent, and that this development was both *inevitable and desirable*. It is inevitable because there is a relentless press for accountability from our public institutions and many more means these days of acting on this interest, including the growing accessibility to information in a technology-based society. It is desirable because in postmodern society you can no longer get the job of education done unless you combine forces. It has become too complex for any one group (like teachers) to do alone. These new ways of partnering are threatening and complex. But we concluded that if the "out there" is going to get you anyway on its terms, why not move toward the danger, and have a chance of getting some of it on your terms. This chapter is about parents and communities, on the one hand, and administrators and teachers, on the other hand, moving toward each other—a process that is a far more dangerous journey at the outset (when you are working from a base of mutual ignorance) than it is once you are underway.

If teachers and administrators who spend 40 to 60 hours a week immersed in the educational world have trouble comprehending the meaning of educational change, imagine what it is like for a parent. Highly educated parents are bewildered; what of the less-well-educated ones who have always felt uncomfortable in dealing with the school?

The question of parent and community involvement in schools

188

has been the subject of hundreds of books and articles over the past 40 years. At first glance this literature appears to be a mass of contradictions, confusion, and hopelessness for understanding—let alone coping with—the relationship between communities and schools. Yet emerging from this research is a message that is remarkable in its consistency: *The closer the parent is to the education of the child, the greater the impact on child development and educational achievement.* Of course, it is not quite that simple, because such a statement encompasses a multitude of variables that make it more or less probable that closeness will occur. And we certainly can imagine situations in which closeness per se could be harmful to the growth of the child. Moreover, decisions about the precise nature of parent involvement must take into account cultural, ethnic, and class differences as well as variations related to the age and gender of students.

In determining under what conditions parent and community involvement is most beneficial, we have to understand the different forms of parent participation and their consequences for the student and other school personnel. Stated another way, why do certain forms of involvement produce positive results, while others seem wasteful or counterproductive? Was Willard Waller (1932) right 75 years ago when he observed:

> From the ideal point of view, parents and teachers have much in common in that both, supposedly, wish things to occur for the best interests of the child; but in fact, parents and teachers usually live in conditions of mutual distrust and enmity. Both wish the child well, but it is such a different kind of well conflict must inevitably arise over it. The fact seems to be that teachers and parents are natural enemies, predestined each for the discomfiture of the other. (p. 203, cited in Hargreaves, 2000)

Is he still right? I think so, but only if things are left to their natural tendencies. This is after all a book about change, so we don't want too many things that are "predestined." Thus, it is going to take some energy and capacity to change things for the better. And much of this redirection must come, at least initially, from the educators.

I start with the role of parents because this is where the most powerful instrument for improvement resides. I also consider the role of school boards and communities.

PARENT INVOLVEMENT IN SCHOOLS

Nowhere is the two-way street of learning more in disrepair and in need of social reconstruction than in the relationship among parents, communities, and their schools. Teachers and principals need to reach out to parents and communities, especially when the initial conditions do not support such efforts. Henry's (1996) study of parent–school collaboration in poor neighborhoods concluded: "Educators have to go out into their communities with empathy, and interact meaningfully with their constituents. Being professional can no longer mean remaining isolated in the school" (p. 132).

This will involve shifts in power and influence. But it is not power in and of itself that counts. It is what new power arrangements can accomplish that matters.

> To seek power is to raise and begin to answer the question: to seek power to change what? Changing the forces of power in no way guarantees that anything else will change. To seek power without asking the "what" question is not only to beg the question but to avoid, and therefore to collude in cosmetic changes. (Sarason, 1995, p. 53)

The "what" question is: "What will it take to mobilize more people and resources in the service of educating all students?" The research is abundantly clear about the answer: Teachers cannot do it alone. Parents and other community members are crucial and largely untapped resources who have (or can be helped to have) assets and expertise that are essential to the partnership. However well or badly they do it, parents are their children's very first educators. They have knowledge of their children that is not available to anyone else. They have a vested and committed interest in their children's success, and they also have valuable knowledge and skills to contribute that spring from their interests, hobbies, occupations, and place in the community.

The research is very clear about the benefits, indeed the necessity, of parent engagement. In Coleman's (1998) study of schools in two districts, he calls this the "power of three" (parent, student, and teacher collaboration). Based on his interviews and surveys of parents, students, and teachers, Coleman argues that

> Student commitment to schooling (or engagement in learning) is primarily shaped by parents through the "curriculum of the home"; but this parent involvement is an alterable variable, which can be influenced by school and teacher practices. (p. 11)

Coleman expounds on this.

> When the development of student responsibility occurs it is a function of the attitudes and practices of all three triad members. The vital elements are: (a) for teachers, beliefs about parental involvement, student capabilities, and the importance of deliberate teaching of responsibility in classrooms; (b) for students, communication with parents about school, confidence in the ability to do the work, valuing school for its importance to the future, and collaboration with teachers; (c) for parents, valuing school, an "invitational" teacher attitude, and communication with students about school. (p. 14)

Coleman concludes that "student commitment can indeed be sustained and strengthened by collaborative teacher attitudes, expressed in and through their practices; strong connections with the home are essential to the task" (p. 139). He argues that "teachers [can] facilitate and encourage parent collaboration through some simple practices, all well-known *but not implemented consistently* in any of our schools (or we believe in many schools anywhere). Most parents," he adds, "are conscious that much more could be done to help their students learn, in classrooms and in the home" (p. 150, emphasis in original).

In the meantime, the research over the years has become more forceful about the need for parent and community involvement. Indeed, the original "correlates of school effectiveness" did not include a reference to parents, but now features parent involvement as a core characteristic. On the research side, Mortimore, Sammons, Stoll, Lewis, and Ecob's (1988) large study of school effectiveness found that parent involvement practices represented one of 12 key factors that differentiated effective from less effective schools.

> Our findings show parent involvement in the life of the school to be a positive influence upon pupils' progress and development. This included help in classrooms and on educational visits, and attendance at meetings to discuss children's progress. The headteacher's accessibility to parents was also important; schools operating an informal, open-door policy being more effective. Parent involvement in pupils' educational development within the home was also clearly beneficial. Parents who read to their children, heard them read, and provided them with access to books at home, had a positive effect upon their children's learning. (p. 255)

Rosenholtz's (1989) research, with which we are familiar, found important differences in how teachers in "moving" versus "stuck" schools related to parents. Teachers from stuck schools "held no goals for parent participation," while teachers from moving schools "focused their efforts on involving parents with academic content, thereby bridging the learning chasm between home and school" (p. 152). Teachers in stuck schools were far more likely to assume that nothing could be done with parents, while teachers in moving schools saw parents as part of the solution.

In the Chicago evaluation conducted by Bryk and associates (1998), those schools that were more successful were found to be committed to developing "the engagement of parents and community resources." In their words:

> Schools pursuing a systemic agenda have a "client orientation." They maintain a sustained focus on strengthening the involvement of parents with the school and their children's schooling. They also actively seek to strengthen the ties with the local community and especially those resources that bear on the caring of children. As these personal interactions expand and become institutionalized in the life of the school, the quality of the relationships between local professionals and their community changes. Greater trust and mutual engagement begins to characterize these encounters. In contrast, schools with unfocused initiatives may set more distinct boundaries between themselves and their neighborhood. Extant problems in these rela-

tionships may not be directly addressed. The broader community resources that could assist improvement efforts in the school are not tapped. These schools remain more isolated from their students' parents and their communities. (pp. 127–128)

Bryk and Schneider's (2002) work on "trust in schools" pursues this theme, showing again its critical importance, and also indicating how difficult it is to establish relational trust between schools and communities—a change in culture right up there with changing school cultures on the scale of difficulty. As noted in Chapter 7, relational trust for Bryk and Schneider consists of four components: respect, competence, personal regard for others, and integrity. High- and low-trust schools were as different as night and day. In low-trust schools

> Teachers criticized parents for their lack of interest in education, family drug dependency, and unemployment. They complained that much in their students' home structures impeded learning, and they took a generally dim view of the quality of parenting that was occurring. (p. 48)

In high-trust schools (similarly disadvantaged, but with different school cultures fostered by school leaders and teachers)

> Teachers constantly spoke about the importance of respecting parents, regardless of their background or education achievement. Although many students came from troubled homes, teachers did not attempt to distance themselves from their students or their families. (p. 84)

And, "teachers' active encouragement of parents, coupled with their demonstrated personal regard for the children, opened up possibilities for teachers and parents to negotiate complementary roles in the children's education" (p. 86).

As Bryk and Schneider emphasize, under conditions of power asymmetry, with poor parents who are vulnerable and unconfident in their relationship to schools, it is incumbent on principals and teachers to reach out, be empathetic, and create nonthreatening possibilities for parent involvement. When they do this, as Bryk and Schneider found, greater connection is made among the triad of student, parent, and school, and achievement goes up.

These findings are corroborated in James and colleagues' (2006) study of 12 "very effective primary schools" in Wales, which I cited in previous chapters. These highly effective schools in disadvantaged communities saw parents and the community as a necessary part of the solution: "The schools knew and worked with the pupils' immediate and extended families to engage their commitment to the work of the school and to help the pupils to learn. They endeavoured to work closely with parents, to promote contact with them and to involve them fully" (p. 112). Among other things:

- Schools' communication with parents was professional, direct and valuing.
- Parents were respected.
- Schools endeavoured to work with *all* families.
- There was a high level of parent support.
- Joint learning schemes for both parents and students were valued, [such as] the family literacy scheme, the family numeracy scheme, and PALS [the Partnership Accelerates Learning Scheme]. (p. 113, emphasis in original)

It is the constellation of things that effective schools do—the characteristics that I identified in Chapters 7 and 8—that enable this synergy of focus. Schools that have their act together have the confidence and competence to reach out to parents; schools that do not have these characteristics play it safe behind the classroom door and school walls, and as a result the distance widens.

I will have more to say about the types of communities in the next section, but for now let us draw the conclusion that part and parcel of professional learning communities is close engagement with parents. In terms of additional resources, the most systematic research and development in this domain have been conducted by Epstein and her colleagues over the past 20 years. In 1988, Epstein had already concluded that

There is consistent evidence that parents' encouragement, activities, interest at home and their participation at school affect their children's achievement, even after the students' ability and family socioeconomic status is taken into account. Students gain in personal and academic development if their families emphasize schooling, let their children know they do, and do so continually over the years. (ch. 1)

Epstein has identified six types of school and parent/community involvement that in combination improve student learning and adult engagement with their children's education.

Type 1—Parent skills
Type 2—Communication
Type 3—Volunteering
Type 4—Learning at home
Type 5—School decision making
Type 6—Collaboration with community agencies (Epstein, 1995; Epstein et al., 2002)

Note that school governance (Type 5) represents only one of six forms, and is not the most important. Most parents do not want to run the school; they want their child to do better. Put another way, it is only when the majority of teachers are collaborating with the majority of parents that any sizable impact on student learning will occur. And this, of course, makes perfect sense even if it is not practiced much.

Over the years Epstein has found that parent involvement is critical to success, but there is no evidence that schools and parents have become substantially closer (except for the minority that have set out deliberately to do this with external training and support). In a statewide survey, Epstein (1986) found that 58% of the parents reported rarely or never having received requests from the teacher to become involved in learning activities at home, while over 80% said they could spend more time helping children at home if they were shown how to do specific learning activities.

In her study, Epstein found significant differences in parent involvement between the teacher leaders and the comparison teachers, even though the two groups were matched on characteristics and type of community. For example, teacher leaders involved parents from differing educational backgrounds compared with the control groups, which reported that parents with little education "could not or would not help at home." Parents of children in the classes of teacher leaders reported significantly more frequent use of 9 of the 12 identified parent involvement practices. The effect on parents was positive and multifaceted. Parents increased their understanding about school most when the teacher frequently used parent involvement practices. Epstein (1986) states:

> What is important in our findings is that teachers' frequent use of parent involvement practices improved parents' knowledge about their child's instructional program, after the grade level, racial composition, and parent education composition of the classroom were taken into account. (pp. 288–289)

Epstein (1986) concludes:

> Parents were aware of and responded positively to teachers' efforts to involve them in learning activities at home. Parents with children in the classrooms of teachers who built parent involvement into their regular teaching practice were more aware of teachers' efforts, received more ideas from teachers, knew more about their child's instructional program, and rated the teachers higher in interpersonal skills and overall teaching quality. Teachers' practices had consistently strong and positive effects on parent reactions to the school program and on parent evaluations of teachers' merits for parents at all educational levels. Teacher practices of parent involvement had more dramatic positive links to parents' reactions than general school-to-home communication or parent assistance at the school. (p. 291)

In related work in eight inner-city schools in Baltimore (five elementary and three middle schools), Epstein and Dauber (1988) concentrated on *teacher attitudes and practices of parent involvement* and *parents' attitudes and practices*. In examining teacher attitudes and practices of 171 teachers, Epstein and Dauber found:

- Almost all teachers express strong, positive attitudes about parent involvement in general. But the strength of school programs and teachers' actual practice vary considerably, with elementary school programs stronger, more positive, and more comprehensive than those in middle grades.
- The individual practices of each teacher at particular grade levels and in particular subject areas are the keystone for strong programs of parent involvement.

- The individual teacher is not, however, the only factor in building stronger programs. Analyses of "discrepancy scores" showed that differences between self and principal, self and teacher colleagues, and self and parents were significantly associated with the strength of schools' parent involvement programs. Programs and practices were stronger in schools where teachers saw that they, their colleagues, and the parents all felt strongly about the importance of parent involvement.
- Without the schools' assistance, parents' knowledge and actions to help their children are heavily dependent on the parents' social class or education. But schools—even inner city schools—can develop strong programs of parent involvement to help more families become knowledgeable partners in their children's education. (pp. 11–12)

Epstein and Dauber also report that teachers with more positive attitudes toward parent involvement report more success in involving "hard-to-reach parents including working parents, less educated parents, single parents, parents of older students, young parents, parents new to the school, and other adults with whom children live" (p. 5).

The work of Epstein and her colleagues in establishing the National Network of Partnership Schools (NNPS) has done a great deal to further both the research knowledge base and the corresponding developmental strategies required to strengthen the family and school connection. Established in 1996, NNPS now includes over 1,000 schools in 11 states in the United States (Epstein & Sanders, 2000; Sanders & Epstein, 2000). Members of the network are provided with tools and strategies to implement their school improvement efforts, according to the six types of involvement. In a second edition of the handbook for network schools, Epstein and colleagues (2002) show how to

- Involve the community in school, family and community partnerships
- Organize more effective Action Teams for Partnerships
- Strengthen partnerships in middle and high schools
- Implement interactive homework for students to show and share their work with family partners
- Organize a program of volunteers in the middle grades

- Conduct state and district leadership activities to assist schools with programs of partnership (p. 2)

As with all forms of collaboration, the process of establishing community/school partnerships is a chicken-and-egg problem. When you have collaborative relationships they produce results, which in turn spurs continued partnership. But if you don't have quality relationships, how do you get started? *The New Meaning of Educational Change* is all about the thinking and actions that break negative cycles in favor of positive ones. I am reminded of Stephen Covey's observation that you cannot talk your way out of situations that you behaved your way into. You need to behave your way into new forms of trust and collaboration—the basis for reflective action we highlighted in Chapter 6.

Up to this point, however, not enough schools have tried to find the particular pathways of involvement appropriate for their setting. Thus, the power of three—student, parent, teacher—remains an unleashed force as far as the majority of schools and communities are concerned.

SCHOOL BOARDS AND COMMUNITIES

The role of school boards (in the United States, usually made up of approximately seven locally elected trustees who are responsible for overseeing the work of schools within the district) is difficult to discern. Danzberger and colleagues (1987) call boards "the forgotten players on the education team." They undertook a national study of local school boards in the United States, in which they surveyed 450 board chairpersons of city districts and 50 of rural districts, and interviewed a variety of local leaders. Danzberger and her colleagues found that state governments were becoming more and more directive, that the role of local boards was unclear, that board members received little preparation and training for their roles, and that only one third of the board chairs surveyed had any process for evaluating or monitoring the board's role. They observed that boards could be crucial agents for school improvement and recommended that state reforms should be concerned with strengthening the capacity of local boards to bring about and monitor change. They further recommended that boards themselves should be engaged in self-improvement through inservice and by establishing systems to assess their own effectiveness.

School boards, depending on their activities, can make a difference. LaRocque and Coleman (1989) investigated the role of school boards in relatively successful compared with less successful districts (as measured by student achievement) in ten districts in British Columbia. On the surface, many of the policies and initiatives were similar across all boards. Through interviews and the examination of specific activities, LaRocque and Coleman found that school trustees in the more successful boards

(a) Were considerably more knowledgeable about district programs and practices;
(b) Had a clearer sense of what they wanted to accomplish, based on a set of firmly held values and beliefs; and
(c) Engaged in activities which provided them with opportunities to articulate these values and beliefs. (p. 15)

Successful boards also worked more actively and interactively with superintendents and the district administration. Greely, quoted in Senge and associates (2000), also talks about "a school board that learns." She notes that there are built-in obstacles to learning.

- External funding from federal and state sources fragments programs and promotes a "command-and-control" mindset;
- Individual board members, elected by constituencies, often do not vote in the interest of the whole community;
- There is large turnover, with new majorities often being established every 2 to 4 years;
- It is hard for school board members to learn as a team because they are frequently in public, political settings. (p. 432)

Greely draws a number of lessons for countering these forces:

- Create a public record of private connections;
- Resist the temptation to involve business examples;
- Keep returning to the observable data;
- Set up alternative meeting formats;
- Practice talking about values;
- Have your behavior model the behavior you want from the schools. (cited in Senge et al., 2000, pp. 436–438)

Hess's (1999) study of school district policymaking indicates that the prevailing system is not likely to improve. As quoted in Hill and associates (2000), school boards often are caught in a "policy churn." Hess (1999) states:

> District policymakers constantly embrace politically attractive changes, producing prodigious amounts of reform at a pace inimical to effective implementation. . . .
> [Districts] recycle initiatives, constantly modify previous initiatives, and adopt innovative reform A to replace practice B even as another district is adopting B as an innovative reform to replace practice A. . . .
> Urban districts appear to do a number of things in a stop-and-start, chaotic fashion that is not part of any clear strategy to improve specific elements of school performance. (p. 5)

Elmore (2000) summarizes Hess.

> Relatively unstable political factors advance new "reforms" as ways of satisfying their electoral constituencies, pausing only long enough to take credit for having acted, and quickly moving on to new reforms, with no attention to the institutionalization or implementation of previous reforms. The political rewards in the pluralistic structure, Hess argues, are in the symbolisms of initiations and enactment of reform, not in its implementation. Among the pathologies the incentive structure creates is high turnover of leadership, both political and administrative. Factions are fickle, political opportunists abound. Board majorities hold onto school superintendents just long enough for them to advance their reform proposals, and at the first sign of opposition, move onto the next superintendent. (p. 19)

On the more optimistic side, McAdams (2006) furnishes a model and some data to show that school board/superintendent rapport is behind every example of district-wide success. He offers a model backed by examples of how boards can be and are instrumental in cases of improving schools across the district. He shows how board and superintendent partnerships have determined success by focusing on:

- Core beliefs and commitments
- Explicit and sound theories of action for change
- Reform policies
- Policy development and oversight
- Reform governance practices
- Clarification of roles, responsibilities, and relationships, which in turn promote civic capacity and transition planning to increase the chances of continuity of good direction

McAdams takes the position that these capacities can be identified and learned, which means that school board members need to receive training in their roles. Understanding the difference between governance and management is at the heart of success, along with a two-way partnership between district leadership and school board leadership. Thus, training and development for school trustees, and models of partnership between school boards and districts are essential.

In those jurisdictions with legal entities at the school level that govern the work of the schools (such as England), the same principles apply (i.e., rapport between the governors and school leaders is central to success). In James and colleagues' (2006) study of the 12 highly effective primary schools in Wales, this rapport is clearly evident. The authors state, "The governing bodies were committed, supportive and engaged" (p. 96). In a list of specific attributes, James and colleagues report that governing bodies

- Were kept informed
- Were encouraged to undertake training and to attend courses
- Provided thoughtful challenge to and validation of the schools' work—especially in promoting pupil attainment and achievement
- Did not have an axe to grind
- Had sound relationships with teachers
- Typically cared strongly about their schools (pp. 96–97)

Granted, close partnership among schools, districts, and their governing bodies is not the norm. Some relationships represent models of policy churn, tumultuous turmoil, and punctuated stalemates. Others suffer from the inertia of laissez faire superficiality. But there are some that operate in a way that brings out the complementary strengths of schools and boards in the service of continuous improvement of students.

IMPLICATIONS

Parents and communities, of course, are not homogeneous and do not represent situations where one size of involvement fits all. The two types of critical characteristics in which communities differ are ethnicity and poverty/affluence (and for many groups there is a strong overlap between the two).

In *Turnaround Leadership* (2006) I demonstrate that the gap of performance between rich and poor is actually widening in the United States, at least since 2000. Pedro Noguera (2003) has made the most compelling case for the deep difficulties faced by schools and communities in U.S. cities. He argues that "until there is a genuine commitment to address the social context of schooling—to confront the 'urban condition'—it will be impossible to bring about significant and sustainable improvements in urban public schools"(p. 62). Noguera tackles a number of fundamental problems, including racial inequality, curbing violence inside and outside the school, motivating alienated youth, and increasing social capital among parents and the community. He calls for increased support for schools in these circumstances to accompany the accountability pressure that these schools are already experiencing. Although intertwined with ethnicity, we also must consider how poverty/affluence influences the matter of parent involvement.

Hubbard and colleagues' (2006) detailed case study of San Diego also concluded that it is a mistake to treat communities as monolithic entities. They found that affluent parents had different concerns and strategies than poor parents.

> Groups from more well-to-do neighborhoods applied political pressure primarily through face-to-face encounters—and they obtained desired results, including the exemption from the district's centralized reforms. Groups from less well-to-do neighborhoods, frustrated by lack of response to their overtures to administrators, resorted to legal and extralegal tactics. They did not often obtain the results they desired. (p. 206)

Jeannie Oakes and her colleagues have been documenting a similar finding for several years, namely, that well-off parents often wear down or block reforms that they perceive will not serve their self-interests (Oakes & Lipton, 2002). Although I mean this facetiously, it is almost as if we need strategies to increase the involvement of poor parents and *decrease* the influence of affluent parents. I don't believe that the interests of the rich and poor are mutually exclusive, but we do have to position reforms so that equity and excellence for all are both winners (Fullan, 2006).

It is not just the needs of the poor that require attention. Indeed, there is evidence that many affluent parents are disinterested or otherwise disengaged from the education and development of their children. Steinberg (1996) notes that despite good intentions, nearly one in three parents in the United States end up being disengaged from their children.

> Disengaged parents have for one reason or another, "checked out" of childrearing. They have disengaged from responsibilities of parental discipline—they do not know how their child is doing in school, have no idea who their child's friends are, and are not aware of how their child spends his or her free time—but they have also disengaged from being accepting and supportive as well. They rarely spend time in activities with their child, and seldom just talk with their adolescent about the day's events. (p. 188)

In all of this there are significant implications for policymakers and other leaders who have the opportunity to alter the larger infrastructure at the district (Chapter 11) and government (Chapter 12) levels. Individuals (and combinations of individuals) also can work in their own ways with a system perspective, that is, from their own vantage point, they can work on developing new relationships between communities and schools. We have seen that the pathways and obstacles to getting there involve working through the discomfort of each other's presence until new patterns of relationships are established.

I also have highlighted that schools must take the initiative, especially in poor communities. Bryk and Schneider (2002) make this point, as do James and colleagues (2006), along with examples of what these initiatives entail. Coleman (1998) summarizes the matter in the following words:

> Teachers must (1) realize that parent efficacy with respect to instructional involvement (collaboration) is dependent upon teacher invitation; (2) legitimize collaboration through an assertion to parents of their rights and responsibilities with respect to collaboration; (3) facilitate collaboration by arranging for parent–teacher conversations of various kinds, and by providing parents with the knowledge of curriculum and methodology they need; (4) encourage collaboration by providing activities that parents and their children can do together; that is, accepting the role of instructional mediator between parents and their children; and (5) acknowledge the results of collaboration by providing adequate and timely information about student performance. (p. 61)

As for parents, I have said that schools do not capitalize enough on the interest in and knowledge of their own children's learning that many parents have. It is also true that many parents are insufficiently involved in the education of their children— poor and affluent parents alike. While schools often have not made parent involvement easy or otherwise have resisted it, many parents may need to act differently as well. Hargreaves and I (1998) suggested the following four guidelines for parents:

1. *Press Governments to Create the Kind of Teachers You Want.* Help make education a sophisticated election issue that goes beyond hackneyed slogans to address how we can make teaching better so that learning will get better too. Demand answers regarding the kinds of resources that will be dedicated to that end. How will we get and keep quality teachers? How will teachers be helped and encouraged to maintain and improve that quality over time? Better learning needs better teaching—how, precisely, will governments bring that about? Push them for answers.

2. *Leave Nostalgia Behind You.* Make more efforts to understand what schools are striving to achieve in today's world. Try and get first-hand knowledge and experience of what your children's school is doing now. Consider the knowledge and skills your children will need as they become citizens and workers in the future, and what kinds of teaching and learning are necessary to create these.

Don't long for your children to have exactly the kind of education you think you remember having yourself, just because that is what's familiar to you. The science of learning is profoundly different today. Find out more about these new developments. What worked in 1965 is unlikely suitable for 1995 or 2005 (Stoll & Fink, 1996). Remember the words of Christopher Lasch (1991)—"nostalgia is the abdication of memory."

3. *Ask What You Can Do for Your School as Well as What Your School Can Do for You.* What can you offer and contribute to support your school? The best place to start is at home. If you expect the school to develop a work ethic in your child, do you also insist on this at home by making sure he or she really does mow the lawn, shovel the snow, complete his or her homework, etc.? The more you give to your school and its teachers, the more responsiveness you are likely to get when you want something in return. Once more, relationships are the key.

4. *Put Praise Before Blame.* If you have criticisms to make of your children's education, remember that the teachers will be as anxious about meeting you as you are about meeting them. Try to put teachers at their ease. Put compliments before criticism. Wherever you can, see what the school is doing firsthand so you know your complaints aren't groundless. Contact teachers and thank them spontaneously when things are going well (which will make the more difficult encounters easier and put them into perspective). Take responsibility to build relationships with your children's teachers *before* problems arise. (pp. 124–125, emphasis in original)

In the meantime, the simple and powerful conclusion of this chapter is threefold. First, the vast majority of parents find meaning in activities related to their own children rather than in school- or systemwide endeavors. Second, educational reform requires the conjoint efforts of families and schools. Parents and teachers should recognize the critical complementary importance of each other in the life of the student. Otherwise, we are placing limitations on the prospects for improvement that may be impossible to overcome. Third, it is also time for system change. The larger infrastructure does make a difference. We start dealing with this infrastructure in Chapter 11 with the district, and then in Part III move to the bigger picture.

The District Administrator

To get the whole world out of bed, and washed, and dressed, and warmed, and fed, Believe me, Saul, costs worlds of pain.
—John Masefield, "The Everlasting Mercy" (1911)

It is possible for an individual school to become highly collaborative despite the district it is in, but it is not likely that it will *stay* collaborative. If the district does not foster collective capacity building by design, it undermines it by default. We now know that schools will not develop if left to their own devices.

Not all systems have school districts, and a local or regional authority in the United States is not the same as one in Canada, or England, or Sweden, or Australia. Nonetheless, it is abundantly clear that if a district is part of the system, it can play a vital role, again, for better or for worse. Just as Chapter 8, on the principal, is a shorthand reference to school leadership, this chapter on the district administrator is meant to encompass district leadership more generally. I comment first on where district administrators are, and then take up the question of what we are learning about the role of districts—moving from the negative to the positive. We are indeed learning a great deal.

WHERE DISTRICT ADMINISTRATORS ARE

District administrators in North America work in school systems ranging in size from fewer than 100 to more than 300,000 students. Districts in provinces in Canada, compared with most states in the United States, tend to be much larger. Ontario, for example, has some 72 districts, while Illinois and Ohio, similar in population to Ontario, have more than 600 each. Thus, the conditions and tasks can vary tremendously. In England it is more complex still. Even prior to the Every Child Matters reform (Department for Education and Skills, 2005), Local Education Authorities (LEAs), as they were called, were part of municipal authorities, and each school had a legally constituted board of governors—a body with considerable authority (to hire school heads and teachers, for example). Since ECM in 2005, education and all children's services (health, social work, etc.) have been placed under one entity called the Local Authority (LA). The chief executive, called the Director for Children's Services, runs the entire operation, with the mandate to integrate schooling and all children's support and development services. Talk about complex, and exciting.

As we consider North America, in small districts, the administrators frequently carry out several functions with few resources, and in large districts, they constantly are dealing with conflicts and crises and large financial and personnel issues through an elaborate bureaucracy of specialists. School superintendents are appointed (and fired) by locally elected school boards. Although there is a fair amount of evidence about the role of the administrator and change (which is the subject of the next section), there is little representative information on what administrators do and think in their total roles. Goldhammer (1977) reviewed the changing role of the American school superintendent from 1954 to 1974 and suggested that the major change over the 20-year period was away from the role of educational spokesperson and executive manager of a relatively homogeneous system, toward one where negotiation and conflict management of diverse interests and groups predominate. School boards have become more politically active, as have teacher unions and community and other special-interest groups. Communities have become more heterogeneous. Federal and state government agencies and courts in the United States have become major participants in educational programming through financial and legislative means. The superintendent, notes Goldhammer, has become more of a negotiator than a goal setter, a reactor and coordinator of diverse interests, and a person who must learn to lead and involve teams of specialists.

Blumberg (1985) studied 25 school superintendents, interviewing them about their roles, responsibilities, and perceptions of impact. Overwhelmingly, his respondents described their role as one of "conflict" and ambiguity mediated by everyday tasks. Blumberg observes that superintendents face

> The necessity of having to live daily with conflictual or potentially conflictual situations in which the superintendent plays a focal role as decision maker, mediator, or simply as a human lightning rod who attracts controversy. Some of the conflicts take on major, systemic proportions, affecting the entire school district. Some are major but affect only individuals. Some are minor. Some relate to the superintendent as a person, some to his job and career, and some to his family. Regardless of the focus or substance, a seemingly absolute condition of the superintendency is that there are only rarely days when the superintendent is not called upon to make a decision that will create some conflict, or is not involved somehow in conflicts of his own making. All of this seems to occur irrespective of the person involved: "it comes with the territory." (p. 1)

In Blumberg's perception, the role of the superintendent is different from that of other chief executive officers, due to

> the public perception of the superintendent as guardian of a sacred public enterprise, the education of the community's children; the politicalness of the relationship between the superintendent and the school board; and the fact that superintendents once held the same job—that of a teacher—as the people over whom they are now expected to exercise authority; the huge number of community and governmental groups with one or another stake in the school; the superintendent's visibility and accessibility as public property. (p. 188)

As one superintendent described it,

> It's always a balancing act because there are so many pressure groups. More so than ever before, and the funny thing is that we have made it happen that way. We have really pushed the idea that everyone should be involved in schools. So now I have so many different constituencies out there with so many differ-

ent interests that my problem is to try and keep them all ap-
peased. (p. 67)

What is most revealing about Blumberg's extensive explora-
tion of the working lives of superintendents is the infrequency
with which curriculum and instruction matters "naturally" arise
in the interviews. Superintendents talk about politics, school boards,
teacher unions, stress, public exposure, conflict, and so on. Curriculum, instruction, and professional development rarely arise in a
prominent way and do not appear at all in the index of Blumberg's book. This is not to say that these 25 superintendents had
no impact on curriculum and student achievement in their districts, only that keeping conflict at bay preoccupies superintendents unless they take extraordinary steps to go beyond it.

Several years ago we conducted an extensive study of "supervisory officers" in Ontario (those above the role of principal in
line positions up to and including the director or chief superintendent). Over 200 supervisory officers were interviewed in 26 school
districts (one quarter of the total) in the province. Three summa-
tive-style dimensions were developed: system-driven versus school-
driven, reflective versus firefighting, and generalist versus special-
ist (Fullan et al., 1987). As might be expected, directors, compared
with other central office superintendents, scored consistently higher
on the system, reflective, and generalist dimensions.

In further analysis of our data focusing on the 22 directors of
education in the study, Allison (1988) identified three distinct sectors of work: board (trustees), system, and community. In comparing the situation of chief executive officers in the United States
with those in Ontario, Allison suggests that the Ontario director-
ship evolved from a more stable tradition. By contrast, Allison states
that the emergence of the superintendent's role in the United
States is characterized by a culture of "conflict, insecurity and uncertainty" (p. 5).

Some specific features provide support for Allison's observation. Compared with their American counterparts, Ontario and,
more broadly, Canadian superintendents are more likely to head
larger, more stable school systems; are less laterally mobile; are
more likely to be appointed from within their own systems; and
have longer tenure as chief executive officers (Allison, 1988; Ful-

lan et al., 1987). Superintendents in Ontario in our study had an average tenure of 7 years. In the United States, it is commonly thought that the average superintendency is about 3 years, but Hodgkinson and Montenegro (1999) and McAdams (2006) report that 5 years is more accurate. Still, turnover in many U.S. districts is very high, leading one wag to observe that the largest group of migrant labor in the country is school superintendents.

In a study of the superintendency, Johnson (1996) followed the work of 12 newly appointed superintendents during the first 2 years of their appointments. She talks about the turmoil and complexity of school district leadership. Based on past experiences, teachers and principals "were skeptical about the promises, intentions and skills of their new superintendent. They withheld their support until they were convinced that these new administrators deserved it; in the end, they judged some to be worthy, others not" (p. 23).

Johnson found that three types of leadership were evident in the work of all the influential superintendents: educational leadership (focus on pedagogy and learning), political leadership (securing resources, building coalitions), and managerial leadership (using structures for participation, supervision, support, and planning). Johnson summarizes:

> When educational leadership was weak, teachers and principals often discredited the superintendent as being misguided and preoccupied with the wrong things. When political leadership was weak, the schools suffered undue financial cuts, became the captives of special interests on the school board, or became the battleground for citizens with competing priorities. When managerial leadership was weak, people became preoccupied with bureaucratic errors, communication among educators faltered, and potential school leaders could not act constructively. (p. 24)

Of the 12 districts, two had sought leaders who could bring about major change, four had looked for leaders who could provide continuity, and six had experienced disruption of such magnitude that their search committees primarily sought candidates "who could stabilize the system" (p. 41). This range is likely not atypical of districts generally. Almost all of these situations involve change in complex circumstances. Even districts seeking stability after disruption still must go through a sophisticated change process, and inevitably they find themselves grappling with student improvement, which is all the more difficult because they often don't have the basic capacity to move ahead.

Johnson concludes that superintendents must be "teachers" in all three domains—educational, political, and managerial—modeling, coaching, and building the capacity of principals, teacher leaders, school board members, and so on. Once again, change with any depth must be cultivated by building relationships while pushing forward. In districts that were on the move, "superintendents were active participants in the change process—raising concerns, voicing expectations, asking questions, offering encouragement, making suggestions, and insisting that change occur" (p. 280).

The major change since 2000 is the growing in-your-face presence of accountability and explicit expectations about improved student achievement. In the United States the federal legislation No Child Left Behind, signed in early 2002, forcefully represents this change of circumstances. By the time you add state standards and accountability (required by NCLB), and local school boards charged with making improvement come true *every year* à la adequate yearly progress (AYP), you have a recipe for "policy churn"— a term that Hess (1999) used to describe the world of school boards pre-NCLB. This phenomenon can only have intensified since his study, although now, as I will show below, we are getting glimpses of what can work (along with the realization that it is a lot harder to crack the instructional core of teaching for continuous improvement).

THE DISTRICT ADMINISTRATOR AND CHANGE

If we take a quantitative approach, the majority of districts are not effective. To be fair, stimulating, coordinating, and sustaining "coherent" development across many schools is exceedingly difficult because it requires balancing top-down and bottom-up forces.

I will trace the evolution of the role of districts in school reform using informal language to capture the three themes: getting somewhere; not so fast; and what's next?

Getting Somewhere

Since about 1990 there has been a growing body of work that points to common characteristics and strategies that successful districts use to raise student achievement. I referred in Chapter 7 to Rosenholtz's (1989) study of 78 elementary schools, which she classified as "stuck," "moving," and "in-between" schools. Rosenholtz also found that a disproportionate number of stuck schools came from certain districts; likewise, moving schools were clustered in certain other districts. This prompted her to write a chapter on stuck and moving districts (two of the eight districts were in the latter category). Rosenholtz comments:

> The contrast between stuck and moving districts, nowhere more apparent than here, underscores how principals become helpful instructional advisors or maladroit managers of their schools. It is also clear that stuck superintendents attribute poor performance to principals themselves, rather than accepting any responsibility to help them learn and improve. This again may indicate their lack of technical knowledge and subsequent threats to their self-esteem. If districts take no responsibility for the inservice needs of principals, of course, principals become less able colleagues, less effective problem-solvers, more reluctant to refer school problems to the central office for outside assistance, more threatened by their lack of technical knowledge, and, most essential, of substantially less help to teachers. Of equal importance, with little helpful assistance, stuck superintendents symbolically communicate the norm of self-reliance and subsequently professional isolation—that improvement may not be possible, or worthy of their time and effort, or that principals should solve their school problems by themselves—lugubrious lessons principals may unwittingly hand down to poorly performing teachers, and thus teachers to students. (p. 189)

Similar findings are contained in LaRocque and Coleman's (1989) analysis of "district ethos" and quality in school districts in British Columbia. The authors compiled performance data by aggregating school results on provincewide achievement tests. They rated the districts according to high, medium, and low performance. They selected ten districts for more detailed analysis, taking into account size and type of school community. LaRocque and Coleman hypothesized that positive district ethos would be characterized by a high degree of interest and concern relative to six sets of activity and attitude "focuses."

1. Taking care of business (a learning focus);
2. Monitoring performance (an accountability focus);
3. Changing policies/practices (a change focus);
4. Consideration and caring for stakeholders (a caring focus);
5. Creating shared values (a commitment focus); and
6. Creating community support (a community focus). (p. 169)

Three of the ten districts were classified as having a strong district presence in the schools, which is described in the following terms:

> The district administrators provided the principals with a variety of school-specific performance data; they discussed these data with the principals and set expectations for their use; and they monitored through recognized procedures, how and with what success the schools used the performance data. . . .
>
> The district administrators used their time in the schools purposefully to engage the principals in discussion on specific topics: school performance data, improvement plans, and the implementation of these plans. . . .
>
> In spite of the emphasis on school test results, the nature of the discussions was collaborative rather than prescriptive. The district administrators acknowledged good performance. They helped the principals interpret the data and identify strengths and weaknesses, and they offered advice and support when necessary. Ultimately, however, plans for improvement were left up to the principal and staff of each school—this point was stressed by the principals—although their progress in developing and implementing the plans was monitored. The features of collaboration and relative school autonomy probably reinforced the perception of respect for the role of the principal and recognition of the importance of treating each school as a unique entity. (p. 181)

All three of these districts had high performance ratings on achievement tests. At the other end of the continuum, three districts were characterized by an absence of press for accountability: Little or no data were provided to the schools, and no structures or processes were established to monitor or discuss progress. All three of these districts were found to be low on achievement results.

As we headed into the new century, evidence appeared to be coalescing around what it would take for districts to get district-wide success, at least in literacy and numeracy. Togneri and Anderson's (2003) study of success in five high-poverty districts found six clear and consistent strategies at work. These districts

1. Acknowledged publicly poor performance and sought solutions (building the will for reform)
2. Focused intensively on improving instruction and achievement
3. Built a system wide framework and infrastructure to support instruction
4. Redefined and distributed leadership at all levels of the district
5. Made professional development relevant and useful
6. Recognized there were no quick fixes (p. 13)

Similar findings were obtained by Snipes, Doolittle, and Herlihy (2002) in their analyses of four successful high-poverty districts—again corroborated in other studies of effective improvement strategies (Council of Chief School Officers, 2002). My colleague Steve Anderson (2006) has just reviewed the research on district effectiveness and named 12 key strategic components.

1. District-wide sense of efficacy
2. District-wide focus on student achievement and the quality of instruction
3. Adoption and commitment to district-wide performance standards
4. Development and adoption of district-wide curricula and approaches to instruction
5. Alignment of curriculum, teaching and learning materials, and assessment to relevant standards
6. Multimeasure accountability systems and systemwide use

of data to inform practice, hold school and district leaders accountable for results, and monitor progress

7. Targets and phased focuses of improvement
8. Investment in instructional leadership development at the school and district levels
9. District-wide, job-embedded professional development focuses and supports for teachers
10. District-wide and school-level emphasis on teamwork and professional community (including in several cases positive partnerships with unions)
11. New approaches to board–district relations and in-district relations
12. Strategic relations with state reform policies and resources

One would think, then, we have a growing consensus and that it is just a matter of going to town on what we know. One would be wrong.

Not So Fast

So, a district should get the standards right, align curriculum to them, conduct assessments on the new alignment, provide solid and continuous professional development on curriculum and instruction, set up a data system that can be used for both assessment "for" and assessment "of" learning, and engage with the local community and state reform policies. It may surprise many readers that these steps by themselves are not sufficient and at best may represent a waste of resources, and at worst do more harm than good.

The experience of the San Diego City Schools District is a good place to start with respect to the "not so fast" theme. Coming off a highly successful experience in District 2 in New York City from 1988–1996, Tony Alvarado was hired as Chancellor of Instruction in 1997 to join a new high-profile superintendent, Alan Bersin, in San Diego. In a sense the question was, if you could take the best knowledge, and add resources and political clout, could you get results in a large urban district within a 4-year period, and then keep going, in this case, moving from success in 45 schools (District 2) to 175 schools (San Diego). The answer, incidentally, is yes, but it requires good strategies and a good deal of finesse.

The San Diego reform story is probably the most closely watched reform initiative in the history of urban school improvement. I draw here on the excellent account by Hubbard and her colleagues (2006). The San Diego strategy was well detailed and explicit from day one. It consisted of the following three main components:

- Improved student learning: closing the achievement gap
- Improved instruction: teacher learning through professional development
- Restructuring the organization to support student learning and instruction

The focus was on literacy, and the strategies, highly specific. Teachers received support from literacy coaches and principals who were positioned to be "leaders of instruction," with day-to-day support, and monthly full-day inservice sessions by area superintendents whose new role (and new people) were re-created as instructional leaders.

We don't have the space to enter a detailed account of the San Diego experience, but the main outcomes and reasons can be identified (for a full account, see Hubbard et al., 2006). To cut to the chase, literacy achievement increased somewhat at the elementary level in the 1997–2001 period, had a limited impact in middle schools, and was a dismal failure in high schools. Momentum was lost by 2001, Alvarado was asked to leave in 2002, and Bersin, after slowing down the nature and pace of reform in 2003–2004, was replaced by the school board when his term expired in June 2005. What happened?

One could say that it was a political problem—the board was divided from the beginning (3–2 in favor of the reform initiative), and the teacher union that opposed the reform from the beginning eventually carried the day. There is some truth to this, but the deeper explanation is closer to the theme of our interest in meaning and motivation relative to pace, the too-tight/too-loose problem, and the depth of instructional change and thinking required to make a difference. Hubbard and colleagues (2006) expressed the basic problem in terms of three challenges that the strategy failed to address: "The need to accomplish deep learning within the constraints of a limited time frame; principals' and coaches' limited understanding of the concepts they were trying to teach; and the difficulty of reaching common ground between school leaders and teachers" (p. 128).

All this despite plenty of classroom visits, walk-throughs involving all schools, frequent problem-solving sessions, and an emphasis on job-embedded professional learning. The San Diego case is an exercise in the dilemmas faced by leaders with an urgent sense of moral purpose and considerable knowledge of what should happen in classroom instruction. But it also points to how the strategies employed must be much more respectful of how deep change happens. Much good was done in improving literacy achievement in elementary schools, but it was not deep enough or owned enough to go further. The San Diego strategy failed because the pace of change was too fast, the strategy was too unidirectional from the top, relationships were not built with teachers and principals, and, above all, the strategies did not really build capacity, which is the development of the collective knowledge and understandings required for ongoing instructional improvement that meets the needs of each child. This is going to be a lot harder than we thought (we have mapped out capacity-building strategies in Fullan, 2006; Fullan et al., 2006).

San Diego is also one of the better examples of attempted reform. Most districts do not focus their efforts on district-wide reform. And when they do, they encounter limits to what can be accomplished despite considerable effort and resources.

Another confirmation of our "not so fast" worry comes from the Cross City Campaign for Urban School Reform (2005), which I referenced earlier and examines major reform initiatives in Chicago, Milwaukee, and Seattle. All three school systems had the attention of political leaders at all levels of the system and focused on many of the "right things," such as literacy and math; all of the systems used current choice strategies such as concentration on "assessment for learning" data, invested heavily in professional development, developed new leadership, and focused on systemwide change.

And they had money—Seattle had $35 million in external

funds, Milwaukee had extra resources and flexibility, and Chicago had multimillions. There was huge pressure, but success was not expected overnight. Decision makers and the public would have been content to see growing success over a 5- or even 10-year period. The upfront conclusion of the case study evaluators, as I mentioned earlier, was that for many of the principals and teachers interviewed, "the districts were unable to change and improve practice on a large scale" (Cross City Campaign for Urban School Reform, 2005, p. 4).

The issues in the Chicago, Milwaukee, and Seattle reforms help to identify the missing ingredient, even though those districts appear to have gotten most components right. Chicago, for example, appeared to have an impressive strategy: Academic standards and instructional frameworks, assessment and accountability systems, and professional development for standards-based instruction are among the tools of systemic reform that are used to change classroom instruction (Cross City Campaign for Urban School Reform, 2005, p. 23).

Here is a "standards-based" systemwide reform that sounds like it should work. The failure, I think, is that the strategy lacks a focus on what needs to change in instructional practice. In Chicago, teachers did focus on standards, but in interviews, they "did not articulate any deep changes in teaching practice that may have been under way" (p. 23). Furthermore, "instructional goals were articulated more often in terms of student outcomes or achievement levels than in terms of instructional quality, that is, *what the schools do* to help students achieve" (p. 29, emphasis in original).

Milwaukee reveals similar problems in achieving instructional improvements while using greater decentralization in the context of system support and competitive choice. The focus was on literacy; a literacy coach was housed in every school in the district and considerable professional development and technical support services were available. Education plans for each school were to focus on literacy standards through (1) data analysis and assessment and (2) subject-area achievement targets, including literacy across the curriculum. Sounds like a convincing strategy. However, what is missing, again, is the black box of instructional practice in the classroom. The case writers observe: "We placed the Education Plan in the indirect category due to its non-specificity regarding regular or desired instructional content and practices" (Cross City Campaign for Urban School Reform, 2005, p. 49).

More generally, the report concludes that while these serious district-wide reform initiatives "appeared" to prioritize instruction, they did so indirectly (through standards, assessment, leadership responsibilities). However, in the experience of principals and teachers, the net effect was that "policies and signals were non-specific regarding intended effects on classroom teaching and learning" (p. 65).

Our third case, Seattle, is a variation on the same theme. The game plan looks good. Standards defined the direction, while the district's Transformational Academic Achievement Planning Process "was designed as a vehicle for helping schools develop their own strategy for (1) helping all students meet standards, and (2) eliminating the achievement gap between white students and students of color" (p. 66). Like Milwaukee, the district reorganized to support site-based management, including the allocation of considerable resources to schools. The case writers observe:

> The recent effort to become a standards-based district was one of the first sustained instructional efforts with direct attention to teaching and learning. However, the conversations district leaders had about standards *were rarely connected to changes in instruction*. (Cross City Campaign for Urban School Reform, 2005, p. 69, emphasis added)

The report continues: "At the school level, finding teachers who understood the implications of standards for their teaching was difficult" (p. 72).

I will cite one more case, which in some ways is more encouraging but still proves my main conclusion that instructional change is going to require different strategies that help develop and shape collective capacity and shared commitment to engage in continuous improvement. As mentioned earlier, Supovitz (2006) conducted an excellent case study of the reform effort in Duval County, Florida. The title of his book captures the emphasis of his analysis—*The Case for District-Based Reform*. Supovitz chronicled the district-wide reform effort from 1999 through 2005. Duval County has 142 schools. The reform strategy is now familiar to us.

1. Develop a specific vision of what high-quality instruction should look like
2. Build both the commitment and capacity of employees across the system to enact and support the instructional vision
3. Construct mechanisms to provide data at all levels of the system that will be used both to provide people with information that informs their practices and to monitor the implementation of the instructional vision
4. Develop the means to help people continually deepen their implementation and to help the district continually refine this vision and understand its implications

With a sustained 5-year focus on the four strategic components, the district made significant gains in student achievement. For example, the number of schools receiving C or better on the state assessment system went from 87 (of 142) in 1999 to 121 by 2003. Also, for the first time in a 7-year period, in 2005 no school in the district received an F on the state accountability system.

The strategy was driven by a strong superintendent who helped to orchestrate the development of district-wide capacity according to the four core components above. The strategy was enacted with considerable action and focus. As Supovitz reports, "Duval County leaders repeatedly stated their vision and the strategies for achieving it in public venues" (p. 43). Supovitz argues that the spread and deepening of district-wide success is as much "gardening" as it is "engineering" (p. 63). And that the balance requires "advocacy without mandate" (p. 66), "fostering urgency" (p. 68), and "building existing proof" of success (p. 69). We see a similar array of strategies as in San Diego, but with less heavy-handedness: direct training of teachers, school standards coaches, district standards coaches, principal leadership development, and district leadership development.

With 6 years of consistent effort and with an explicit emphasis on professional learning communities as a strategy, Supovitz comments: "The possibilities of professional learning communities— rigorous inquiry into the problems and challenges of instructional practice and the support of that practice—seemed only to be occurring in pockets of the district" (p. 174). Much was accomplished in Duval County, but it was by no means deep or durable after 6 years. So our "not so fast" observation is an apt worry. Even with comprehensive strategies and relentless focus over a 5- or 6-year period, we are still not getting it right.

What's Next?

We have seen that even the most ambitious efforts fall short, and these initiatives involve only a small minority of districts. Most are not nearly so active. I believe we are on the right track, but the approach needs considerable refinement. To state what is needed up front, we do need a focus on instruction, standards, assessment, continuous feedback and use of data, and instructional leadership at the district and school levels. But we also need a process of interactive capacity building and commitment building within and among schools, and between schools and the district. Above all, this increasingly must deprivatize teaching so that learning in context can occur, and the district must "stay the course" over a period of 10 or more years. This work does not necessarily require the same superintendent over two or more terms, but does require continuity of good direction over two or three superintendencies. I cite here three examples, from three different countries, of what this means in practice.

York Region District School Board just outside Toronto, Ontario, is a multicultural district with a growing and diverse population, and over 100 different languages spoken in the schools. There are 140 elementary schools and 27 secondary schools. We have been working in partnership with York for the past 5 years, including monitoring the processes and results as we go (see, for example, Sharratt & Fullan, 2006). The focus is on literacy in an initiative called the Literacy Collaborative (LC). The basic approach is designed to shape and reshape district-wide continuous improvement, what I call *capacity building with a focus on results*. Key features of the approach include

- A clearly articulated vision and commitment to literacy for all students, which is continually the subject of communication in the district
- A systemwide comprehensive plan and framework for continuous improvement

- Using data to inform instruction and determine resources
- Building administrator and teacher capacity to teach literacy for all students
- Establishing professional learning communities at all levels of the system and beyond the district

All schools, including all secondary schools, joined the LC in a phased-in fashion, with school-based teams being the focal point for capacity building. At the elementary level, teams consisted of the principal (always the principal), the lead literacy teacher (a leadership role within the school, with a teacher released for .50 to 1.0 time to work with principals and teachers), and the special education resource teacher. High school teams were slightly larger and focused on literacy, especially in grades 9 and 10. The LC model has evolved to contain 13 parameters, which I will not list here but which include embedded literacy teachers, timetabled literacy blocks, a case-management approach focusing on each student, cross-curricular literacy connections, and so on (see Sharratt & Fullan, 2006). There is constant interaction, action research and capacity building through formal monthly sessions, and many learning-in-context interactions carried out daily by school and district leaders within and across schools.

The results, as measured by provincewide assessments, were significant after a 3-year period (2001–2004), but not as substantial as district leaders had hoped. On a closer examination of the initial cohort of 17 schools, it was found that nine of the schools had implemented the 13 parameters more deeply compared with the other eight. When the latter schools were separated, the results showed that the nine schools, despite starting below the York Region and Ontario provincial average in 2001, had risen above both averages by 2004. In the meantime, the district was working with all 167 schools. Provincewide results in 2005 showed that York Region increased by a full 5%, on the average, in literacy across its 140 elementary schools. High schools also did well for the first time on the grade 10 literacy test. Reflecting a theory of action that I will soon spell out, in 2006 the district identified 27 elementary schools and six high schools that were still underperforming and designed an intensive capacity-building interaction for the 2005–2006 school year (as work with all schools continued).

In terms of what's new, we can consider the theory of action reflected in the approach in York Region. First, we have many of the elements we have seen previously—standards, assessment of and for learning, instructional leadership, and so on—but we also see two new significant emphases. One is that the leaders have taken a long-term perspective. They realize that it takes a while for change to kick in. They frequently speak of "staying the course," and "persistence but flexibility." The pace is steady, even pushy, but not overwhelming. They expect results, not overnight, but also not open-ended. The other new aspect is that leaders are careful not to judge slow or limited progress in given schools. They take what I call a "capacity building first, judgment second" stance as they have with the 33 lower performing schools. Large-scale change is all about moving the whole system so that more and more leaders permeate the system and take daily actions that build capacity and ownership.

This is a whole district that is on the move. There has been one director (superintendent), Bill Hogarth, throughout the 8-year process, and a strong rapport between the board and the district leadership. Because a strong collaborative culture has been built, the chances of continuing this direction when he leaves (sometime in the next 2 years) are greatly increased. As I said, you don't need the same superintendent over 8 to 12 years, but you do need continuity and deepening of "good" direction.

A second good example is the decade-long reform initiative of the 58,000 student Boston Public Schools (BPS) under the leadership of Superintendent Tom Payzant. McLaughlin and Talbert (2006) describe the basic plan as based on six essentials: effective instruction as the core essential, student work and data, professional development, shared leadership, resources, and families and community. Again the words are familiar, but it is the theory of action, and careful cultivation over a decade, that is the real story. Professional development, for example, takes place at the school level and features a coaching strategy involving collaborative teaching groups. In collaborative coaching, teachers learn by analyzing one another's work under the guidance of skilled coaches. The idea is not just to observe one another's teaching and share ideas, but to critique lessons in a way that links to improving student learning. As with the York Region, a well-supported and easy-to-access database on student learning is used to help teachers examine their teaching in light of ongoing results, integrating data into professional learning. Substantial outreach to parents and community is a major component of all teachers' and schools' work.

Education Week published a profile on BPS and Payzant on the occasion of his announcing his retirement in 2007 after 11 years as superintendent ("Time on His Side," 2006). In addition to reporting on the activities and approach just described, *Education Week* gets beneath the strategy.

> Mr. Payzant did not bring the Boston schools to this point overnight. He rolled out initiatives not all at once, but only when they made sense. The ideas was to start small, test things out, and retool them. And he focused on building consensus. All were radical notions in an era of hard-charging, quick turnaround leaders. (p. 31)

The impact of the Boston strategy brought significant results in student achievement. In grade 10 English language arts and in grade 10 mathematics, scores have increased steadily since 1999 for all four race and ethnicity groups (Black, White, Asian and Hispanic), with some leveling off in the 2004 and 2005 years (a point to which I will return shortly). McLaughlin and Talbert (2006) summarize the positive impact in these words.

> Multiple evaluations show that Boston's approach to instruction [and] to collaborative coaching and learning are benefiting students and teachers. Student outcomes have improved, as have relationships between teachers and students and among teachers. Boston sees other positive system-level consequences of their strategy—enhanced coherence, increased accountability at all levels, and increased buy in from district educators. (pp. 126–127)

Again we see a more sophisticated theory of action carrying the day. Not that we are seeing flawless strategies. The pace of change was likely not fast enough in Boston. Put another way, few superintendents would be allowed to take this amount of time in

2007. But my point remains. Too fast is a more likely negative scenario. Balancing pace—press for improvement with corresponding capacity building—carefully assessed as you go, is required. Payzant's own reflective lessons are revealing. He says he left some areas of work "too much to chance." He said he should have allowed fewer programs for teaching literacy. Likewise, he said it was a mistake to let high schools come up with their own plans for creating more personalized learning environments for students ("Time on His Side," 2006).

The performance in Boston, along with substantial improvements, also reveals a plateauing effect in the last 2 years, a phenomenon that is normal, not to be lamented, but requiring new, deeper strategies. Elmore (2004) and I (Fullan, 2006) have both commented on the plateau effect as a natural and (depending on what you do next) a valuable opportunity to consolidate and then go deeper. Also, while all four race and ethnicity groups have gained, the gap has not closed and in some cases has increased. The next critical question for Boston is who will be Payzant's successor. I have said that in these cases of being on the right track, it is crucial for districts to hire for continuity and deepening of good direction. We shall see.

We move to England for our third example, which does have continuity of good direction over two directors of education. Knowsley Local Education Authority (since 2005 called Local Authority) is a metropolitan district just east of Liverpool. It is defined as the sixth most-deprived authority in the country. In 1999 Knowsley consisted of 59 primary schools, 11 secondary schools, and 7 special schools. The district was audited in that year as part of the national inspection scheme conducted by the Office for Standards in Education (OFSTED). The assessment found serious weaknesses on most basic dimensions of performance: student achievement, capacity to improve, relationships between the district and the schools, and linkage to the community. A new Director of Education, Steve Munby, was appointed in 1999. A second inspection was conducted in 2003, which found major improvements. What happened in 4 years to transform a very low-performing, disadvantaged, discouraged system into one vastly improved and ready to do more?

We can begin with OFSTED's 2003 findings.

> Recent developments and the implementation of well thought
> through initiatives have resulted in Knowsley establishing itself
> as an LEA of some significance. It has improved over the past
> three years and shown how vision and leadership together with
> excellent relationships with schools, can revive an education
> service. (p. 2)

As OFSTED further noted, both literacy and numeracy scores increased at a time when national averages were flatlined. OFSTED
also observes that "the new adminstration has taken partnerships
and collaborative working to an unusually high level." And,
"headteachers of individual schools see themselves as part of a
wider team with responsibility for the education service throughout the borough" (p. 2).

Steve Munby (2003) states that the drivers for change are low
student performance, new leadership, external funding, and a
moral commitment to narrowing the gap between the highest and
lowest performing schools. Munby then lists what he calls his
"priorities for sustainability":

- Establishing an innovative, coherent, and comprehensive policy
  framework that provides direction for instruction and professional learning
- The training of "lead learners" to support school learning
- Deploying lead learners to work with clusters of schools to embed
  new practice
- Cluster-based work—action learning, observing and sharing
  learning, supporting small-scale action research to provide evidence of impact on pupil motivation, and engagement with the
  learning process
- Encouragement and support of the further development and em-
  bedding of a culture of co-planning, co-teaching, co-review, and
  co-coaching in schools, everyone a leader of learning (p. 2).

In January 2005, Munby was appointed CEO of the National
College of School Leadership (see Chapter 14). Time for continuity
of good direction. The new director, Damian Allen, was appointed
from within Knowsley, having been deputy director. Because
Munby had employed a strategy of co-development of leadership,

Allen was already immersed in the strategy, and in fact had helped shape it. By the time he was appointed in January 2005, the new Every Child Matters agenda had become a reality, with all children's services, including schools, coming under the Local Authority (LA). Allen became the first Executive Director, Children's Services. Knowsley has continued with the directional strategy of having an ambitious agenda for children, but forging ahead with co-leadership and capacity building. The district proceeded to introduce a remarkable secondary school reform that involved closing all 11 high schools, and reopening them with eight brand-new schools, complete with new state of the art buildings called "learning centers." Knowsley did this without any rancor and indeed considerable enthusiasm, partly because of the co-leadership strategy, partly because new national money was available for new buildings, and partly because it was already experiencing success (for example, the percentage of 15-year-olds passing five or more GCSEs—a mark of advanced placement courses for further education—had doubled from 22% in 1998 to 45% in 2005, while the national average moved from 47% to 57%).

Ever conscious of the theory of action that had gotten them there, Allen (2006) made a presentation at a national meeting in which he compared the Knowsley strategy with the strategy embedded in the recent white paper from the government (Department for Education and Skills, 2005). After pointing out the inconsistencies in the white paper, he noted the following comparisons (Knowsley on left; white paper on right):

Co-leadership between LA and schools	Vs.	Individual independent specialisms
Collaboration and federation as standard	Vs.	Collaboration and federation as a response to weakness
System performance	Vs.	Individual school performance
Failure driven out by challenge and support	Vs.	Failure driven out by early intervention and closure
Development of co-leadership	Vs.	Schools need autonomy
High support and engagement with schools	Vs.	Light-touch monitoring

Well, you get the picture. What's new, in my view, is the creating of partnerships of engagement that mobilize the entire system (see Fullan, 2006). It is still early in Knowsley's journey, but one can see a consistent, adaptable strategy in which successive leaders build on good direction, interacting with internal and external contexts. We see this in our own work in Ontario in which we are helping districts develop effective strategies to bring about systemwide reform—a strategy I describe in Chapter 12 (see also Campbell & Fullan, 2006; Fullan, 2006).

IMPLICATIONS

Anyone close to the scene of action can bear witness to the fact that the role of the local district is subject to hot debate and enormous gyrations. Districts shift from tightly focused prescription to empowered decentralization and all variations in between. I have tried in this chapter to uncover what is effective and ineffective, and why when it comes to the role of the district it is neither centralization nor decentralization, but both. Strong presence of the center is required in order to establish conditions for collective focus and commitment, where educators feel and act responsibly for the system of schools, not just their corner of the action. Some guidelines can be generated.

1. *Choose a district in which change has a chance of occurring or do not expect much change.* Some communities are dominated by a power structure that is more interested in the status quo; other communities are so fractious that the superintendent is the inevitable victim; still others expect administrators to lead change. Although the classification is greatly oversimplified, the main message is sound—the interest in change, or leverage for change, in a district must be at least minimally present. Without that, the chief executive officer is as powerless as anyone else, and in fact will likely become the convenient scapegoat. Other district administrators (below the level of the CEO) will have to make similar choices and also will have to determine whether the superintendent with whom they will be or are working is knowl-

edgeable and actively supportive of change—ideally, someone who can teach them something about how to implement change effectively.

2. *Once in a district, develop the management capabilities of administrators—other district administrators and principals—to lead change.* Using a combination of promotion criteria, inservice training emphasizing development and growth, and replacement of administrators through attrition or forced resignation (in extreme cases), the goal is to develop incrementally the district's administrative capability to lead and facilitate improvement. Among other things, the district administrator must require and help principals to work with teachers, which means that he or she must have the ability and willingness to work closely with principals. Co-leadership (co-determination) by school and district levels is key.

3. *Invest in teacher development from recruitment to professional development throughout the career, with a strong emphasis on "learning in context"* (see Chapters 13 and 14).

4. *Focus on instruction, teaching, and learning, and changes in the culture of schools.* Both short-term and long-term strategies should be used consistently and persistently to establish norms and the capacity for collaboration and continuous improvement in the learning environments of students and educators. This is deep cultural change involving deprivatizing teaching in a way that motivates teachers to improve as part of the collective action within and across schools.

5. *Monitor the improvement process.* The need for monitoring is never ending. The information-gathering system to assess and address problems of implementation must be institutionalized. The more horizontal and vertical two-way communication that exists, the more knowledge there will be about the status of change. Benchmarks, transparent information, and intervention in persistently failing schools are all part of the monitoring process. Action research with respect to instruction, and in regard to the efficacy of change strategies, is a must.

6. *Foster an identity with the district.* Principals and teachers who are interested in only whether their own school does

well and are not interested in other schools in the district will not find themselves in supportive districts in the long run. Superintendents can change that by developing district-wide identity in the service of individual school development for all schools. System coherence occurs when peers (e.g., principals across schools) identify with one another, as well as experience a true partnership with district leadership.

7. *Move toward the danger in selectively forming external partnerships* with the community, city, and other agencies in order to further the work of the schools in the district.

8. *Above all, work on continually conceptualizing the purpose, design, and process of continuous district reform.* The best leaders evolve, articulate, and reflect on their theories of action/change. For example, most districts need to be reorganized in order to function in the new way, but a superintendent would be at sea without a conception of what design principles should drive the new organization, and what theories of action are likely to go deep and sustain focus and the pursuit of improvement.

In sum, I want to emphasize how very fundamental the change we are talking about is relative to the current cultures of schools and districts. Most school systems are still "loosely coupled," despite top-down efforts to the contrary. When things are tightened, as in San Diego, good efforts can backfire. What is necessary, as Elmore (2000) also argues, is a change in the organization itself—in its very culture.

> Improvement at scale is largely a *property of organizations*, not of the pre-existing traits of the individuals who work in them. Organizations that improve do so because they create and nurture agreement on what is worth achieving, and they set in motion the internal processes by which people progressively learn how to do what they need to do in order to achieve what is worthwhile. (p. 25, emphasis in original)

And

> It seems clear that administrators in the districts that are improving avoid pointless and distracting arguments about cen-

tralization and decentralization. Instead, they spend a lot of time building a sense of urgency and support in specific schools and communities around issues of standards and performance. It also seems clear that if they communicate that urgency to principals and teachers, as well as to schools collectively, they will have to accept a high degree of responsibility for the detailed decisions. (p. 33)

Elmore (2004, 2006) has continued to insist that administrators at the school and district level are responsible for creating and nurturing, and propelling the conditions necessary to support, sustained individual and collective engagement in improvement. In the same way that effective principals "cause" teachers' work to improve, effective superintendents, as we have seen, affect the work of schools through the strategies they pursue and the specific mechanisms on the ground associated with such strategies. You can get short-term results through heavy-handed methods, but they are surface gains, and they are extracted at a high price. Besides, "why get better at a bad game?" (Block, 1987, p. 9). Why not change the game? In a word, the role of the superintendent is to help lead the way in changing the game for the better.

PART III

EDUCATIONAL CHANGE AT THE REGIONAL AND NATIONAL LEVELS

CHAPTER 12

Governments

> *The state is an incredibly blunt instrument; it gets hold of one overarching idea and imposes it without any sensitivity to local context. [And there] is the desperate craving of politicians for a magical solution.*
> —Micklethwait and Wooldridge (1996, p. 294)

It will be a wise and courageous politician who declares that capacity building is more important than accountability (and it will take a wise and courageous teacher union leader to declare that professional learning communities take precedence over individual teacher autonomy; see Chapter 14). A decade ago Andy Hargreaves and I wrote the *What's Worth Fighting for* trilogy on the assumption that on any given day, the "system" might not know what it is doing. Thus, we tried to equip teachers and principals with insights and action guidelines so that they could make headway despite the system. This is still valuable advice. But what if the system did know what it was doing by way of creating meaning, commitment, and impact on a large scale? This chapter explores the ins and outs of this question.

   Only small-scale, nonlasting improvement can occur if the system is not helping. My *Change Forces* trilogy focused on the system, using chaos or what is now called complexity theory. I argued that the complex nonlinear forces in dynamic systems could be better understood and acted upon if people at all levels worked on building learning organizations. This led to the conclusion, first introduced in *Change Forces with a Vengeance* (Fullan, 2003), that we need to base our future on trying to accomplish trilevel reform, namely, what has to happen at (1) the school and community level, (2) the district level as the mid-part of the tri, and (3) the state or national level. The goal is not to strive for alignment, but rather to establish *permeable connectivity*. This means that there would be plenty of two-way interaction and mutual influence within and across the three levels. Much of our recent work focuses on this ambitious but crucial goal.

Governments face a dilemma, as Micklethwait and Wooldridge pointed out above. Their world is one of wanting quick solutions for urgent problems. Yet bringing about change on a large scale is enormously complex. If it is difficult to manage change in one classroom, one school, one school district, imagine the scale of the problems faced by a state or province or country in which numerous agencies and levels and tens or hundreds of thousands of people are involved. It is infinitely more difficult for that government if its personnel do not venture out to attempt to understand the culture and the problems of local school people.

If we are to achieve large-scale reform, governments are essential. They have the potential to be a major force for transformation. The historical evidence to date, however, suggests that few governments have gotten this right. In this chapter I take up the role of governments in three ways. First, I address what we know about their effect on local implementation. Second, I use the National Literacy and Numeracy Strategy in England as a case example to illustrate many of the issues that will require attention, and the more recent case of Ontario, Canada, to show what is involved in trying to get it right. Third, I draw out the implications for what governments need to do if they are interested in greater improvement across all or most schools. The issues at stake are what governments are doing and what they can do to make a difference.

THE ROLE OF GOVERNMENTS

By "governments" I mean federal and state governments in the United States, provinces in Canada (because there is virtually no federal policy presence in education), and national governments in countries that are governed as one system. I want to provide an advance organizer. Governments can push *accountability*, provide *incentives* (pressure and supports), and/or foster *capacity building*. We will see that if they do only the first and second, they can get some short-term results that, I will argue, are real but not particularly deep or lasting. If they do all three, they have a chance of going the distance. Many governments have put all their eggs in the accountability basket; a few have been good at integrating pressure and support; and none have seriously affected capacity, although several are now working on it.

In the United States, starting with the publication of *A Nation at Risk* (National Commission on Excellence in Education, 1983), attention shifted to what governments should do to accomplish badly needed large-scale reform. By and large, the efforts of the decade following 1983 concentrated on beefing up accountability expectations and requirements. These early policy initiatives, focusing only on accountability, did more damage than good. They put tremendous pressure on local systems, while providing little help, and actually increased the overload and fragmentation of effort.

Firestone, Rosenblum, and Bader (1992) studied the evolution of reform in six states—Arizona, California, Florida, Georgia, Minnesota, and Pennsylvania—over a 7-year period between 1983 and 1990. They make a similar observation.

> Government fragmentation runs from central agencies to peripheral ones—that is, from federal and state governments to districts, schools, and ultimately classrooms. The study of policy implementation since the 1960s has been a history of efforts to identify ways for agencies at one level to influence those at the next level down; authoritative directions and responsive compliance turn out to be the exception. The best that can usually be expected of efforts to get districts to implement state and federal policy is mutual adaptation through which central expectations adapt to local preferences at least as much as the opposite occurs. High-quality implementation is the exception. (p. 256)

In addition to the fragmentation in the above vertical relationships, there are also enormous horizontal disconnections. Countless agencies, many of them government entities or government-sponsored groups, fail to coordinate their work, so that multiple initiatives collide in a haphazard fashion. Let us not forget that governments also live in a world of "adoption," not implementation—the time line for implementation is always longer than the next election. Related to this, is that it is easier to adopt *structural* changes than it is to engage in the hard work of *cultural* changes in relationships, capacity, and motivation. Most policies (e.g., vouchers, charters, and site-based management), argues Elmore (2000), "are quintessential structural changes in that they imply absolutely nothing about either the content or quality of instruction" (p. 10).

Lusi's (1997) detailed case studies of the role of State Departments of Education (SDEs) in Kentucky and Vermont confirm that accountability-driven strategies by themselves can never work because you cannot "change the practice of a large number of practitioners over whom [you] have little control and no proximity" (p. 11). I will return later to new work that states have begun to do to enhance the likelihood of widespread reform at the local level. In any case, in complex systems heavy-handed accountability schemes can never work because they cannot create the beliefs and behaviors necessary for success. The next logical step, then, is to add incentives (an amalgamation of pressure and support). The history of policymaking over the past decade concerning teacher quality is very instructive.

A good summary is provided by Darling-Hammond from the work of the National Commission on Teaching and America's Future.

> Of the 50 states, North Carolina and Connecticut undertook the most substantial and systematic investments in teaching during the mid-1980's. Both of these states, which share relatively large high poverty student populations, coupled major statewide increases in teacher salaries and improvements in teacher salary equity with intensive recruitment efforts and initiatives to improve preservice teacher education, licensing, beginning teacher mentoring, and ongoing professional development. Since then, North Carolina has posted the largest student achievement gains in mathematics and reading of any state in the nation, now scoring well above the national average in 4th grade reading and mathematics, although it entered the 1990s near the bottom of state rankings. Connecticut has also posted significant gains, becoming one of the top scoring states in the nation in mathematics and reading (ranked first at the 4th grade level in mathemat-

ics and reading, and in the top five at the 8th grade level),
despite an increase in the proportion of low-income and limited
English proficiency students during the time. (Darling-Hammond,
2000b, p. 13)

Even more revealing is Darling-Hammond's comparison of
states that employed accountability-only strategies versus those
that combined accountability with incentives (skill training, rewards, etc.).

State reform strategies during the 1980s that did not include
substantial efforts to improve the nature and quality of classroom work have shown little success in raising achievement,
especially if the reforms relied primarily on student testing
rather than investments in teaching. For example, the two states
to reorganize their reforms around new student testing systems
were Georgia and South Carolina. These states developed extensive testing systems coupled with rewards and sanctions for
students, teachers, and schools. Although both states mandated
tests for teachers, they did not link these assessments to emerging knowledge about teaching or to new learning standards,
nor did they invest in improving schools of education or ongoing professional development. (2000a, pp. 14–15)

In comparing student achievement in geographically proxi-
mate states that used different strategies (Connecticut vs. New Jer-
sey; North Carolina vs. Georgia; and West Virginia vs. Virginia),
Darling-Hammond concluded:

Although the states that have aggressively pursued investments
in teacher knowledge and skills have equal or higher levels of
student poverty than nearby states that pursued other distinc-
tively different strategies, their students now achieve at higher
levels. (2000a, p. 15)

It appears that the more successful states have indeed invested in *capacity building*, but I am going to conclude later that
these are really baby steps, more in line with what incentives will
produce—some degree of commitment and achievement, but not
very deep. Nonetheless, it is a start. A principal from Kentucky in

Goertz's (2000) study of local accountability in nine states puts it this way.

> [The state assessment program] has probably been driving everything we've done. You can say you're doing it to raise students' achievement. To be honest you're doing it because of accountability and assessment. I don't know if the whole accountability piece with rewards and sanction is still the deal. It was at the beginning. Now it's a matter of pride. Before, we didn't want the scores to slip; now it's self-examination. Without the state assessment, I don't think that would have come into play. We may have been able to make some changes, maybe start some good things. But the degree and speed we have changed never would have happened. (p. 12)

In the United States accountability got another boost in 2002 with the passage of No Child Left Behind. This legislation required all states to establish, no later than 2005–06, annual reading and mathematics tests for all students in grades 3 through 8, and reading and mathematics tests in grades 10, 11, or 12. Tests must be administered to at least 95% of students enrolled in a given grade level. The specific assessments and tests are left up to the states, but they must be standardized statewide—all students must take the same tests in the same way.

The law also requires every school in the state to demonstrate every year adequate yearly progress. By 2013–14, every child must attain "proficiency" in every test. Schools and districts set AYP targets annually on their way to 100% proficiency. From day one, if a school fails to meet its targets for 2 consecutive years, it is designated as "in need of improvement." Parents in those schools have the right to transfer their children to other, successful schools in the district. Schools that fail to make AYP for 4 years in a row are identified as in need of "corrective action." Schools that fail for 5 years are placed in a "restructuring" category and may be taken over by the state, operated by a private management firm, or converted into a charter school.

Additional actions and requirements accompany or spin off from NCLB. The law also mandated that, by 2005–06, every classroom in the country must have a "qualified teacher" (see Chapter

13 for a review of teacher education policies). In addition to training the spotlight on every school, districts quickly become implicated. Entire districts with too many "failing schools" are being taken over by city mayors, or states—not a requirement of the federal law but a natural consequence of rampant AYPism.

NCLB certainly has brought matters of performance and progress out in the open. It does some good in focusing attention on the problems we have been discussing in this book. But in its present form, NCLB cannot possibly succeed. James Popham (2004) has rendered a devastating chapter and verse critique of NCLB, showing that the law is practically and politically impossible and that the majority of schools will be labeled as failing under the criteria provided, with little opportunity and time to address the issues. Richard Elmore (2004) makes the definitive case that no external accountability scheme can succeed in the absence of internal (to the school/district) accountability, which he defines as the capacity (knowledge, skills, resources) of the entity for individual and collective responsibility to engage in daily improvement practices. In other words, heavy-handed accountability systems omit or seriously underestimate capacity building. Without equal attention to the latter, all is lost. This is why, for example, the governor of Maine in January 2006 declared a moratorium on local assessments. The state still must meet federal requirements, but it had taken NCLB seriously and established, in cooperation with districts, an elaborate and comprehensive system of local assessments of learning in virtually all subjects and all grades. The result was that entire districts were grinding to a halt under the weight of conducting ubiquitous assessments. Put another way, they were spending all their resources and energy on assessments, with little left for doing the actual work of improvement.

It is not that NCLB is entirely wrong, but more that it is fatally flawed by failing to concentrate on capacity building. To make my point, capacity building is more important than accountability because the former is the route to the latter. Clearly you need both. Finding the right combination and integration of the two is the trick. The dilemma for well-intentioned governments is considerable. If they trust local entities to take policies seriously, to take advantage of resources, only a few will do it systematically.

If they force the issue by increasing accountability, they at best can make minor and superficial differences. And certainly in the United States the gap between high and low performance has widened since 2000, precisely the opposite of what NCLB so forcefully intended (Fullan, 2006). Let us now turn to two statewide cases where governments did take capacity building more seriously—England, and Ontario, Canada.

THE CASE OF THE NATIONAL LITERACY
AND NUMERACY STRATEGY

A new government came into power in England in 1997, and the Secretary of State declared that his three priorities were "education, education, education." We had heard that before, but this government went further. It said that the initial core goal was to raise the literacy and numeracy achievement up to age 11. To accomplish its ambitious goals, it established a National Literacy and Numeracy Strategy, as I mentioned in Chapter 1. The government set specific targets. It observed that the base line percentage of 11-year-olds scoring 4 or 5 on the literacy test was 63% in 1997 (level 4 being the level at which proficient standards are met); for numeracy, the base line was 62%. The minister announced that the targets for 2002 were 80% for literacy and 75% for numeracy. He made a commitment that he would resign if those targets were not met—a commitment that implicated 20,000 primary schools and 7 million students.

The leaders of the initiative set out to "use the change knowledge base" to design a pressure and support set of strategies to accomplish this remarkable feat. Finally, they knew they were going to be watched carefully as this highly political and highly explicit initiative unfolded, and they added an external evaluation component. A team of us at the University of Toronto was contracted to monitor and assess the entire NLNS strategy as it unfolded over the 1998–2002 period.

This is not the place to tell the full story (see Barber, 2000; Earl et al., 2003), but the essence of it can be told in two brief stages: the strategy and its impact in what I will call phase one (1997–2002), and phase two (2003–2006).

Phase One Strategy

The main elements of the implementation strategy in phase one were summarized by Michael Barber (2000), the head of the government initiative.

- A nationally prepared project plan for both literacy and numeracy, setting out actions, responsibilities, and deadlines through to 2002;
- A substantial investment sustained over at least 6 years and skewed toward those schools that need most help;
- A project infrastructure involving national direction from the Standards and Effectiveness Unit, 15 regional directors, and over 300 expert consultants at the local level for each of the two strategies;
- An expectation that every class will have a daily math lesson and daily literacy hour;
- A detailed teaching programme covering every school year for children from ages 5 to 11;
- An emphasis on early intervention and catch up for pupils who fall behind;
- A professional development programme designed to enable every primary school teacher to learn to understand and use the proven best practice in both curriculum areas;
- The appointment of over 2,000 leading math teachers and hundreds of expert literacy teachers, who have the time and skill to model best practice for their peers;
- The provision of "intensive support" to circa half of all schools where the most progress is required;
- A major investment in books for schools (over 23 million new books in the system since May 1997);
- The removal of barriers to implementation (especially a huge reduction in prescribed curriculum content outside the core subjects);
- Regular monitoring and extensive evaluation by our national inspection agency, OFSTED;
- A national curriculum for initial teacher training requiring all providers to prepare new primary school teachers to teach the daily math lesson and the literacy hour;
- A problem-solving philosophy involving early identification of difficulties as they emerge and the provision of rapid solutions or intervention where necessary;

- The provision of extra after-school, weekend, and holiday booster classes for those who need extra help to reach the standard. (pp. 8–9)

Barber (2001) characterized the theory of action behind the strategy as high challenge–high support in relation to six key elements: ambitious standards, good data and clear targets, devolved responsibility, access to best practice and quality professional development, accountability, and intervention in inverse proportion to success (low-improving schools receive extra attention).

Phase One Impact

The impact of the strategies on achievement, as a percentage of pupils reaching levels 4 or 5, is, in many ways, astounding (recall that 20,000 schools are involved). Table 12.1 displays the results up to 2002. Two main things stand out. First, it is possible to take a very large system and achieve substantial results over a reasonably short period (within one election period, as we say). Second, the results plateaued or flatlined by the fourth year. Plateauing is an interesting and complicated problem. I will pursue this question in the next section, but one of the main points is that it is partly a function of not reaching deeply enough into the hearts and minds of principals and teachers, which is one of our evaluation findings (Earl et al., 2003). More complicated is Elmore's

TABLE 12.1. Percentage of 11-Year-Olds Achieving Level 4 or 5 on the National Tests for Literacy and Numeracy

	Literacy*	Numeracy
1997	63	62
1998	65	59**
1999	70	69
2000	75	72
2001	75	71
2002	75	73

* Reading increased substantially, while writing improved marginally
** A new mental arithmetic component was added

(2004) finding that periodic plateaus are normal and not a bad thing. They represent periods where new practices are being consolidated and additional strategies must be developed to get to the next stage of accomplishments. Let's consider this a moot point, and ask the question, what needs to be done to go further?

Phase Two

David Hopkins (2006), who served as chief adviser on school standards to the Secretary of State, recently updated the strategies being employed in England beginning in 2003. He presents the results beyond 2002 (our Table 12.1 above). Literacy moved off the plateau from 75% (2003) to 77% (2004), and 79% (2005). Similarly, numeracy moved up slightly from 73% to 74% to 75%, respectively. In effect the challenge to go beyond plateaus is to use strategies that build the motivation and commitment capacity of collective groups (see Chapter 3). Let me be specific. Once you have a good focus and as people across a large system begin to make improvements, you need to have strategies that draw on the "wisdom of the crowd" (Surowiecki, 2004). We call this strategy "lateral capacity building," which is any strategy that deliberately enables (requires) schools and/or districts to learn from one another. For example, England introduced a new strategic component in 2004, as part of the primary strategy, that funded and supported 1,500 groups of six schools each. They were charged with learning best practices from one another (and from outside the cluster) in order to improve literacy. In my view, it is strategies like this that got England beyond the plateau.

Hopkins, in fact, identifies four "drivers." One is networks and collaboration such as the one I just described. A second is moral purpose coupled with personalized learning and assessment for learning in order to meet the needs of individual learners. A third is a focus on improving teaching, and a fourth is what he calls *intelligent accountability*, in which external accountability becomes less onerous (but still explicit and present), while internal accountability gets built up. These are significant shifts in trying to get the too tight/too loose balance right through better two-way partnerships with schools and local authorities.

The situation in England, as I write, is much more complicated than we can address here. As I noted in Chapter 11, there is the Every Child Matters agenda, which is incredibly ambitious and based on integrating all children's services in a district under a single director (Department for Skills and Education, 2003). Second, an aggressive and controversial white paper, after much debate and modification, has found its way into legislation (Department for Education and Skills, 2005). It is rife with contradictions and ambiguity. Containing many good ideas for pursuing ECM priorities, it also calls for competitive marketing proposals of federations of schools and school trusts, along with collaboration. It has a sink-or-swim (improve or be closed) mindset more than a capacity-building emphasis. We saw in Chapter 11 one director of Children's Services who named the contradictions as he experienced them at the local level (Allen, 2006). Secondary school reform remains a big priority of unfinished business. And we have increasing political instability within the Labour government as Prime Minister Tony Blair, in his third term, faces unpopularity within his own party. In September 2006 he announced that he would resign in a year. In any case, my main point in this chapter is to begin to identify what large-scale reform strategies look like when you try to combine accountability and capacity building. A second example, based on the lessons learned from England, gives us another opportunity to delve explicitly into the issues we have been discussing. We go now to Ontario, Canada.

THE ONTARIO LITERACY AND NUMERACY STRATEGY

We have England to thank for starting us down the path of whole-system reform using a deliberate knowledge-based strategy. We have the chance in Ontario to learn from the English experience, to design and carry out our own Ontario-based system reform. In April 2004, I was appointed by the premier of Ontario, Dalton McGuinty, as a special adviser to him and to the minister of education. The task is to create a strategy that will substantially improve literacy and numeracy, within one election period for all 72 school districts and all 4,000 or so elementary schools in the province. We are attempting to do just that in all districts: 12 francophone districts, 28 Catholic, and 32 public, all fully publicly funded.

There are three main differences from the English strategy. First, the English strategy fixated on targets. The system was to move from 62% literacy in 1997 to 80% by 2002 (recall they reached 75%). Second, England has an inspection agency called the Office for Standards in Education (OFSTED), which in the early stages carried out a name-and-shame regimen of identifying failing schools for immediate intrusive intervention (OFSTED currently has a more balanced approach). Third, the literacy and numeracy curriculum and teaching practices to be followed were specified, while in Ontario we have allowed for a greater range of teaching practices.

My point here is not so much to judge the limitations of the English strategy as to stress the differences from the Ontario strategy. What I discuss in this section is our actual strategy, and the results we are getting so far. I offer the Ontario case not as an example to be copied but rather as a concrete case of what the full strategy looks like in actual practice. This is a strategy that is based on the theories of action I discussed in Chapter 3. In brief, the approach is based on "capacity building with a focus on results," using policies and strategies designed to motivate the whole system to engage in deliberate improvement actions.

There are eight interlocking strategies that we are putting into place. As I describe them briefly here, recall from Chapter 3 that the main measure of an overall strategy is whether it is *motivational*—mobilizing a large number of people to spend their energy and otherwise invest in what will be required to reap and sustain major improvements. The key in large-scale reform is whether the strategy can get a large number of leaders (change agents) within and across the three levels—school, district, and state—to jointly own the enterprise. There are eight components to the overall strategy.

1. Establishing a guiding coalition to be constantly in communication
2. Developing peace and stability with labor unions and addressing other "distractors"
3. Creating a Literacy and Numeracy Secretariat

4. Negotiating aspirational targets
5. Building capacity in relation to the targets
6. Growing the financial investment
7. Evolving positive pressure
8. Connecting the dots with key complementary components

I take up each of these strategies in the following pages, showing how they build on one another.

Establishing a Guiding Coalition

A guiding coalition is concerned with whether the small number of key leaders consistently communicate among themselves and with all other stakeholders; and further that they have the same message, which is capacity building with a focus on results through all eight strategic elements. In Ontario's case, the Guiding Coalition includes the premier, the minister, the deputy minister (chief civil servant), the CEO of the secretariat (see below), and me as special adviser, along with the relevant policy advisers. They need to meet often enough (in subgroups and as a whole) to continually agree on the nature of the strategy at work and to address problems being encountered, progress being made, and additional actions required. They also need to meet with constituent groups—parents, teacher unions, administrator associates, school board trustees, and others—formally, which we do through partnership tables, and informally through the many opportunities created by working with schools and districts in the course of implementing the other seven strategies. The Guiding Coalition must listen as well as promulgate the strategy.

A good hypothetical test of whether the coalition has its act together is to imagine that five newspaper reporters asked five members of the coalition the same question (such as, "What is the role of targets in your strategy?") on the same day and at the same time. The responses should be essentially consistent and specific across the five individuals. They would not have a chance to check with one another, and it would not occur to them that this would be necessary. This is not groupthink at work; the strategy is deeply understood (and in fine detail) as it is implemented and refined.

Addressing "Distractors"

Peace and stability with the teacher unions is the second element. A deliberate part of our strategy is to address the distractors— anything that takes you away from continuous focus on teaching and learning and student achievement. A big distractor prior to 2003 was constant labor strife between unions and districts or the government. Countless days and energy were lost to strikes and work-to-rule in the 1997–2002 period. Closing the gap is a system problem that needs a system solution, which you cannot reach if people are constantly sniping at one another.

To make an intense political story short, the minister of education, in partnership with unions and districts, created a framework to guide the establishment of new collective bargaining agreements and then rode herd on completing the agreements within a specified time line. The result was that by June 2005 122 four-year agreements had been signed across the 72 districts— providing a significant period of potential labor stability, which I should add must not be taken as a given but pursued into implementation. For whole-system reform, the energies of all parties must be devoted to addressing the core task of improving teaching, learning, and achievement. Labor-related distractions are especially debilitating. It is important to note that once the framework of collective agreements is decided upon, it is necessary to monitor implementation as new ideas and interpretations arise in the heat of everyday action. Hence, we have established a Provincial Stability Commission whose job it is to provide a normative framework and mechanism to resolve any problems between unions and management that surface during the course of everyday business. In its first 4 months of operation, the commission reduced the number of potential grievances from 815 to 50.

We continue in the Ontario strategy to work to reduce or eliminate other distractors that take up time and energy at the expense of student learning. In our case these include reducing the amount of bureaucracy and unnecessary paperwork faced by districts and schools; simplifying a teacher appraisal scheme that consumes a large amount of time on the part of principals without yielding positive results; and determining what can be done to help principals cope with the managerial side (budget, plant, and personnel) of their role so that they can devote time to the core work of building cultures that focus on learning and results. In short, if you are serious about closing the gap, you have to make it possible to do so. Managing distractors is another of those issues that amount to taking excuses off the table.

Creating a Literacy and Numeracy Secretariat

The third element in the strategy was the creation of a Literacy and Numeracy Secretariat. Ontario chose to focus on literacy and numeracy in order to establish foundational literacies. There is some work on what I refer to as the third basic, well-being, but much more focus is necessary in the near future on this component. In the cognitive domain, it is not that other parts of the curriculum are unimportant, but rather that literacy and numeracy are a special priority. They are pursued in their own right, and in relation to the rest of the curriculum. Because capacity building (knowledge, resources, and motivation necessary to improve literacy and numeracy) is a core part of our overall strategy, we created a brand-new unit within the Ministry of Education called the Literacy and Numeracy Secretariat. The CEO was hired from one of the 72 districts, where she was employed as director (superintendent) of education. The secretariat was established in 2004 and became fully staffed in 2005 with approximately 80 individuals. Most were hired from "the field," where they were leading literacy and numeracy superintendents, consultants, or other administrators. The goal was to create a new, innovative unit highly respected for its qualities by schools and districts and that would work interactively with the latter to achieve results, especially concerning strategies four (aspirational targets) and five (capacity building). The secretariat is organized into seven regional teams (about six to a team), which are responsible for working with the districts (typically 10–12 districts in a given region). In addition to the seven regional teams, there is a research team, an equity team, a capacity-building coordinating team, and an administrative support team.

The goals of the secretariat are to stimulate and keep engagement going across the province, to be responsive, and to initiate deeper strategies for reform. The secretariat is to be a proactive force to increase two-way development between districts and the government, and to stimulate lateral interaction across districts in seeking most effective practices.

Negotiating Aspirational Targets

Fourth, targets have been introduced for the first time. Targets can be controversial. Certainly England's were. As part of the election platform, Premier McGuinty, noting that Ontario's 12-year-olds were scoring about 54% on literacy and numeracy in 2002 and had been flatlined in previous years, announced a target of 75% for both literacy and numeracy by 2008. Incidentally, absolute scores should not be compared across countries (except as part of the same testing regimen, as with the Organization for Economic Cooperation and Development's [OECD] Programme for International Student Assessment [PISA]) because standards and cutoff points vary. Ontario has an independent assessment agency (Education Quality and Accountability Office, or EQAO) that conducts annual assessments in literacy and numeracy at grades 3 and 6. Ontario's standard of proficiency within its own assessment system is high, requiring substantial comprehension and performance in literacy and numeracy.

In any case, we entered the strategy with an overall target set at 75%. My colleagues, Hargreaves and Fink (2006), are against externally imposed targets, arguing that they are not owned and result in superficial actions and mistrust. Their argument seems to be around whether the targets are experienced as externally imposed; as they say, "People can and sometimes should set targets together as part of a shared commitment" (p. 48).

Our practice in Ontario is to negotiate targets with each of the 72 districts by discussing starting points and negotiating the next year's target as part of rolling reform. We have found that because these discussions take part in the context of the other seven strategy components, they are not problematic. Most educators think that 75% as a 5-year goal is reasonable for the province to aspire to; most think moving up 5 percentage points, say, from 61 to 66%, is a desirable and achievable stretch for the next year, given the additional resources embedded in many of the elements of the strategy. Although I believe these directional goals and the strategy as a whole appear to be receiving widespread endorsement by educators, I am conscious of the fact that we are at the early stages of the initiative and that we don't yet have full appreciation of the experiences of the everyday classroom teacher. As we proceed, the strategy needs (and will benefit from) a stronger infusion of teacher perspectives. A basic premise of the overall strategy is to be evidence-based, to learn as we go. Commitment to research and inquiry, and timely action and correction are crucial to all large-scale change efforts.

Annual targets, in any case, are negotiated in interaction with the secretariat; the first ones were for the end of school year 2004, and so on. We are careful not to detach targets from other key components such as capacity building. There is now engagement on the part of districts and schools to work on strategies in relation to literacy and numeracy, and excitement to see how they do when EQAO results are released annually. If you were to ask the 72 directors of education and the 4,000 school principals whether they feel the targets are jointly owned, I believe that the vast majority would say yes.

Building Capacity

The fifth component, capacity building, is multifaceted because it involves everything you do that affects new knowledge, skills, and competencies; enhanced resources; and stronger commitments. These are the main capacity-building components in our case.

- Initiating ongoing professional development for the staff of the secretariat. If they are going to help in capacity building, they have to engage in it themselves.
- Interacting with districts to strengthen the capacity-building improvement plans each district prepares in relation to aspirational targets. There is an emphasis on keeping paper to a minimum. The purpose is to increase reflective action—strategizing more than strategy.
- Identifying and sharing effective practices in relation to both content (literacy and numeracy instruction) and strategy (change strategies that increase quality and extent of

implementation). Each regional area receives money to engage in lateral learning and capacity building.

- Developing resource materials for targeted issues such as boys and literacy, English as a second language, special education, and Aboriginal students.

- Conducting case studies of districts that (1) seem to have good strategies and (2) get good results (see Campbell & Fullan, 2006). The research arm of the secretariat, in partnership with selected districts, has just completed case studies in eight districts representing the whole range of circumstances in the province (a multicultural large urban district in the south; a huge, dispersed geographical sprawl with high Aboriginal population in the north; a francophone district in the east; a Catholic county district in the west; and so on). These case studies are fed back to districts so that all can learn and spawn cross-district visits and learning exchanges. The findings are consistent with the conclusion we came to in Chapter 11. To use the language of our report, districts that do well have a bias for action, which is based on four major interrelated strategic themes, namely (1) leading with purpose and focusing direction; (2) designing a coherent strategy and coordinating implementation and reviewing outcomes as they go; (3) developing precision in knowledge, skills, and daily practices for improving learning; and (4) sharing responsibility through building partnerships (Campbell & Fullan, 2006).

- Building up the capacity for "assessment literacy," which is our term to encompass both assessment for and assessment of literacy. We have invested heavily in developing the high-yield capacity of assessment for learning at the school and district levels.

- Creating a system of lead literacy and lead numeracy teachers in all 4,000 schools. Our research has found that "second change agents" (in addition to the principal) are crucial. They work inside the school with other teachers to demonstrate new techniques, offer instructional resources, and link to other teachers' classrooms in the school and in other schools. In the most disadvantaged schools, lead literacy teachers are released full-time to work across the school.

- Establishing ongoing professional development in summers and evenings to constantly update teachers, with a growing emphasis on working with teams, and lending support to teachers so they can learn in context as they apply the ideas in their own schools.
- Incorporating a turnaround school program. This is a small but important part of the overall strategy in which low-performing schools in highly challenging circumstances *voluntarily* join a program of intensive support and development, run by the Ministry of Education using external expert coaches to work with selected schools over a 3-year period. Because the program is voluntary, there is less stigma attached to it (all schools in the province are implicated anyway in the overall strategy). The turnaround program was introduced by the previous government but was a detached, stand-alone initiative. We are now able to incorporate it with district work in the context of an integrated strategy. We have just established a more comprehensive strategy called the Ontario Focused Intervention Partnership, in which over 800 underperforming schools are scheduled to receive additional capacity-building support. The secretariat works with the districts to develop specific intervention activities tailored to the needs of the schools.
- Reducing class size in the early years (up to grade 3) to a limit of 20 (many classrooms had reached 30-plus students). We have been careful to go about this not as an end in itself but as part of a strategy to improve instruction: reduce class size *and* teach differently to be more effective.

The very use of the term *capacity building* has made a big difference. The term now is used readily and easily by everyone from the premier of the province to classroom teachers. Capacity building means something because there are so many concrete examples of it in practice. People know it and value it because they are experiencing it.

Growing the Financial Investment

The sixth element is to increase the financial investment. Money per se is not the answer, but the Education Trust's (2005) report on the funding gap got it right in the conclusion: "It is unfortunate that the debate over education funding is dominated by extreme views—with some claiming that money doesn't matter at all and others claiming reforms are impossible without additional dollars. Neither argument makes sense but both postpone the day when we will give poor students of color the education they deserve and need" (p. 9). Even though Ontario was in a serious budget deficit situation when the new government came into power, the premier made it clear that education and education spending were a priority. To make the point, in public speeches he frequently says that "if given the choice of spending my next dollar on health or on education, I will choose education every time." Funding, especially directed at capacity building, has increased substantially.

The budget for education in Ontario in 2002–03 (that is, prior to the new strategy) was $14.8 billion (all figures expressed in Canadian dollars). In the first 3 years of the new initiatives, the budget increased to over $18.4 billion. Cumulative new expenditures represent an increase of $8.3 billion over this period, or, expressed as an increase from the base, growth of some 22%, some 12% increase in constant dollars after discounting inflation. Much of the new money is devoted to capacity building, with all those in challenging circumstances receiving additional earmarked resources. All this as the government is working to reduce an overall budget deficit.

The logic and strategy of growing the financial investment go like this: Invest substantially at the front end to get the process kick-started, and to show goodwill and seriousness of commitment. Make it a quid pro quo proposition. As the government does its part, it in effect asks the field to do its share (in partnership, as I have stressed) by using the money to focus on priorities and by leveraging it into additional investments of energy, skill development, and commitment. As results move upward, use the momentum as a lever to obtain more dollars from the treasury and elsewhere. This year's gains chase next year's additional money. Don't make literal judgments year by year, because trends take time and must be judged over 3-year cycles. As Kanter (2004) states, "winning streaks attract investments" (p. 341).

The fundamental premise underlying the overall strategy is to raise the bar and close the gap. If done well, these investments are financially lucrative for society. They produce direct economic development and benefits; they save money by reducing the bill in education with respect to later remedial costs for failing students, and by affecting costs related to crime, health, and other aspects of well-being (see Fullan, 2006).

Evolving Positive Pressure

I call the seventh component the evolution of positive pressure. Positive pressure is nonpejorative at the outset, treats people with respect and dignity, appreciates and is empathic to challenging circumstances, furnishes assistance and support in the form of resources and capacity building, and helps take all of the excuses off the table; then it turns ugly, so to speak, in cases of persistent low performance. There are, of course, situations so egregiously wrong that tough, decisive action must be taken right away. But for large-scale system change, you need to motivate a large number of people. Positive pressure is designed to do that. If resources are provided and excuses are eliminated one by one, persistent good performance is going to be noticed in another light. So are situations where things fail to improve despite new investments. Peers are more likely to think that maybe it is poor teaching and leadership, bad attitudes, low expectations, lack of care, and the like. Leaders will find it easier to have pointed discussions that most would find fair and reasonable. In the end, positive pressure is inevitable and irresistible.

Let me give an example of assessment both for and of learning, dealing with the online database we are just establishing. Using Statistics Canada data, we have grouped the approximately 4,000 elementary schools into four bands according to the percentage of students living in low-income households, which we call the low-income cutoff point (LICO). There are 1,552 schools in the 0–5% LICO category, 1,393 schools in the 6–15% LICO group, 612 at 16–24% LICO, and 497 schools with more than 25% of the students in low-income households. All 4,000 schools by name (and by a variety of indicators), along with their reading, writing, and math scores for grades 3 and 6, are in the database. The system will soon be online for all to access.

In addition, schools also are classified according to whether they are extremely far from the provincial target, far from it, somewhat near, or above it. The database tracks improvement or lack thereof, which we view over 3-year cycles according to several categories of schools expressed in terms of whether the school is high or low in performance, as well as whether it is declining, stagnant, or improving (in relation to the 3-year trend). Well, you can see where we are going with positive pressure. System leaders, for example, could look at the 1,552 schools with few poverty households (no apparent excuses) and ask by name why 200 schools in that category are "extremely far" or "far" from the provincial target. What if many of these schools were clustered in certain districts? When you do fair comparisons, apples to apples, people can learn from others in similar circumstances, and if you don't do anything to improve your situation, the pressure mounts.

This analysis has led us to identify low-performing schools according to their LICO comparators. As I said above, we are now working with over 800 schools to furnish greater capacity-building support, along with pressure to make gains in student achievement according to their own starting points and the performance of their comparators.

As far as I know, we are the first to put the spotlight on the cruising schools as a group—those schools not facing difficult circumstances, but not moving forward. This leads to focusing on advantaged schools that are doing especially well compared with their peers in order to learn valuable lessons from them; and inevitably to schools that despite their initial advantage are not showing commensurate performance. Then we will probe why they are not on the move and what can be done to ignite the stagnant situations. Reeves (2006) captures the array of situations when he identifies schools that have favorable circumstances but fail to take advantage of them, and those that face difficult challenges and are trying to do something about it. He calls the former group (high initial advantage) "lucky." These schools may take advantage of their initial good circumstances or they may cruise along resting on the laurels of the students they inherited—akin to the person who was born on third base and thought he had hit a triple.

In addition to system use of the data profile, we are heading toward making the database available for individual schools. An individual school, for example, could use the Schools Like Me option and find by name the (let's say) 168 schools with similar profiles—for example, the same LICO category, whether urban or not, similar size—and see where it fit in achievement, expecting to learn from those doing better.

None of this is literal. You do need to know your stuff. You do need to appreciate the dynamics of all eight strategies in action. In Ontario, as a policy matter we have three very important motivationally oriented ground rules (or, rather, means of minimizing the demotivators). First, we explicitly and categorically have rejected using league tables ranking all schools, regardless of contextual circumstances. League tables represent negative, unhelpful pressure. You have to start with comparing apples to apples and then move to gap closing. Second, we have taken the policy position that interpreting any single year's results could be misleading (odd blips occur, impact of strategies takes time, and trends cannot be discerned); thus we treat only 3-year rolling trends as legitimate. Third, when we see low performance, we first take a capacity-building attitude, and second make a judgment, again because it is a better way to improve motivation.

In all of this, the goal at the end of the day is to establish the conditions for discussions about performance that would be seen as reasonable and fair—to be able to have telling and revealing discussions with certain principals, directors of education, and others. If the overall strategy fails to produce widespread improvement, these telling discussions turn to the minister and the special adviser, and from the public to the premier. Positive pressure all around is the way it should be for an agenda so crucial to society.

Finally, another face of positive pressure is to compare one's own progress on an ongoing basis according to national and international standards. As noted earlier, OECD conducts excellent assessments in literacy, math, and science, with carefully developed instruments and protocols. As it progresses, Ontario will want to compare itself with the performance of Alberta, the leading province in Canada, and Finland, which recently has been leading the pack of the 32 OECD countries.

Connecting Complementary Components

The eighth and final aspect of the strategy we call connecting the dots with key complementary components. You cannot do everything at once, which is why we have prioritized literacy and numeracy as the first order of business. As you go, however, it is necessary to begin working on linking to other key components that surround literacy and numeracy. I have already mentioned well-being as an essential element of the initial three basics. Other main complementary components are high school reform, early childhood programs, teacher education, and leadership development.

High school reform is obviously important in its own right, but also because you want to build on the new increases in literacy and numeracy at the elementary level. In this third year of the literacy and numeracy strategy, additional strategies are being added to work on high school reform. At the provincial level, a goal has been set to cut the high school dropout rate in half, from 30 to 15%. Each district has been funded to appoint a "student success" educator, who works in the district to provide more targeted support to students on the verge of dropping out. Programs are being revamped for more options for students who may be less interested in a university track. All over the developed countries, secondary school reform has lagged behind and is now getting the attention it deserves as part of the reform package.

Early childhood programs are a natural ally for our three basics of literacy, numeracy, and well-being. Diagnostic and intervention programs are being put in place, for example, to assess 4-year-olds prior to entry to school. Early childhood is finally getting some attention, but the attention needs to be more prominent, stronger, and more specific as an articulated link to success at the elementary level.

Teacher education is another underdeveloped part of the reform picture (see Chapter 13). In England, the Teacher Training Agency has been successful in strengthening the focus on literacy and numeracy in initial education, and in attracting new people to the profession through incentives related to the profession as a whole and with respect to the supply of teachers for certain subject areas, as well as for geographical areas in the country. Ontario is now turning its attention to teacher education by way of new requirements and resources to support teachers in the induction period.

Leadership development is most obviously the key. Many of our strategies are based on leaders developing other leaders so that there is a greater critical mass of distributed leaders in the first place and a built-in pipeline of future leaders. Something direct must be done about the principalship, in which new expectations have been added for the principal as leader of leaders in improving learning and closing the gap, *without* taking away or extending support for the managerial and community relations side of the role. In Ontario we have just issued a discussion paper with the principals' associations to concentrate on the tasks of reducing the distractors, adding more support for management tasks, and increasing the focus on development of collaborative school cultures, as well as increasing the expectation and means for principals to be system leaders, that is, learning from and contributing to other schools, and contributing to and influencing system priorities. Similar developments even further along can be found in the new corporate plan for the National College for School Leadership in England (NCSL, 2005).

Summing Up

The eight strategic components currently are being coordinated and implemented in Ontario, and early results are promising. After only 2 years, there is enormous goodwill, commitment, and excitement at all levels of the system. In terms of student achievement, if we take grade 6 reading, for example (the pattern is essentially the same for grade 6 writing and math, and grade 3 reading, writing, and math), after being flatlined at 54% proficiency for 5 years prior to 2003–04, there was an increase of 3% in 2004–05 and a further 5% in 2004–05. In effect, we have gone from 54 to 62% in 2 years (with the 2004–05 increase the largest single-year jump since EQAO began its assessments in 1997). Subanalyses also confirm that relevant gaps are closing slightly—such as between low- and high-performing districts, low- and high-performing schools, and boys and girls—as everyone moves up. The 2005–2006 results show an increase of 1–2% in all categories of grades 3 and 6 (reading, writing, and math), reflecting continuous progress, but also a need to persist with and deepen the strategy.

This is no time to claim success. We are aware of Kanter's (2004) law that everything can look like a failure in the middle, or its corollary, "early success is fragile"; small initial victories do not yet represent a trend. Much hard work remains, and it would not take many missteps for goodwill to dissipate. Will people be able to stay the course and develop greater capacity as the problems become harder? The external confidence of parents, the community, business leaders, and the media may have increased slightly, but it remains tentative. Teacher unions are still wary after years of conflict with the previous government and are tentatively supporting the direction (whereas going the distance requires strong teacher union leadership). We also need to look for other jurisdictions where strong successful partnerships are developing with teacher unions. Teacher unions as well as governments have their work cut out in gaining public confidence, and I believe that it is in their best interests to partner in the agenda laid out in this book.

The whole arena of public confidence, as Kanter notes, is essential to sustaining a winning streak. There are few winning streaks as crucial to society as establishing momentum for people to invest their energies and resources in raising the bar and reducing the income and education gap in society.

Ontario is a work in progress, but it represents a good example in which we are trying to combine all our knowledge of change to bring about reform in the system as a whole—to raise the bar and close the gap in literacy and numeracy. It is an example of trying to learn from others as we contribute our lessons learned to the global community of system reformers.

IMPLICATIONS

Radical experiments are now surfacing in many places as policymakers know that virtually all strategies over the past decades have failed to achieve needed breakthroughs. Centralized high-stakes accountability schemes have failed to produce ownership, as has decentralized site-based mangement.

The solution, in my view, is to develop strategies that integrate top-down and bottom-up forces in an ongoing dynamic manner, achieving what I call "permeable connectivity." We saw one version of this in the Ontario case just presented. Permeable connectivity requires a sophisticated and delicate balance because to work it requires all three levels—school–community, district, and state—to interact regularly across and within levels. We don't want the inadequacies of tightly controlled centralization being replaced with the equal flaws of school and community autonomy. The answer is to have state interests present in local settings, while local interests are reflected in state thinking and action. Instead of local autonomy we need clusters of schools engaged in lateral capacity building incorporating state and local agendas. The clustering of networks of schools is essential to the future because they compensate for the dangers of isolated autonomy without succumbing to top-down running of schools. The Ontario case represents some aspects of this model, although likely not the full solution that should evolve in the next stages of reform.

The clear advice in this chapter, indeed this book, is that governments must go beyond standards and accountability and focus on capacity building linked to results, engaging all three levels of the system. Elmore's (2000) argument for building a new structure for school leadership is similar. In complex systems, he claims, you need standards: a set of expectations for what students should know and be able to do, and a teaching force held accountable for its contribution to student learning. *But*, Elmore says, as I have been saying, that solving problems in complex systems is not accomplished by having great standards, but has to be addressed everyday as a continuous learning proposition.

> Instructional improvement requires continuous learning. Learning is both individual and a social activity. Therefore, collective learning demands an environment that guides and directs the acquisition of new knowledge about instruction. (p. 20)

Capacity building at its heart is a system of guiding and directing people's work, which is carried out in a highly interactive professional learning setting. All else is clutter. Policies need to be aligned to minimize distractions and mobilize resources for continuous improvement. This is obviously a tall order, but failure to do it means that we will continue to have small-scale successes that even in the best cases have little likelihood of lasting. A major part of this tall order is figuring out how to attract, prepare, and nurture the education force that can work in this new way. The preceding chapters have set the stage that will enable us to tackle this question more productively—the subject of Chapters 13 and 14.

CHAPTER 13

Professional Preparation of Teachers

The fact is that our primary value concerns our need to help ourselves change and learn, for us to feel that we are growing in our understanding of where we have been, where we are, and what we are about, and that we are enjoying what we are doing. To help others to change without this being preceded and accompanied by an exquisite awareness of the process in ourselves is "delivering a product or service" which truly has little or no significance for our personal or intellectual growth.

—Sarason (1982, p. 122)

Recall from Chapter 6 that success is associated with a bias for action. Reform in teacher education has proven to have a bias for inertia! That is why in this chapter I want to focus not only on attracting good people to the profession but also on providing them with the best possible initial preparation. This would be no mean feat, as solid teacher preparation programs are in the minority. Then in Chapter 14 I will take up the next piece of the educational-change equation—ensuring that teachers have a place to work that enables them to learn and develop on the job. Most macro strategies to improve the profession are *individualistic* in the sense that they try to generate more and more people with the skills, knowledge, and dispositions to do the things we have been talking about in this book. These strategies by themselves will never work.

The call for reform in teacher education mostly has fallen on deaf ears, although there are currently pockets of action that represent excellent examples of what is needed. But we have been there before. Let us start with the five strategies for policymakers set out by the Education Commission of the States (ECS) in its report *In Pursuit of Quality Teaching* (2000).

> *Strategy 1:* Ensure a diverse and high-quality approach to teacher preparation that involves solid K–12/postsecondary partnerships, strong field experience, and good support for new teachers.
>
> *Strategy 2:* Ensure that teacher recruitment and retention policies target the areas of greatest need and the teachers most likely to staff them successfully in the long run.
>
> *Strategy 3:* Ensure that all teachers are able to participate in high-quality professional development so they can improve their practice and enhance student learning.
>
> *Strategy 4:* Redesign teacher accountability systems to ensure that all teachers possess the skills and knowledge they need to improve student learning.
>
> *Strategy 5:* Develop and support strong school and district leadership statewide focused on enhancing the quality of student learning and instruction.

These goals are laudable, but they are not going to be achieved because the strategies won't generate what they set out to produce. It is not that the strategies are misguided but rather that they are underguided. All five strategies focus on improving the skills, knowledge, and dispositions of individuals—teachers and leaders alike. What they don't do is address the core of school capacity—the reculturing we saw in a minority of schools in Chapters 7 and 8. Elmore (2000) identifies the fatal flaw in these strategies.

> Many well-intentioned reformers argue that large-scale improvement of schools can be accomplished by recruiting, rewarding, and retaining good people and releasing them from the bonds of bureaucracy to do what they know how to do. . . . What's missing in this view is any recognition that improvement is more a function of learning to *do the right thing in the setting where you work.* (p. 25)

This is a very powerful insight and we need to be crystal clear about what it means. The logic goes like this:

1. We are trying to accomplish deeper learning in the new pedagogies of constructivism.
2. Students' and others' motivation depends on the quality of local context.
3. Problems are so complex and context-dependent to solve that they must be worked on all the time—this is fundamentally what is meant (but not understood except as a cliché) by the learning organization. Learning on the job is the *sine qua non* of improvement.
4. Better recruitment strategies and better ongoing professional development will *temporarily* increase motivation, but it soon will dissipate in the face of underdeveloped learning communities.
5. The more that people realize number four, the less likely they will be attracted in the first place, even though new policies offer incentives to enter teaching.

Fast forward to the present and we have the final report of The Teaching Commission (2006), which is entitled *Teaching at Risk: Progress and Potholes*. This commission calls for reform in four domains: transforming teacher compensation, reinventing teacher preparation, overhauling licensing and certification, and strengthening leadership and support. Mostly the commission concludes that results have fallen far short of what is needed. They do cite some promising examples, and I will refer to some of these in the next chapter. Still, my overall conclusion is that concentrating on getting and retaining *individuals* is not sufficient. I am not saying don't pursue the five ECS strategies or the four Teaching Commission recommendations. I am saying they represent only a part of the solution, and the harder work is to change schools into learning *organizations*; that is, the policy considerations in this chapter and the subsequent one must be integrated with the strategies contained in previous chapters, especially Chapters 7 through 11. With this in mind, we can now delve into the problem and recent promise of the preparation, hiring, and induction of teachers.

THE PREPARATION OF TEACHERS

We did a review, for the Ford Foundation, of the Holmes Group, and more broadly teacher education covering the 1986–1996 decade. We entitled our report, not facetiously, *The Rise & Stall of Teacher Education Reform* (Fullan, Galluzzo, Morris, & Watson, 1998). The 1986–1996 decade started with great fanfare. In 1986 the Holmes Group—an alliance of 100 major research universities dedicated to joining with schools to produce deep improvements in the education of teachers—produced its first book, *Tomorrow's Teachers*. The Carnegie Forum released its report at the same time— *A Nation Prepared: Teachers for the 21st Century* (1986). Also, in that year, Sarason and his colleagues published a revised edition of their 1962 book, *The Preparation of Teachers: An Unstudied Problem in Education* (Sarason, Davidson, & Blatt, 1986), noting that the relationship between the preparation of teachers and the realities they experience in their careers is a question "as unstudied today—as superficially discussed today—as in previous decades" (p. xiv).

Especially for the Holmes Group, the 5 years following 1986 was a period of great excitement, considerable debate, and activity concerning the reform of teacher education. This period encompassed the release of *Tomorrow's Schools* (Holmes Group, 1990), the second in the Holmes Group trilogy. Over the next 4 or 5 years, however, the intensity of the debate began to wane. The energy and enthusiasm of those working on the complex problems of implementing reform on behalf of the group had been heavily taxed. During these years, the Holmes Group collective entered a phase of soul-searching, realizing that it was losing ground. In particular, we witnessed the loss of momentum in the period 1993–1995. It was a time when the Holmes Group faced the question of what must be done to recapture and revitalize an agenda that had barely begun. By the time the third monograph— *Tomorrow's Schools of Education*—was released in 1995, the initial momentum for reform had become more diffuse.

Why do even the best attempts fail? It is a big problem primarily related to the fact that most societies do not treat teacher education as a serious endeavor. As we said in *Rise & Stall*, society has failed its teachers in two senses: It gives teachers failing grades for not producing better results; at the same time, it does not help improve the conditions that would make success possible.

Despite the rhetoric about teacher education in today's society, there does not seem to be a real belief or confidence that investing in teacher education will yield results. Perhaps deep down many leaders believe that teaching is not all that difficult. After all, most leaders have spent thousands of hours in the classroom and are at least armchair experts. And they know that scores of unqualified teachers are placed in classrooms every year and required to learn on the job. In addition, investing in teacher education is not a short-term strategy. With all the problems facing us demanding immediate solutions, it is easy to overlook a preventive strategy that would take several years to have an impact. When a crisis occurs, you have to deal with it. A course of action that is aimed at preventing a crisis, despite being much less expensive in the mid to long term, is much harder to come by.

Critiques of Teacher Preparation Programs

The problem begins with teacher preparation programs. Howey and Zimpher's (1989) detailed case studies of six universities in the United States enabled them to generate key attributes that would be necessary for program coherence, which they find lacking in existing programs, such as:

- Programs based on clear conceptions of teaching and schooling
- Programs that have clear thematic qualities
- Faculty coalescing around experimental or alternative programs that have distinctive qualities
- The formation of student cohort groups
- Adequate curriculum materials and a well-conceived laboratory component
- Articulation between on-campus programming and field-based student teaching
- Direct linkage to research and development knowledge bases
- Regular program evaluation

Goodlad (1990) is even more damning in his comprehensive investigation of 29 universities. Among his main findings:

1. The preparation programs in our sample made relatively little use of the peer socialization process employed in some other fields of professional preparation. There were few efforts to organize incoming candidates into cohort groups or to do so at some later stage. Consequently, students' interactions about their experiences were confined for the most part to formal classes (where the teaching is heavily didactic). The social, intellectual, and professional isolation of teachers, so well described by Dan Lortie, begins in teacher education. This relatively isolated individualism in preparation seems ill-suited to developing the collegiality that will be demanded later in site-based school renewal.

2. The rapid expansion of higher education, together with unprecedented changes in academic life, have left professors confused over the mission of higher education and uncertain of their role in it. Although the effects of these changes in academic life transcend schools and departments, the decline of teaching in favor of research in most institutions of higher education has helped lower the status of teacher education. In regional public universities, once normal schools and teachers colleges, the situation has become so bad that covering up their historic focus on teacher education is virtually an institutional rite of passage. Teaching in the schools and teacher education seem unable to shake their condition of status deprivation.

3. There are serious disjunctures in teacher education programs: between the arts and sciences portion and that conducted in the school or department of education, from component to component of the so-called professional sequence, and between the campus-based portion and the school-based portion. It is also clear from our data that the preparation underway in the programs we have studied focused on *classrooms* but scarcely at all on *schools*.

4. Courses in the history, philosophy, and social foundation of education . . . have been seriously eroded. (pp. 700–701, emphasis in original).

As the momentum for reform in teacher education receded in the mid-1990s, along came the National Commission on Teaching and America's Future (NCTAF, 1996). The commission found:

- In recent years, more than 50,000 people who lack the training required for their jobs have entered teaching annually on emergency or substandard licenses. [In 1990–1991, 27.4% of all newly hired teachers in the nation had no or substandard emergency licenses.]

- Nearly one-fourth (23 percent) of all secondary teachers do not have even a college minor in their main teaching field. This is true for more than 30 percent of mathematics teachers.
- Among teachers who teach a second subject, 36 percent are unlicensed in the field and 50 percent lack a minor.
- 56 percent of high school students taking physical science are taught by out-of-field teachers, as are 27 percent of those taking mathematics and 21 percent of those taking English. The proportions are much higher in high-poverty schools and in lower track classes.
- In schools with the highest minority enrollments, students have less than a 50 percent chance of getting a science or mathematics teacher who holds a license and a degree in the field he or she teaches. (pp. 15–16)

The litany of problems, although familiar, is dramatically disturbing.

1. Low expectations for student performance;
2. Unenforced standards for teachers;
3. Major flaws in teacher preparation;
4. Painfully slipshod teacher recruitment;
5. Inadequate induction for beginning teachers;
6. Lack of professional development and rewards for knowledge and skills;
7. Schools that are structured for failure rather than success. (NCTAF, 1996, p. 24)

All this from a commission friendly to the teaching profession! When John Goodlad read the draft of *The Rise & Stall*, he was aware of the new momentum from NCTAF and his own National Network of Educational Renewal. He thought perhaps the title should be altered to *The Rise, Stall, and Re-rise of Teacher Education Reform*. There is some truth to this, but in 2006 the jury is still out on this question. Society has never yet sustained an interest in teacher education reform, and until it does, there is no chance for meaningful educational improvement.

But where are we in the year 2006? Recall the starting point. Most teacher education programs are not coherent within the university campus, let alone between the university and the school. Even in content terms, teacher education contains huge gaps in the very things needed to work in professional learning communities—how to work with parents, assessment literacy vis-à-vis the standards movement, constructivists' pedagogies, understanding diversity, learning to be collaborative.

Research Knowledge Base

Recently research and program development (still in the minority of cases), and more significantly *new action* through Carnegie's (2001, 2006) *Teachers for a New Era* (TNE) initiative, are providing pressure and positive role models for the future. Let us first consider the research knowledge base and then the action. I start with the case for teacher expertise.

> Teacher expertise—what teachers know and can do—affects all the core tasks of teaching. What teachers understand about content and students, for example, shapes how judiciously they select from texts and other materials and how effectively they present material in class. Teachers' skill in assessing their students' progress also depends on how deeply teachers know the content and how well they understand and interpret student [work]. Nothing can fully compensate for the weakness of a teacher who lacks the knowledge and skills needed to help students master the curriculum. (Darling-Hammond & Ball, 1999, pp. 1–2)

NCTAF reviewed all the studies they could find on the relationship between teacher qualification and student learning. Two studies in particular provide a good summary of these results. First, Ferguson (1991) found that teacher expertise (as measured by teacher education, licensing, examination scores, and experience) accounted for a large variation in student achievement (over 40%). Second, Greenwald, Hedges, and Laine (1996) reviewed over 60 studies and found that teacher education and teacher ability, along with small schools and lower teacher–pupil ratios, are associated with significant increases in student achievement. In investment terms, the authors display achievement gains by type of investment, finding that "increasing teacher education" is a major component.

Pushing further, Darling-Hammond and Ball (1999) found that "teacher knowledge of subject matter, student learning and development, and teaching methods are all important elements of teacher effectiveness" (p. 3); and that "teachers who are fully prepared and certified in both their discipline and in education are more highly rated and more successful with students than are teachers without preparation, and those with greater training are found to be more effective than those with less" (pp. 3–4). With respect to the latter, NCTAE's review found that "graduates of five or six year programs that include an extended internship tied to coursework are more successful and more likely to enter and remain in teaching than graduates of traditional undergraduate programs" (p. 4).

What should a strong teacher education program look like? Darling-Hammond and her colleagues identified and conducted case studies of seven exemplary teacher education programs— defined as programs that have a consistently high reputation among those hiring their graduates (Darling-Hammond, 2000a, 2000b, 2000c). The following quotes capture the reputation:

> When I hire a Trinity graduate I know [he or she] will become a school leader. These people are smart about curriculum, they're innovative. They have the torch (principal);
>
> I'd grab all the Trinity graduates for jobs [if I could]. They have both a depth of content knowledge and the ability to continue to learn (superintendent);
>
> Integrating new teachers into the staff from Alverno is so much easier, because of their high ability to be self-reflective, their personally wide experiences with performance assessment . . . and their ability to apply critical research bases to their classroom experiences (principal);
>
> They are highly collegial, unafraid to seek out all they need to know from mentors and staff around them (principal);
>
> I had a very challenging classroom with many diverse needs in my first year of teaching. I feel that because of my education at Wheelock, I was able to be successful (graduate).

Darling-Hammond (2000a) concluded that all seven programs, while designed differently in a number of ways, had six common features.

- a common, clear vision of good teaching that is apparent in all coursework and clinical experiences;
- well-defined standards of practice and performance that are used to guide and evaluate coursework and clinical work;
- a curriculum grounded in substantial knowledge of child and adolescent development, learning theory, cognition, motivation, and subject matter pedagogy, taught in the context of practice;
- extended clinical experiences (at least 30 weeks) which are carefully chosen to support the ideas and practices presented in simultaneous, closely interwoven coursework;
- strong relationships, common knowledge, and shared beliefs among school- and university-based faculty; and
- extensive use of case study methods, teacher research, performance assessments, and portfolio evaluation to ensure that learning is applied to real problems of practice. (p. x)

On a more definitive note, the National Academy of Education sponsored a comprehensive compendium of the needed teacher education curriculum (Darling-Hammond & Bransford, 2005; National Academy of Education, 2005). In 28 detailed chapters, Darling-Hammond, Bransford, and their colleagues map our what teachers of the present need to know and be able to do with respect to knowledge of learners, knowledge of subject matter and curriculum, and knowledge of teaching. The National Academy of Education published a brief version of this work.

We have the usual strong set of recommendations for systematically strengthening teacher education. As part and parcel of the required reforms, much work needs to be done on linking arts and science to teacher education (Goodlad, 1994) and on forming partnerships with schools.

Action-Based Initiatives

Carnegie's TNE initiative is the most promising action-based work in the United States. Along with the Annenberg Foundation and the Ford Foundation, Carnegie set out to provide substantial funds to selected universities to develop and disseminate excellent teacher education programs that produce caring, competent, effective teachers. The ultimate goal of the TNE initiative, as stated in the prospectus, reads:

> At the conclusion of the project, each of these institutions should be regarded by the nation as the locus for one of the best programs possible for the standards primary route to employment as a beginning professional teacher. [Graduates from these programs] will be competent, caring, and qualified [and they] will be actively sought by school districts and schools and will be known for the learning gains made by their pupils. (Carnegie Foundation, 2001, p. 1)

The design principles in the prospectus called for proposals that had three fundamental characteristics: (1) a teacher education program guided by a respect for evidence, (2) faculty in disciplines of the arts and sciences that were fully engaged in the education of prospective teachers, and (3) an understanding that education is an academically taught, clinical-practice profession.

Through the TNE initiative, 11 institutions have received $5 million each for a 5-year period. The first four—Bank Street College of Education in New York; California State University, Northridge; Michigan State University; and the University of Virginia—received their grants in 2002. Another seven institutions were added in a second round: Boston College, Florida A&M University, Stanford, the University of Connecticut, the University of Texas at El Paso, the University of Washington, and the University of Wisconsin–Milwaukee. As a condition of the grant all institutions are required to receive technical assistance from the Academy of Education Development, an independent technical assistance agency. In addition to the 11 institutions receiving full grants, TNE has established a TNE Learning Network in which 30 institutions were invited to join and have full access to the entire network of resources. The whole enterprise is being evaluated by the Rand Corporation. We can look for good ideas coming from TNE, but it is still a drop in the bucket (albeit a good one) given the thousands of approved teacher preparation programs in the United States.

While the TNE initiative is promising, initial teacher education as a whole remains highly problematic. The Teaching Commission (2006) gave a grade of D in its section on "Reinventing Teacher Preparation." The commission concludes that there are few incentives to improve initial teacher education. There is little political incentive to tackle the problem seriously, universities by and large have failed to mobilize their institutional resources to revamp teacher education, graduates still get hired, and so on. "If teacher preparation institutions are failing," says the commission, "they are failing quietly" (p. 40).

NCLB's requirement to have a qualified teacher in every classroom by 2005–06 is far from being realized in terms of quantity, even without quibbling about definitions of what represents quality. I have not addressed the proliferation of alternative certification programs. Such programs now represent 20% of all new hires in the United States (The Teaching Commission, 2006, p. 50). The evidence is that they are no better and no worse than traditional programs. Put positively, we need standards and strong developmental experiences for teachers in all types of programs. The problem is especially acute in the United States given the sheer size of the teaching force and the fact that its teachers on the average are less well qualified than is the case in many of their OECD counterpart countries.

These concerns are further reinforced by Arthur Levine's recent report, *Educating School Teachers* (Education School Project, 2006). Levine concludes that many teacher education graduates are inadequately prepared to meet the demands of today's classroom because faculties, curriculum and research are disconnected from school practice. Levine states, "There are wide variations in program quality, with the majority of teachers prepared in lower quality programs" (p. 1). The American Association of Colleges for Teacher Education responded that the conclusions were too sweeping and that in fact the issues raised by Levine are the very ones that the AACTE and its members are working on (AACTE, 2006). Still, almost everyone agrees that much of the work of reform in teacher education in the United States remains unfinished.

I must say as far as Canada is concerned, initial teacher education does not appear to be on anyone's radar screen. It proceeds quietly with only periodic attempts to raise the profile, but no sustained effort to make improvements. There are good programs here and there, such as the one I am most familiar with at OISE, University of Toronto (OISE/UT, 2005; Rolheiser & Evans, 2006). We have been especially interested in integrating university work with school work. As much as possible, we prefer to work with cohorts of students (30 to 60), teams of instructors (university- and school-based leaders), and clusters of partner schools. As is the case with all strong programs, partnerships between schools and districts, and the university are crucial. The best way of characterizing school–university partnerships is to say that in these arrangements, schools become just as committed to teacher education as they are to school improvement; and universities become just as committed to school improvement as they are to teacher education. If a whole district is using teacher education as a strategy for reform, it can make a substantial difference.

England is having good success with its Teacher Training Agency (TTA, 2005), because it made initial teacher training and continuous development of teachers a priority as an integrated part of the national school reform strategy. To begin with, the mandate of the agency is comprehensive, encompassing as strategic aims (1) to ensure schools have an adequate supply of good-quality newly qualified teachers, (2) to enable schools to develop the effectiveness of their support staff, (3) to enable schools to develop the effectiveness of their teachers and keep their knowledge and skills up-to-date, and (4) to support schools to be effective in the management of the training, development, and remodeling of their workforce. Only the first one concerns us here, but note the comprehensiveness of the brief of TTA (which recently has been renamed the Training and Development Agency).

The TTA has worked directly with teacher education institutions to revise the teacher education curriculum to reflect, for example, new developments in literacy and numeracy reform in schools. The agency also has used various financial incentives to attract new candidates to the profession, including areas facing shortages like mathematics, science, and so on. They now have a record number of candidates applying for teacher education programs in the country. The TTA also monitors the quality of programs and holds a standard that at least 85% of newly qualified teachers rate the quality of their training as good or better.

Standards

We need to get ahead of ourselves here in order to frame where I am going with this analysis. I already have mentioned that standards are difficult to formulate and enforce in initial teacher education, although the field is moving in that direction. Two other sets of standards also have evolved, one pertaining to the licensing and certification of new teachers, and the other related to the continuous development of teachers. In the United States, the National Board for Professional Teaching Standards (NBPTS), which we will discuss in Chapter 14, was the catalyst for focusing on ongoing professional development, creating thousands of National Board Certified Teachers. The NBPTS also stimulated backward mapping in order to frame requirements for beginning teachers and for teacher education programs. The assessment of what "teachers need to know and be able to do" involves a variety of methods to profile teachers' work with students, knowledge of subject, expertise in student assessment, and their own professional development (see especially Darling-Hammond & Bransford, 2005). NCTAF (1996) argued that

> Standards for teaching are the lynchpin for transforming current systems of preparation, licensing, certification, and ongoing development so that they better support student learning. [Such standards] can bring clarity and focus to a set of activities that are currently poorly connected and often badly organized. Clearly, if students are to achieve high standards, we can expect no less from their teachers and from other educators. Of greatest priority is reaching agreement on what teachers should know and be able to do to teach to high standards. (p. 67)

The NBPTS (1993) has organized its assessment around five major propositions.

1. Teachers are committed to students and their learning;
2. Teachers know the subject they teach and how to teach those subjects to students;

3. Teachers are responsible for managing and monitoring students' learning;
4. Teachers think systematically about their practice and learn from experience;
5. Teachers are members of learning communities.

Of course, these are just words, and we will get to their implementation import in Chapter 14. In the meantime, there is policy pressure on schools of education and better frameworks of assessment to guide their work. I cannot say that there is a great deal of *capacity building* going on beyond the minority of universities that are taking up special initiatives (much the same problem, as I observed earlier, occurs when only a minority of schools and districts are engaged in substantial reform.

To understand the themes of the previous chapters is to understand that revamping initial teacher preparation is part of any solution. You cannot develop professional learning communities if you have a weak foundation to begin with. It is easy to see why one might be tempted to give up on initial teacher education. The cultures of universities represent huge barriers to reform (for positive examples, see Carnegie Foundation, 2001, 2006; Thiessen & Howey, 1998), and more schools than not are powerful but *negative* socializing agents in this equation.

The biggest barrier, however, is that initial teacher education is always an afterthought in any reform effort. The critical shortage of teachers and the growing research knowledge base that having "three good teachers in a row" can determine the direction of a student's life are causing new (and nervous) attention to be paid to the whole area of teacher education reform. With Carnegie's TNE and England's TTA, one could say that we are witnessing a "rise, stall, and re-rise" phenomenon. It won't go anywhere this time either, however, unless it receives intensive development work in its own right, and unless it is closely integrated with and congruent with other parts of the solution, like how to hire and support beginning teachers. I still consider teacher education to be simultaneously "the worst problem and best solution in education" (Fullan, 1993, p. 105).

HIRING AND INDUCTION

The National Commission on Teaching and America's Future issued its second major report, entitled *No Dream Denied*, in 2003. In it, unlike the 1996 report, NCTAF concluded that we don't have a recruitment problem in education as much as we have *retention problem*. Actually we have both, but retention is more serious. Here is where we bridge the university and the school. In fact, in its 1993 report NCTAF identified five areas of recommendations, the last of which was "improve the working conditions of teachers." No one touched this recommendation. Let me put it dramatically: in the United States 46% of newly hired teachers leave in the first 5 years of teaching, 33% after 3 years (The Teaching Commision, 2006). You know the old song, "How are you gonna keep them down on the farm once they see Paree?" Well, this is, "How are you going to keep them down on the farm once they've seen the *farm*?" We need better farms. As I will argue later, changing the farm—improving the working conditions of teachers—may turn out to be the most effective route to reforming initial teacher preparation as well—a kind of push-back phenomenon. Changing the farm, for starters, means changing hiring and induction practices.

It should be abundantly clear by now that learning to teach effectively takes time, and the way in which one gets started on the job dramatically affects the rest of one's career, including driving out potentially good teachers in the early years. Hiring practices themselves, combined with the presence or absence of induction programs, are an indication, usually negative, of whether teaching is a worthwhile, developmental profession. Here is where some very positive developments have occurred in the past 5 years. Think of it this way: If districts established efficient and effective hiring practices coupled with solid mentoring/induction programs, they could cut the attrition rate of 33 or 46% in half, and get better career-long teachers. We can take as an example what has happened in New York City over the past 5 years.

New York is the largest urban district in the United States, and one where hiring practices traditionally bring a high proportion of unqualified teachers into the system. In 1992, only one third of new teachers hired were fully qualified. Yet the problem had less to do with a lack of supply and more to do with poor hiring procedures; a study by the New York Education Priorities Panel discovered that a substantial number of well-qualified new recruits were dissuaded from looking for work in New York City by excessively bureaucratic application procedures, inability to get information, inability to speak to hiring officers, and long delays.

New York has taken these criticisms to heart and has changed hiring processes. Darling-Hammond (1999) reports that the city has undertaken the following initiatives to improve hiring practices:

- bring city recruiters directly to students in local preparation programs each spring;
- offer interviews and tests on-site at college campuses;
- recruit teachers in high-need areas like bilingual and special education through scholarships, forgivable loans, and strategically located recruitment fairs;
- work with universities and local districts to bring well-trained prospective teachers into hard-to-staff schools as student teachers, interns, and visitors;
- make offers to well-qualified candidates much earlier in the year;
- streamline the exchange of information and the processing of applications. (p. 21)

The result of these initiatives was that by 1997, two thirds of new teachers had full qualifications when they were hired; in absolute terms, this is still a poor record, but the improvement from 1992 is significant. Building on this, in 2004 New York expanded its support for new teachers with a $36 million mentoring program that provides 300 mentors for the approximately 5,000 teachers hired annually (The Teaching Commission, 2006). The mentoring model shows an attrition rate of 12% after 6 years of teaching, compared with the national rate, as we have seen, of 46% leaving within the first 5 years. New York's new induction model is based on six basic principles:

1. Build political will for reform of induction systems
2. Ensure that all mentoring programs develop and maintain a high-quality selection process
3. Identify and support successful program standards
4. Align mentoring programs and general induction activities

with district and regional programs related to teacher development

5. Address systemic and infrastructure issues that affect new teachers (e.g., new teacher workload, student data systems)
6. Leverage systems of change by building on mentor skills, knowledge, and experience (New Teacher Center, 2006)

The value of improving hiring and support practices is also evident in New Haven, Connecticut, a school district that has made a remarkable turnaround in the past 2 decades. The district has brought about dramatic improvements by focusing on improving the quality of its teachers through a combination of recruitment, standards, development, and school organization. A key element in this strategy has been the development of recruitment strategies that target good teachers and that use a process of support and assessment to work with beginning teachers over the first 2 years of their careers, to ease them into the profession, and to provide support for their development. The district's recruitment strategy is to catch the interest of exceptional teachers and then invest in resources to hire and keep such people in the system.

> New Haven does not have large-scale recruitment crises annually because of the low attrition rate in their new and experienced teachers. Clearly, one of the major recruitment efforts is the district's internship program; 38 of 80 [newly hired teachers] had worked as part-time interns in the district internship program. (Snyder, 1999, p. 13)

In all these cases jurisdictions are developing standards of practice for beginning teachers. The NBPTS referred to above have been "backward mapped" to guide the work of the Interstate New Teacher Assessment and Support Consortium (INTASC).

> [INTASC is] a consortium of 33 states working together on "National Board-compatible" licensing standards and assessments for beginning teachers both before they enter teaching and during their first two years on the job. This effort, in time, has informed the work of the National Council for Accreditation of Teacher Education (NCATE), which has recently incorporated the performance standards developed by INTASC for judging preservice teacher education programs. (Darling-Hammond, 2000a, p. 10)

All in all promising, but one can see how very far we have to go. If most schools and districts are not good learning organizations (or good professional learning communities), this means they are not good employers. They are especially not good employers for teachers who want to make a difference. In sheer quantitative terms, having a 40% or more attrition rate in the first 5 years, when by changing practices you could reduce it to less than half that rate, doesn't make good business sense. In quality terms, if you want improvement, you have to attract talented people and then foster their collective development on the job from day one. Indeed, if you do the latter, you are more likely to attract good people in the first place.

Another key aspect of teacher development involves attracting teachers to serve in the most challenging schools. The current incentive system, as we will see in the next chapter, serves to do the opposite (Fullan, 2006). As Berry and Ferriter (2006) say in their work with National Board Certified Teachers: "Financial incentives alone will not lure these accomplished teachers to low-performing schools. Other factors such as strong principal leadership, a collegial staff with a shared teaching philosophy, adequate resources necessary to teach, and a supportive and active parent community were far more important determinants" (p. 4).

We of course have come full circle. Better teacher preparation, hiring, and induction are not a set of structural reforms. We are talking about reculturing the teaching profession as a whole. And we are talking again about better farms. No matter how good a job you do on initial teacher preparation and induction, it is all for nought if you don't also improve the working conditions of teachers. In their major study of teachers, Johnson and Kardos (2005) made the key discovery that "having a mentor in itself has no statistical relationship to new teacher job satisfaction, whereas working in a school with an integrated professional culture is strongly positively related to job satisfaction" (p. 12; Johnson, 2004, chap. 9). Thus, the ideas in this chapter do not stand alone. They must flow with career-long continuous professional development, and the latter in turn is more than quality workshops and standards—an issue to which we now turn.

CHAPTER 14

Professional Learning of Educators

A profession is not created by certificates and censures but by the existence of a substantive body of professional knowledge, as well as a mechanism for improving it, and by a genuine desire of the profession's members to improve their practice.
— Stigler and Hiebert (1999, p. 146)

We have come a certain distance from the time a few years ago when I listened to a teacher in Baton Rouge, Louisiana, make a representation to a Blue Ribbon Commission on the Teaching Profession. The teacher said, "When I die I hope it is during a professional development session because the transition from life to death will be so seamless." Note also the title of this chapter. I refer deliberately to professional *learning*, not professional development.

Professional learning is not about workshops and courses, or even meeting high standards and qualification frameworks. If done well, these are all important inputs, but they represent only a portion of the solution, let's say, 30%. The other 70% concerns whether teachers are learning every day, continuously improving their craft collectively. The development of habits of learning can occur only if they present themselves day after day.

Put another way, the agenda for transforming the professional learning of educators consists of two fundamental, interrelated parts: overhauling the standards, incentives, and qualification systems (what I called 30% of the solution), and remodeling the working conditions of teachers (the 70%).

To define the problem, we need to return to the themes we pursued in earlier chapters. In their observations of the Chicago Public Schools (CPS), Smylie, Bay, and Tozer (1999) remind us:

> Only about one-third of teachers in the system engage in regular dialogue about instruction. One-quarter work in schools where teachers and administrators disagree about school goals and norms of practice. Half fail to see any real coherence and continuity across programs in their schools. Most believe that their schools have so many programs coming and going that they cannot keep track of them all.
>
> Given these situations, it is not surprising that approaches to improvement in many schools lack coherence. In the early 1990s, 31 to 39 percent of CPS elementary schools had unfocused approaches to school improvement. Another 20 to 35 percent had more coherent approaches but these could not be considered systemic. More recent evidence of fragmentation has been found in a study of the Chicago Annenberg Challenge. Among the major challenges to school improvement reported by principals and external partners was the lack of coherence among multiple programs and innovations at their schools. These data indicate that multiple programs often compete for teachers' time and attention, pull faculties in different directions, and limit teachers' ability to fully participate in any program. (p. 39)

The question, then, is what policies and practices stand a chance of changing this deeply ingrained dysfunctional culture. The answer is that it will take a set of policies based on standards of new practice, combined with opportunities to learn new ways of working together. Elmore (2000) makes this key observation.

> People make these fundamental transitions by having *many* opportunities to be exposed to the ideas, to argue them into their own normative belief systems, to practice the behaviors that go with these values, to observe others practicing those behaviors, and, most importantly, to be successful at practicing in the presence of others (that is, to be seen to be successful). In the panoply of rewards and sanctions that attach to accountability sys-

tems, the most powerful incentives reside in the face-to-face relationships among people in the organization, not in external systems. (p. 31, emphasis in original)

We also must realize that it is not collaboration per se that counts. Collaboration is powerful, which means that people can do powerfully wrong things together. McLaughlin and Talbert (2001), it will be recalled, found that some strong high school communities reinforced traditional teaching and ended up failing large proportions of students. Collaboration makes a positive difference only when it is focused on student performance for all and on the associated innovative practices that can make improvement happen for previously disengaged students.

In terms of need, The Teaching Commission's (2006) final report frankly states that in the United States "teacher evaluation and on-the-job training are arcane and largely ineffective; novice teachers are usually left to sink or swim; far too many sink" (p.16). Let us start with standards and qualification frameworks.

STANDARDS OF PRACTICE

Most professional development experiences for teachers fail to make an impact. Almost 30 years ago I conducted a review of "in-service," as it was called then, and concluded that one-shot workshops were ineffective, the topics were selected by people other than those receiving the in-service, and follow-up support for implementation was rare (Fullan, 1979). Almost 15 years later, Little (1993) drew the same conclusion, adding that "the dominant training model of teachers' professional development—a model [at best] focused on expanding an individual repertoire of skills— is not adequate to the ambitious visions of teaching and schooling embedded in present reform initiatives" (p. 129). Reform initiatives, as I concluded earlier, are even more ambitious now, both in depth and in terms of being large scale.

Enter new standards of practice, themselves more ambitious. I referred in the previous chapter to the work in the United States of the National Board of Professional Teacher Standards. The

NBPTS has developed standards and assessment procedures in 30 subject-matter disciplines, organized around five major propositions. The five domains, stated here in full, are:

1. *Teachers are committed to students and their learning.* National-Board certified teachers are dedicated to making knowledge accessible to all students. They treat students equitably, recognizing individual differences. They adjust their practice based on observations and knowledge of their students' interests, abilities, skills, knowledge, family circumstances, and peer relationships. They understand how students develop and learn. They are aware of the influence of context and culture on behavior. They develop students' cognitive capacity and their respect for learning. Equally important, they foster students' self-esteem, motivation, character, civic responsibility and their respect for individual, cultural, religious and racial differences.

2. *Teachers know the subject they teach and how to teach those subjects to students.* National-Board certified teachers have a rich understanding of the subject(s) they teach and appreciate how knowledge in their subject is created, organized, linked to other disciplines and applied to real world settings. Accomplished teachers command specialized knowledge of how to convey and reveal subject matter to students. They are aware of the preconceptions and background knowledge that students typically bring to each subject and of strategies and instructional materials that can be of assistance. Their instructional repertoire allows them to create multiple tasks with knowledge, and they are adept at teaching students how to pose and solve their own problems.

3. *Teachers are responsible for managing and monitoring students' learning.* National-Board certified teachers create instructional settings to capture and sustain the interest of their students and to make the most effective use of time. Accomplished teachers command a range of instructional techniques, know when each is appropriate, and can implement them as needed. They know how to motivate and engage groups of students to ensure a purposeful learning environment, and how to organize instruction to allow the schools' goals for students to be met. They understand how to motivate students to learn and how to maintain their interests even in the face of temporary failure. Board certified teachers regularly assess the progress of individual students as well as that of the class as a whole. They employ multiple methods for mea-

suring student growth and understanding and can clearly explain student performance to parents.

4. *Teachers think systematically about their practice and learn from experience.* National-Board certified teachers exemplify the virtues they seek to inspire in students—curiosity, tolerance, honesty, fairness, respect for diversity and appreciation of cultural differences—and the capacities that are prerequisites for intellectual growth: the ability to reason and take multiple perspectives, to be creative and take risks, and to adopt an experimental and problem-solving orientation. Striving to strengthen their teaching, Board certified teachers critically examine their practice, seek the advice of others, and draw on educational research and scholarship to expand their repertoire, deepen their knowledge, sharpen their judgment and adapt their teaching to new findings, ideas and theories.

5. *Teachers are members of learning communities.* National-Board certified teachers contribute to the effectiveness of the school by working collaboratively with other professionals on instructional policy, curriculum development and staff development. They can evaluate school progress and the allocation of school resources in light of their understanding of state and local educational objectives. They are knowledgeable about specialized school and community resources that can be engaged for their students' benefit, and are skilled at employing such resources as needed. Accomplished teachers find ways to work collaboratively and creatively with parents, engaging them productively in the work of the school. (NBPTS, 1993, pp. 1–3)

By the end of 2000, the NBPTS had certified over 5,000 teachers; by 2006, the number had jumped to 47,500 certified in some 25 fields of teaching. Research on the impact of NBPTS-certified teachers is gradually accumulating. What is available is encouraging: "Teachers report that the process of analyzing their own and their students' work in light of standards enhances their abilities to assess student learning and to evaluate the effects of their own actions" (Darling-Hammond, 2001, p. 15).

In an early pilot study of the portfolio in the Stanford Teacher Assessment Project, "teachers reported that they improved their practice as they pushed themselves to meet specific standards that had previously had little place in their teaching" (Darling-Hammond, 2001, p. 15). In a more detailed study, Bond, Smith,

Baker, and Hattie (2000) found that NBPTS-certified teachers were more expert than noncertified teachers and were "producing students who differ in profound and important ways from those taught by less proficient [non-Board-certified] teachers" (p. x).

The NBPTS standards are being used in more and more states. All 50 states have offered some kind of endorsement of the credential, and 30 states provide financial incentives, which include higher salaries for all certified teachers meeting the qualification. Several states use NBPTS certification as a criterion for appointing teachers to mentor and other lead teacher positions. A recent report raised doubts about whether certified teachers were better at increasing student achievement, but the value of increased NBPTS qualifications still is widely seen as essential for focusing on teacher quality over a career (NBPTS upgrades profession, 2006).

The National Staff Development Council (NSDC) has provided yeoman service in raising the standards of professional development, addressing head-on the experiences of the Louisiana teacher quoted at the beginning of this chapter. NSDC's Standards of Practice for Professional Development (2005) are stated in three main categories—context, process, and content standards that improve the learning of all students:

Context Standards:
- Organizes adults into learning communities whose goals are aligned with those of the school and the district.
- Requires skillful school and district leaders who guide continuous instructional improvement.
- Requires resources to support adult learning and collaboration.

Process Standards:
- Uses disaggregated student data to determine adult learning priorities, monitor progress and sustain continuous improvement.
- Uses multiple sources of information to guide improvement and demonstrate its impact.
- Uses learning strategies appropriate to the intended goals.
- Applies knowledge about human learning and change.
- Provides educators with the knowledge and skills to collaborate.

Content Standards:
- Prepares educators to understand and appreciate all students (equity).

- Deepens educators' content knowledge, provides them with research based instructional strategies to assist students in meeting rigorous academic standards, and prepares them to use various types of classroom assessments appropriately.
- Provides educators with knowledge and skills to involve families and other stakeholders. (pp. 1–2)

These are all laudable and effective standards for raising awareness of professional development practice, for exposing poor practice, and for improving professional development, but of course they don't change cultures, a point to which I will turn shortly.

Similar developments for improving professional development practices are underway in England, Canada, and other jurisdictions. One of the four main strategic aims of England's Teacher Training Agency (2005) focuses directly on improving professional development. Strategic Aim 3 is: "To enable schools to develop the effectiveness of their teachers and keep their knowledge and skills up-to-date." The English refer to ongoing professional development as continuous professional development or CPD. TTA states: "Our new role will mean taking the lead in national, regional, and local partnerships in order to bring greater coherence to teachers' CPD and to shape future strategy and priorities" (p. 8).

All of this leads to the thorny area of recertification, performance-based compensation, and the like. Certainly individual merit pay, career ladders, and similar schemes have failed miserably. Odden (1996) cites research from a wide variety of American sources, describing the unsuccessful efforts throughout the 20th century to implement these mechanisms. He concludes that such attempts, designed for manufacturing industries, are inappropriate for a system that does not produce discrete products. He recommends that a new system of rewards and career paths be designed and lays out a framework for teacher compensation focusing on "tools for assessing the knowledge and skills" of (1) beginning teachers, (2) mid-career teachers, and (3) experienced teachers, with corresponding forms of compensation (Odden, 2000).

And indeed there are in 2006 a number of new developments underway. I have already referred to the TTA's ambitious agenda in England. In the United States the initiatives are more uneven, depending on the state. The Teaching Commission (2006) cites a number of examples, such as Minnesota's Quality Compensation plan. Every district is required to submit plans that must include five core components: "(1) a career ladder for teachers; (2) ongoing training that is linked to improving the quality of the work that teachers do on a daily basis; (3) instructional observations and standards-based assessments; (4) measures to determine student growth; and (5) alternative compensation and performance pay linked to those observations and assessments" (p. 29).

Although I will have more to say about teacher unions in the concluding section of this chapter, there are instances of major barriers, along with examples of significant new partnerships between unions and districts aimed at improving standards. Relative to barriers to improvement, we can take Levin, Mulhern, and Schunck's (2005) study of union contracts in five school districts. The authors identify three factors—(1) vacancy policies, (2) staffing rules favoring seniority, and (3) late budget timetables—that produce four negative consequences.

1. "Urban schools are forced to hire large numbers of teachers they do not want and who may not be a good fit for the job and their school" (p. 5). In their study, 40% of school-level vacancies were filled by voluntary transfers or excess teachers over whom schools had no choice at all or had limited choice.
2. "Poor performers are passed around from school to school instead of being terminated" (p. 5).
3. "New teaching applicants, including the best, are lost to late hiring" (p. 6), as transfers and other adjustments have to be addressed first.
4. "Novice teachers are treated as expendable regardless of their contribution to their school" (p. 6).

There are individual positive exceptions to these harmful practices. The Teaching Commission (2006), while observing that there are "far too many counterproductive protections for teachers across the country" (p. 61), cites new contracts in New York City, Chicago, and Philadelphia that provide more flexibility for hiring. And the Teacher Union Reform Network has been operating for about a decade (Urbanski & Erskine, 2000). The network consists of 21 urban districts in the United States. "The primary goal," say Urbanski and Erskine, "is to promote new union models that can take the lead in building and sustaining high achieving schools through improving the quality of instruction" (pp. 367–368). They continue:

> The culture of labor/management relations in the education community must change to one of shared responsibility, characterized by cooperation to improve instruction, rather than one of traditional polarized roles and adversarial relationships. (p. 368)

Taking all the above developments together, new standards of practice and related policies are providing stronger avenues for the professional development of teachers. Aside from problems of implementation, and there are plenty of these, even the best of these solutions are incomplete because they rest on the assumption that we should improve *individuals*. *The New Meaning of Educational Change* argues that we also must simultaneously and more fundamentally change the *cultures or working conditions* within which educators work.

CHANGING CULTURES AND WORKING CONDITIONS

To be effective, even the best set of "standards of practice" must be evident in the daily organization and culture of schools. It seems obvious to state, but we need to be explicit here. In our book *Breakthrough*, Hill, Crévola, and I (2006) argued that the new goal for public education in the 21st century must be to serve successfully 95%+ of the school population. In order to do this, we said, it will be necessary to build an instructional system that is based on personalization (connecting to the unique needs of each student) and precision (connecting in a way that is geared specifically to the student's needs in a timely fashion). There was a third P, which we called "professional learning." We made the case that the first two Ps could not be served unless *each and every teacher was learning virtually every day in concert with other teachers*. Elmore

(2000) has made a similar claim. When a culture for learning in context is established:

> Experimentation and discovery can be harnessed to social learning by connecting people with new ideas to each other in an environment in which the ideas are subjected to scrutiny, measured against the collective purposes of the organization, and tested by the history of what has already been learned and is known. (p. 25)

In the absence of such cultures, no incentive or qualification scheme by itself can possibly carry the day. Much in the previous chapters of this book is about changing the cultures and working conditions of educators. Put positively, when standards of practice and cultural change are working together, we will create powerful mutually connected forces of change.

Changing working conditions, in common with all successful organizational change, involves two components, structure and culture. The former is important but also the easier of the two. Thus, providing more time for teachers to work together during the day, as many jurisdictions are doing, is necessary but not sufficient. If the capacity (culture) is not evident in these situations, the new time will be squandered more times than not. We have seen some successful examples of cultural change in earlier chapters, such as in the Knowsley, Boston, and York Region school districts. But these are clearly in the minority and not necessarily well established themselves.

In England the National Remodelling pilot project is an example of the kind of bold experiment that meets many of the objectives I have mentioned, although this is such new, complex, and fundamental territory, it is going to take many years to make substantial progress. Arising from a national work force agreement in 2003 between the government and the teacher union, a pilot initiative was established under the direction of a National Remodelling Team (NRT). The executive director describes the focus.

> Remodelling at the school level is designed to enhance the status and work/life balance of all who work in our schools. It enables teachers to focus more effectively on their teaching and provides every pupil with a chance to achieve greater success.

> It presents new opportunities to our support staff. . . . Remodel-
> ling encourages collaboration *within* and *between* schools. (Col-
> larbone, 2005, p. 5, emphasis in original)

Starting with 1,500 schools in 2003–04, the number expanded to 14,000 schools by 2004–05. I don't think for a moment that this particular initiative by itself will change working conditions across the country. The needed change is too deep, and there are too many other things going on in England right now—some compatible with NRT, others not—but it does furnish an excellent example of focusing directly on improving the working conditions and cultures of schools.

In sum, new policies that promulgate high standards of practice for all teachers invite the possibility of large-scale reform. A corresponding set of policies is required to create many opportunities, in fact requirements, for people to examine together their day-to-day practice. It is through local problem solving with expanded horizons that new solutions can be identified and implemented. This represents a huge cultural change for schools, and as such it is going to require sophisticated new leadership.

THE ROLE OF LEADERSHIP

A front-page article in the January 12, 2000 issue of *Education Week* is headlined "Policy Focus Converges on Leadership." Its first two paragraphs commence:

> After years of work on structural changes—standards and test-
> ing and ways of holding students and schools accountable—the
> education policy world has turned its attention to the people
> charged with making the system work.
>   Nowhere is the focus on the human element more preva-
> lent than in the recent recognition of the importance of strong
> and effective leadership. (p. 1)

Indeed I do mark 2000 as a turning point in the resurgence of leadership; "what standards were to the 1900s, leadership is to the 2000s" (Fullan, 2003, p. 91). I could repeat in detail the same analysis here as I did for the professional learning of teachers, namely,

the system of standards and certification of leaders requires attention, as does what we have called "learning in context." Instead I
will provide just the highlights.

In the United States, the Interstate Leaders Licensure Consortium (ISLLC) has established a comprehensive set of standards for
principals, and roughly 200 indicators that help define those standards. Their six standards are as follows (2000):

1. A school administrator is an educational leader who promotes
   the success of all students by facilitating the development, articulation, implementation, and stewardship of a vision of learning
   that is shared and supported by the school community;
2. A school administrator is an educational leader who promotes
   the success of all students by advocating, nurturing, and sustaining a school culture and instructional program conducive to student learning and staff professional growth;
3. A school administrator is an educational leader who promotes
   the success of all students by ensuring management of the organization, operations, and resources for a safe, efficient and effective
   learning environment;
4. A school administrator is an educational leader who promotes
   the success of all students by collaborating with families and
   community members, responding to diverse community interests
   and needs, and mobilizing community resources;
5. A school administrator is an educational leader who promotes
   the success of all students by acting with integrity, fairness and
   in an ethical manner;
6. A school administrator is an educational leader who promotes
   the success of all students by understanding, responding to, and
   influencing the larger political, social, economic, legal and cultural context. (Murphy, Yff, & Shipman, 2000, pp. 7–8)

The consortium has linked these standards to professional development and training, licensure, and assessment for school leaders.
ISLLC standards have been adopted by many states, either in full
or in part.

These positive developments were overshadowed by Arthur
Levine's (2005) devastating critique of how school leaders are educated in the United States. Perhaps somewhat overstated, Levine
charges that the quality of preparation of the nation's school leaders ranges from "inadequate to appalling" and that programs are
marked by "low standards, weak faculty and irrelevant curricu-

lum." Incidentally, Mintzberg (2004) has made a similar critique of MBA programs, concluding that they produce superficial generalists who know nothing about the contexts in which they work. The direction of his solution, which I take up below, is similar to my own argument.

Levine (2005) identifies the work of the National College for School Leadership (NCSL) in England as representing "a promising model." I agree. When the mandate for NSCL was set out at its founding in 2000, one of the government's chief strategists, Michael Barber (2000), stated, "Our tasks as a government are to attract and develop a new generation of school leaders and to enable the present generation to adapt to this radically new and demanding world" (p. 1). To do so, Barber said, the government has:

- created a new qualification for aspiring principals (the National Professional Qualification for Headship) which sets new standards and combines workplace learning with scholarship;
- provided all newly appointed headteachers with a £2000 voucher to spend on professional development, invited them every year to a spectacular conference in London and linked them to an online learning community in which they can debate among themselves and with internationally-known education experts;
- established a new qualification for mid-career principals (the Leadership Programme for Serving Heads) which requires them to engage in vigorous, externally validated self-assessment;
- announced the intention to establish a new National College for School Leadership which will become operational later this year, have a new state of the art building on a university campus, develop an online as well as traditional presence, and will link our school principals to leaders in other sectors and their peers in other countries;
- worked with business to provide business mentors for thousands of school principals;
- improved principals' pay and capacity to earn performance bonuses;
- created a new leadership tier in each school;
- established a £50 million fund to enable the removal or retirement of principals who are not ready for the new challenge. (p. 3)

Now in its seventh year of operation, NCSL, with a new director, Steve Munby (whom I introduced earlier as director of Knowsley), appointed in 2005, has reviewed its work and strengthened its focus. In *Charting a Course*, NCSL (2005) identifies four main goals. NCSL is committed to

1) transform achievement and well-being through excellent school leadership
2) develop leadership within and beyond the school
3) identify and grow tomorrow's leaders
4) create a "fit for purpose" national college (making sure we are properly geared to deliver what school leaders want from us) (p. 15)

Among other things, NCSL currently is working on a National Programme for Qualifications of Heads, which soon will become mandatory for all new school heads; succession practices to ensure the continual cultivation and flow of new leaders; and the fostering of habits and practices that envision school heads as "system leaders," an argument that I made in relation to establishing conditions for sustainability (Fullan, 2005).

I return again to the import of all this. The solution lies in combining stronger qualification standards, *along with* experiences in which aspiring and existing leaders develop themselves and new cultures simultaneously. This is not an abstract proposition. I have already quoted Elmore several times to the effect that we must learn new things in the context in which we work. Perkins (2003) makes a similar point: "Vision and policy from the top as well as formal training can help to foster progressive transformation. They may be essential to getting it started. But they do not do the actual work of transformation. *This is done by developmental leaders* [on the job]." (p. 224, emphasis in original)

Mintzberg (2004) arrives at the same conclusion about developing business leaders. Becoming effective leaders "is as much about doing in order to think as thinking in order to do" (p. 10). And, "successful managing is not about one's own success but about fostering success in others" (p. 16). Then Mintzberg hits a home run when he says we need "programs designed to educate practicing managers in context; [such leadership] has to be learned, not just by doing it but by being able to gain conceptual insight while doing it" (p. 200). The goal, according to Mintzberg, is not just to develop better leaders, but also to develop the organization and to improve the larger system. There we have it. Changing and developing individuals, and changing and developing cultures suited to the 21st century *is the same work*. We need to design policies and practices relative to the professional learning of education based on this absolutely crucial assumption.

TO RE-CREATE A PROFESSION

If you read this book carefully, the biggest revolution I am talking about is *changing the teaching profession*, which includes standards, qualifications, and the conditions and cultures within which educators work. If you examine the underlying message of even the most supportive government commissions on teaching, you are compelled to conclude that teaching as a profession has not yet come of age. It needs reform in recruitment, selection, status, and reward; redesign of initial teacher education and induction into the profession; continuous professional development; standards and incentives for professional work; and, most important of all, changes in the daily working conditions of teachers. Yet there appears to be little political will to launch sustained reforms in teacher development and in the organization of the teaching profession more widely. Changing the teaching profession, of course, is not an end in itself. Every teacher learning, every day, individually and collectively, is the *sine qua non* of transforming schools for educating all and for sustaining society (Fullan, 2006; Fullan et al., 2006).

As teachers work more and more with people beyond their own schools, a whole gamut of new skills, relationships, and orientations will fundamentally change the essence of their profession. This new professionalism is collaborative, not autonomous; open rather than closed; outward-looking rather than insular; and authoritative but not controlling.

Teachers of today and tomorrow need to do much more learning on the job, or in parallel with it—where they constantly can test out, refine, and get feedback on the improvements they make. They need access to other colleagues in order to learn from them. Schools are poorly designed for integrating learning and teaching on the job. The teaching profession must become a better learning profession.

Finally, I hope it is obvious that leadership must come from many sources. The teacher in a collaborative culture who contributes to the success of peers is a leader; the mentor, the grade-level coordinator, the department head, the local union representative are all leaders if they are working in a professional learning community. Our sixth and last guideline for teachers in *What's Worth Fighting for Out There* is "Help to Recreate Your Profession" (Hargreaves & Fullan, 1998, p. 102). Recreating the profession, as I have said, will require leadership at all levels of the system—leadership that fosters capacity building with a focus on results.

Rise, stall, rise, stall—is this a perpetual cycle or is there something qualitatively different this time?

CHAPTER 15

The Future of Educational Change

The future isn't what it used to be.

—Anonymous

There is something different in this fourth edition of *The New Meaning of Educational Change*. It has become more obvious that the approaches that have been used so far to bring about educational change are not working and cannot work. Accountability-focused schemes fail to move the sticks forward, as do empowering based site-based management and all variations in between. But necessity isn't always the mother of invention, so why would it be different now? Two reasons: One is that we do have a clearer sense of the theories of action that will be required, what I have called broadly, "capacity building with a focus on results"; the other reason is that most of the elements needed for success have been developed and are in use in one place or another. Just as Senge (1990) observed that after the first air flight, it took many more specific inventions over several decades before modern jet travel was possible, breakthrough forces in educational reform now seem to be in our midst (see also Wilson & Barsky, 2006).

What we know is, first, it is going to be a lot harder than we thought, and second, it will require some bold experiments that generate new powerful forces, including, for example, teachers' energies and commitments unleashed by altered working conditions and new collective capacities, and students' intellectual labor in collaborating with other students to do the work of learning. The breakthrough solutions will need to be efficient because the energy required for the results to which we aspire is enormous. Thus we need simultaneously to stop wasting our energies on failed change attempts and to find and forge new sources of energy. Mintzberg (2004) captures what I have in mind beautifully in these words.

> Leadership is not about making clever decisions. . . . It is about energizing other people to make good decisions and do better things. In other words it is about helping people release the positive energy that exists naturally within people. Effective leadership inspires more than it empowers; it connects more than it controls; it demonstrates more than it decides. It does all this by *engaging* —itself above all, and consequently others. (p. 143, emphasis in original)

Thus, do not go into the future of educational change unless you have a plan to locate and unleash new forms of energy. We have used existing sources of energy to the limit, so that the only solution is to find different, additional forms of energy that are cheap in that they are potentially plentiful, renewable, and low cost. Such energy can be only human and social capital. We need theories of action that tap into this reservoir of meaning—no other form of energy can do the work of change.

The ideas for mobilizing meaning are contained in each chapter of this book, but I see these ideas as representing initiation or readiness steps prior to more radical transformation. Many more people must get familiar with these ideas before we can expect breakthroughs, which could come rapidly once we reach a critical mass. So the message is not to jump in the deep end, but to work on meaning and capacity building. The initial invitation for each reader is threefold:

1. Get a better understanding of your own role, and be liberated by the insights and possibilities for growth you see in the most successful examples; do not self-limit.
2. Work hard at understanding the situation of other roles with which you have the most contact, and alter your approach to them accordingly. Empathy does not mean agreement, but it is an essential component of any strategy that depends on developing the new relationships necessary for success.
3. As difficult as it seems, get a sense of "the big picture."

> Place your work in the context of society. If there ever was
> a societal function that has global consequences for human-
> kind, it is the education of us all. (Fullan, 2006)

Twenty-five years ago, *The Meaning of Educational Change* had
a one-level message: If people don't find meaning in reform, it can
never have an impact. There is now much more comprehensive
confirmation of this stance. Cognitive scientists have made it powerfully clear that learning is meaning making, which requires a
radically new way of approaching learning—one that guides the
development of individual minds through many minds working
together.

Just as learning will go nowhere if educators do not have a
deep theoretical understanding of the first principles of pedagogy,
improvement will not happen if leaders and others do not have a
deep theoretical grasp of the first principles of change—what I have
called theories of action. Theories of pedagogy and theories of action must be integrated again and again in each action setting.

Existing strategies will not get us to where we need to go, if
we want large-scale, lasting reform. In this sense the research can
be misleading. If research shows, for example, that successful
schools have school principals with "vision," it would be wrong
to think that getting more principals with vision is the answer (or,
if you prefer, it would be wrong to think that you could multiply
their numbers). The answer to large-scale reform is not to try to
emulate the characteristics of the minority who are getting somewhere *under present conditions*; if the conditions stay the same, we
will always have only a minority who can persist (for short periods of time) against many odds. Rather, we must change existing
conditions so that it is normal and possible for a majority of people to move forward.

The "learning organization" is more than a cliché. The phrase
"learning organization" is one of the most used and most superficially understood terms in the change business. How many of us
have read a book or article on the learning organization, agreed
with everything we read, and then had no clue about what to do?
I think here is where the new insights of cognitive scientists and
organization theorists converge. Just as the former have discov-

ered that learners must learn in context (because of their individuality and the uniqueness of their situations), the latter have concluded that improvement occurs only when you change context.

So, what is the real reason that learning organizations are required? The answer is contained in Elmore's (2004b) statement, "improvement is . . . a function of learning to do the right thing *in the setting where you work*" (p. 73, emphasis added). When enough people start doing the right thing in the setting in which they work, they end up changing their very context. When they do this by becoming engaged with other settings, as I have advocated for lateral capacity building, many contexts get changed.

Advocates of school reform cannot be blamed for being impatient with the excruciatingly slow pace of reform. For some, the alternative to get action is a market model in which public money is dispensed directly to consumers to purchase education based on their preferences. This model has some merit: it is efficient; it allows for choice; it generates competition. However, it radically misses a fundamental matter, namely, that a strong public school system and societal development are closely connected (Fullan, 2006). There are deep theoretical and evolutionary reasons to believe that society will be stronger if education serves to enable people to work together to achieve higher purposes that serve both the individual and the collective good. When you boil it all down, there are two social forces that cause continuous improvement. One pertains to ongoing knowledge creation and use; the other, to ever-deepening and -widening moral purpose and commitment. Both these forces, to flourish, require a strong public school system.

Personal and social betterment are intimately interconnected. The line of thinking goes like this:

1. Large-scale change cannot be achieved if teachers identify only with their own classrooms and are not similarly concerned with the success of other teachers and the whole school.
2. Large-scale change cannot be achieved if principals identify only with their own school and are not similarly concerned with the success of other principals and schools in the district.

3. Large-scale change cannot be achieved if school districts identify only with their own district and are not similarly concerned with the success of other districts.
4. Large-scale change cannot be achieved if individual states identify only with their own states and are not similarly concerned with the success of other states and the country as a whole. And so on.

Put in terms of responsibility, individual classroom teachers cannot opt out of school reform; individual schools cannot opt out of district reform; individual districts cannot opt out of state reform; and individual states cannot opt out of global reform. Small-scale improvement will not last if we do not identify with and help improve the surrounding system. Thus, we have both selfish and altruistic reasons for wanting to see the overall system get better.

This book has been a very long journey into complex space. We have seen that there is a deep reciprocity between personal and social (shared) meaning. One contributes to the other; each is weakened in the absence of the other. The ultimate goal of change is for people to see themselves as shareholders with a stake in the success of the system as a whole, with the pursuit of meaning as the elusive key. Meaning is motivation; motivation is energy; energy is engagement; engagement is life.

References

Abrahamson, E. (2004). *Change without pain*. Boston: Harvard Business School Press.

Allen, D. (2006, January 2006). *A new role for local authorities—from direct provider to strategic commissioner*. Paper presented to Capita White Paper conference, London.

Allison, D. J. (1988). *Ontario directors and American superintendents: A study of contrasting cultures and contexts*. London, Ontario: Division of Educational Policy Studies, University of Western Ontario.

American Association of Colleges for Teacher Education. (2006). *Response to* Educating school teachers. Washington, DC: Author.

American Institutes of Research. (1999). *An educators' guide to school-wide reform*. Washington, DC: Author.

Anderson, S. (2006). The school district's role in educational change. *International Journal of Educational Reform, 15*(1), 13–37.

Ashton, P., & Webb, R. (1986). *Making a difference: Teachers' sense of efficacy and student achievement*. New York: Longman.

Ball, D., & Cohen, D. (1999). Developing practice, developing practitioners: Towards a practice-based theory of professional education. In L. Darling-Hammond & G. Sykes (Eds.), *Teaching as the learning profession* (pp. 3–32). San Francisco: Jossey-Bass.

Barber, M. (2000). *High expectations and standards*. Unpublished paper, Department for Education and Further Employment, London.

Barber, M. (2001). *Large scale reform in England*. Paper prepared for the school development conference, Tartu University, Estonia.

Barber, M., & Fullan, M. (2005, March 2). Tri-level development: It's the system. *Education Week*, pp. 15–16.

Bate, P., Bevan, H., & Robert, G. (2005). *Toward a million change agents: A review of the social movements literature*. London: National Health System.

Bender Sebring, P., & Bryk, A. (2000, February). School leadership and the bottom line in Chicago. *Phi Delta Kappan, 81*(6), 440–443.

Berends, M., Bodilly, S., & Kirby, S. (2002). *Facing the challenges of whole school reform*. Santa Monica, CA: Rand Corporation.

Berends, M., Chun, J., Schulyer, G., Stockly, S., & Briggs, R. (2002). *Challenges of conflicting school reforms*. Santa Monica, CA: Rand Corporation.

Berger, P., & Luckmann, T. (1967). *The social construction of reality*. New York: Anchor Books.

Berliner, D. (2005). Our impoverished view of education reform. *Teachers College Record, 107*(3), 1–36.

Berman, P. (1980). Thinking about programmed and adaptive implementation: Matching strategies to situations. In H. Ingram & D. Mann (Eds.), *Why policies succeed or fail* (pp. 205–227). Beverly Hills, CA: Sage.

Berman, P., & McLaughlin, M. (1977). *Federal programs supporting educational change: Vol. 7. Factors affecting implementation and continuation*. Santa Monica, CA: Rand Corporation.

Berman, P., & McLaughlin, M. (with Pincus, J., Weiler, D., & Williams, R.) (1979). *An exploratory study of school district adaptations*. Santa Monica, CA: Rand Corporation.

Berry, B., & Ferriter, B. (2006). *Every child deserves our best: Lessons from North Carolina's National Board Certified Teachers on how to support and staff high-needs schools*. Chapel Hill, NC: Center for Teacher Quality.

Black, P., Harrison, C., Lee, C., Marshall, B., & Wiliam, D. (2003). *Assessment for learning*. Philadelphia: Open University Press.

Block, P. (1987). *The empowered manager*. San Francisco: Jossey-Bass.

Blumberg, A. (1985). *The school superintendent: Living with conflict*. New York: Teachers College Press.

Bodilly, S. (1998). *Lessons from New American Schools' scale-up phase*. Santa Monica, CA: Rand Corporation.

Bodilly, S., & Berends, M. (1999). *Necessary district support for comprehensive school reform*. Cambridge, MA: Harvard Civil Rights Project.

Bond, L., Smith, T., Baker, W., & Hattie, J. (2000). *The certification system of the National Board for Professional Teaching Standards*. Greensboro: Center for Educational Research and Evaluation, University of North Carolina at Greensboro.

Bowles, S., & Gintis, H. (1976). *Schooling in capitalist America*. New York: Basic Books.

Boyd, W. (1978). The changing politics of curriculum policy making for American schools. *Review of Educational Research, 48*(4), 577–628.

Bransford, T., Brown, A., & Cocking, K. (Eds.). (1999). *How people learn: Bridging research and practice*. Washington, DC: National Academy Press.

Bridge, G. (1976). Parent participation in school innovations. *Teachers College Record, 77*(3), 366–384.

Brown, S., & Eisenhardt, K. (1998). *Competing on the edge.* Boston: Harvard Business School Press.

Bryk, A., & Schneider, B. (2002). *Trust in schools.* New York: Russell Sage.

Bryk, A., Sebring, P., Kerbow, D., Rollow, S., & Easton, J. (1998). *Charting Chicago school reform.* Boulder, CO: Westview Press.

Bussis, A., Chittenden, E., & Amarel, M. (1976). *Beyond surface curriculum.* Boulder, CO: Westview Press.

Campbell, C., & Fullan, M. (2006). *Unlocking the potential for district-wide reform.* Unpublished paper, Ontario Literacy Numeracy Secretariat, Toronto.

Campbell, E. (2005). Challenges in fostering ethical knowledge as professionalism within schools as teaching communities. *Journal of Educational Change, 6*(3), 207–226.

Carnegie Forum on Education and the Economy. (1986). *A nation prepared: Teachers for the 21st century.* Report of the Task Force on Teaching as a Profession. New York: Author.

Carnegie Foundation of New York. (2001). *Teachers for a new era.* New York: Author.

Carnegie Foundation of New York. (2006). *Teachers for a new era: Technical support and capacity building.* New York: Author.

Charters, W., & Jones, J. (1973). *On the neglect of the independent variable in program evaluation.* Unpublished paper, University of Oregon, Eugene.

Clark, D., Lotto, S., & Astuto, T. (1984). Effective schools and school improvement. *Educational Administration Quarterly, 20*(3), 41–68.

Cohen, D., & Hill, H. (2001). *Learning policy.* New Haven, CT: Yale University Press.

Coleman, P. (1998). *Parent, student and teacher collaboration: The power of three.* Thousand Oaks, CA: Corwin Press.

Collarbone, P. (2005, January). Remodelling leadership. Presented at the North of England Conference, Belfast.

Consortium of Educational Change. (2000). *Annual report.* Oakbrook Terrace, CA: Author.

Cross City Campaign for Urban School Reform. (2005). *A delicate balance: District policies and classroom practice.* Chicago: Author.

Council of Chief School Officers. (2002). *Expecting success: A study of five high performing, high poverty schools.* Washington, DC: Author.

Cowden, P., & Cohen, D. (1979). *Divergent worlds in practice.* Cambridge, MA: Huron Institute.

Daft, R., & Becker, S. (1978). *The innovative organization.* New York: ElsevierNorth-Holland.

Danzberger, P., Carol, L., Cunningham, L., Kirst, M., McCloud, B., &

Usdan, M. (1987). School boards: The forgotten players on the education team. *Phi Delta Kappan, 68*(1), 53–59.

Darling-Hammond, L. (1999). *Solving the dilemmas of teacher supply, demand, and standards.* New York: Columbia University, National Commission on Teaching and America's Future.

Darling-Hammond, L. (Ed.). (2000a). *Studies of excellence in teacher education: Preparation in undergraduate years.* Washington, DC: American Association of Colleges of Teacher Education.

Darling-Hammond, L. (Ed.). (2000b). *Studies of excellence in teacher education: Preparation in a five-year program.* Washington, DC: American Association of Colleges of Teacher Education.

Darling-Hammond, L. (Ed.). (2000c). *Studies of excellence in teacher education: Preparation at the graduate level.* Washington, DC: American Association of Colleges of Teacher Education.

Darling-Hammond, L. (2001). *Reshaping teaching policy, preparation and practice.* Washington, DC: Accountability on Teaching.

Darling-Hammond, L., & Ball, D. (1999). *Teaching for high standards: What policymakers need to know and be able to do.* Philadelphia: CPRE, National Commission on Teaching for America's Future.

Darling-Hammond, L., & Bransford, J. (Eds.). (2005). *Preparing teachers for a changing world.* San Francisco: Jossey-Bass.

Datnow, A. (2000). Implementing an externally developed school restructuring design. *Teaching and Change, 7*(2), 147–171.

Datnow, A., Hubbard, L., & Mehan, H. (2002). *Extending educational reform: From one school to many.* London: RoutledgeFalmer Press.

Datnow, A., & Kemper, E. (2003, April). *Connections between federal, state and local levels in the implementation of comprehensive school reform.* Paper presented at the annual meeting of the American Educational Research Association, Chicago.

Datnow, A., & Stringfield, S. (2000). Working together for reliable school reform. *Journal of Education for Students Placed at Risk, 5*(1–2), 183–204.

Day, C., Harris, A., Hadfield, M., Toley, H., & Beresford, J. (2000). *Leading schools in times of change.* Buckingham, UK: Open University Press.

Department for Education and Skills. (2003). *Every child matters.* London: Author.

Department for Education and Skills. (2005). *High standards for all: More choice for parents and pupils.* London: Author.

Deutschman, A. (2005, May). Change or die. *Fast Company, 94,* 53–57.

Donovan, M. S., Bransford, J. D., & Pellegrino, W. (Eds.). (1999). *How people learn: Bridging research and practice.* Washington, DC: National Academy Press.

Drucker, P. (1985). *Innovation and entrepreneurship.* New York: Harper & Row.

Dryden, K. (1995). *In school.* Toronto: McClelland.

Duke, D. L. (1988). Why principals consider quitting. *Phi Delta Kappan, 70*(4), 308–313.

Dufour, R., Dufour, R., Eaker, R., & Many, T. (2006). *Learning by doing: A handbook for professional learning communiites at work.* Bloomington, IN: Solution Tree.

Dufour, R., Eaker, R., & Dufour, R. (Eds.). (2005). *On common ground.* Bloomington, IN: National Education Services.

Earl, L., Fullan, M., Leithwood, K., & Watson, N. (2003). *Watching & learning: OISE/UT evaluation of the national literacy and numeracy strategies.* London: Department for Education and Skills.

Earl, L., & Lee, L. (1999). Learning for change: School improvement as capacity building. *Improving Schools, 3*(1), 30–38.

Education Commission of the States. (2000). *In pursuit of quality teaching.* Denver: Author.

The Education Schools Project. (2006). *Educating school teachers.* Washington, DC: Author.

Education Trust. (2005). *The funding gap 2005: Low income students short changed in most states.* Washington, DC: Author.

Elmore, R. (1995). Getting to scale with good educational practice. *Harvard Educational Review, 66*(1), 1–26.

Elmore, R. (2000). *Building a new structure for school leadership.* Washington, DC: Albert Shanker Institute.

Elmore, R. (2004a). The hollow core of leadership in practice. Unpublished paper. Cambridge, MA: Harvard University Graduate School of Education.

Elmore, R. F. (2004b). *School reform from the inside out: Policy, practice, and performance.* Cambridge, MA: Harvard University Press.

Elmore, R. (2006). *Leadership as the practice of improvement.* Paper presented at the OECD Conference on Improving Leadership, London.

Elmore, R., & Burney, D. (1999). Investing in teacher learning. In L. Darling-Hammond & G. Sykes (Eds.), *Teaching as the learning profession* (pp. 236–291). San Francisco: Jossey-Bass.

Epstein, J. L. (1986). Parents' reactions to teacher practices of parent involvement. *Elementary School Journal, 86*(3), 277–294.

Epstein, J. L. (1988). Effects on student achievement of teachers' practices for parent involvement. In S. Silvern (Ed.), *Literacy through family, community, and school interaction* (pp. 73–88). Greenwich, CT: JAI Press.

Epstein, J. (1995). School/family/community partnerships. *Phi Delta Kappan, 76*, 701–712.

Epstein, J. L., & Dauber. S. L. (1988, April). *Teacher attitudes and practices of parent involvement in inner-city elementary and middle schools.* Paper presented at the annual meeting of the American Sociological Association, San Francisco.

Epstein, J., & Sanders, M. (2000). Connecting home, school and community. In M. Hallinan (Ed.), *Handbook of the sociology of education* (pp. 285–306). New York: Kluwer/Plenum.

Epstein, J., Sanders, M., Simon, B., Salinas, K., Jansorn, N., & Van Voorhis, F. (2002). *School, family and community partnerships: Your handbook for action* (2nd ed.). Thousand Oaks, CA: Corwin Press.

Erickson, F., & Shultz, J. (1992). Students' experience of curriculum. In P. W. Jackson (Ed.), *Handbook of research on curriculum* (pp. 465–485). New York: Macmillan.

Evans, C. (1995, June). Leaders wanted. *Education Week*, p. 1.

Ferguson, R. (1991, Summer). Paying for public education: New evidence on how and why money matters. *Harvard Journal on Legislation, 28*, 465–498.

Fielding, M. (2001). Students as radical agents of change. *Journal of Educational Change, 2*(2), 123–141.

Firestone, W., Rosenblum, S., & Bader, B. (1992). Recent trends in state educational reform. *Teachers College Record, 94*(2), 254–277.

Fullan, M. (1979). *School-focused in-service education in Canada.* Report prepared for the Centre for Educational Research and Innovation (OECD), Paris.

Fullan, M. (1985). Change process and strategies at the local level. *The Elementary School Journal, 84*(3), 391–420.

Fullan, M. (1991). *The new meaning of educational change* (2nd ed.). New York: Teachers College Press.

Fullan, M. (1993). *Change forces: Probing the depths of educational reform.* London: Falmer Press.

Fullan, M. (1997). *What's worth fighting for in the principalship?* (2nd ed.). Toronto: Elementary Teachers Federation of Ontario; New York: Teachers College Press.

Fullan, M. (1999). *Change forces: The sequel.* Philadelphia: Falmer Press/Taylor & Francis.

Fullan, M. (2000). The return of large scale reform. *The Journal of Educational Change, 1*(1), 1–23.

Fullan, M. (2001). *Leading in a culture of change.* San Francisco: Jossey-Bass.

Fullan, M. (2003). *Change forces with a vengeance.* London: Falmer Press.

Fullan, M. (2005). *Leadership and sustainability.* Thousand Oaks, CA: Corwin Press.

Fullan, M. (2006) *Turnaround leadership.* San Francisco: Jossey-Bass.

Fullan, M., Bertani, A., & Quinn, J. (2004) Lessons from district-wide reform. *Educational Leadership, 61*(6), 42–46.

Fullan, M., & Eastabrook, G. (1973). *School change project.* Unpublished report, Ontario Institute for Studies in Education, Toronto.

Fullan, M., Eastabrook, G., & Biss, J. (1977). The effects of Ontario teachers' strikes on the attitudes and perceptions of grade 12 and 13 students. In D. Brison (Ed.), *Three studies of the effects of teachers' strikes* (pp. 1–170). Toronto: Ontario Ministry of Education.

Fullan, M., Galluzzo, G., Morris, P., & Watson, N. (1998). *The rise & stall of teacher education reform.* Washington, DC: American Association of Colleges for Teacher Education.

Fullan, M., & Hargreaves, A. (1992). *What's worth fighting for? Working together for your school.* Toronto: Elementary Teachers Federation of Ontario; New York: Teachers College Press.

Fullan, M., Hill, P., & Crévola, C. (2006). *Breakthrough.* Thousand Oaks, CA: Corwin Press; Toronto: Ontario Principals' Council.

Fullan, M., Park, P., Williams, T., Allison, P., Walker, L., & Watson, N. (1987). *Supervisory officers in Ontario: Current practice and recommendations for the future.* Toronto: Ontario Ministry of Education.

Fullan, M., & Pomfret, A. (1977). Research on curriculum and instruction implementation. *Review of Educational Research, 47*(1), 335–397.

Fullan, M., & St. Germain, C. (2006). *Learning places.* Thousand Oaks, CA: Corwin Press; Toronto: Ontario Principals' Council.

Gardner, H. (1999). *The disciplined mind.* New York: Simon & Schuster.

Gardner, H. (2004). *Changing minds.* Boston: Harvard Busines School Press.

Gaynor, A. (1977). A study of change in educational organizations. In L. Cunningham (Ed.), *Educational administration* (pp. 28–40). Berkeley, CA: McCutchan.

Gilligan, J. (1996). *Violence: Our deadly epidemic and its causes.* New York: Putnam.

Gitlin, A., & Margonis, F. (1995). The political aspect of reform. *The American Journal of Education, 103,* 377–405.

Goertz, M. (2000, April). *Local accountability: The role of the district and school in monitoring policy, practice and achievement.* Paper presented at the annual meeting of the American Educational Research Association, New Orleans.

Gold, B., & Miles, M. (1981). *Whose school is it anyway? Parent–teacher conflict over an innovative school.* New York: Praeger.

Goldhammer, K. (1977). Role of the American school superintendent. In L. Cunningham et al. (Eds.), *Educational administration* (pp. 147–164). Berkeley, CA: McCutchan.

Goleman, D. (1995). *Emotional intelligence.* New York: Bantam Books.

Goleman, D. (1998). *Working with emotional intelligence.* New York: Bantam Books.

Good, R. H., & Kaminski, R. A. (Eds.). (2002). *Dynamic indicators of basic early literacy skills* (6th ed.). Eugene, OR: Institute for the Development of Educational Achievement.

Goodlad, J. (1984). *A place called school: Prospects for the future.* New York: McGraw-Hill.

Goodlad, J. I. (1990). *Teachers for our nation's schools.* San Francisco: Jossey-Bass.

Goodlad, J. (1994). *Educational renewal: Better teachers, better schools.* San Francisco: Jossey-Bass.

Goodlad, J., Klein, M., & Associates. (1970). *Behind the classroom door.* Worthington, OH: Charles Jones.

Gordon, M. (2005). *Roots of empathy: Changing the world child by child.* Toronto: Thomas Allen.

Greenwald, R., Hedges, L., & Laine, R. (1996, Fall). Interpreting research on school resources and student achievement: A rejoinder to Hanushek. *Review of Educational Research, 66*(3), 411–416.

Gross, N., Giacquinta, J., & Bernstein, M. (1971). *Implementing organizational innovations: A sociological analysis of planned educational change.* New York: Basic Books.

Grove, A. (1996). *Only the paranoid survive.* New York: Doubleday.

Hargreaves, A. (1994). *Changing teachers, changing times.* New York: Teachers College Press.

Hargreaves, A. (2000). Professionals and parents: Personal adversaries or public allies? *Prospects, V.XXX*(2), 201–213.

Hargreaves, A. (2003). *Teaching and the knowledge society.* New York: Teachers College Press.

Hargreaves, A., & Fink, D. (2006). *Sustainable leadership.* San Francisco: Jossey-Bass.

Hargreaves, A., & Fullan, M. (1998). *What's worth fighting for out there.* New York: Teachers College Press; Toronto: Elementary School Teachers' Federation; Buckingham, UK: Open University Press.

Hatch, T. (2000). *What happens when multiple improvement initiatives collide.* Menlo Park, CA: Carnegie Foundation for the Advancement of Teaching.

Heifetz, R. (1994). *Leadership without easy answers.* Cambridge, MA: Harvard University Press.

Heifetz, R., & Linsky, M. (2002). *Leadership on the line*. Boston: Harvard Business School Press.

Henry, M. (1996). *Parent–school collaboration*. Albany: State University of New York Press.

Hess, F. M. (1999). *Spinning wheels: The politics of urban school reform*. Washington, DC: Brookings Institute.

Hill, P., Campbell, C., & Harvey, J. (2000). *It takes a city*. Washington, DC: Brookings Institute.

Hill, P., & Celio, M. (1998). *Fixing urban schools*. Washington, DC: Brookings Institute.

Hill, P., & Crévola, C. (1999). The role of standards in educational reform for the 21st century. In D. Marsh (Ed.), *Preparing our schools for the 21st century* (pp. 117–142). Washington, DC: Association for Supervision and Curriculum Development.

Hodgkinson, H., & Montenegro, Y. (1999). *The U.S. school superintendent*. Washington, DC: Institute for Educational Leadership.

The Holmes Group. (1986). *Tomorrow's teachers*. East Lansing, MI: Author.

The Holmes Group. (1990). *Tomorrow's schools*. East Lansing, MI: Author.

The Holmes Group. (1995). *Tomorrow's schools of education*. East Lansing, MI: Author.

Hopkins, D. (2006). *Every school a great school*. Paper presented at the meeting of the London Centre for Leadership and Learning, London.

House, E. (1974). *The politics of educational innovation*. Berkeley, CA: McCutchan.

Howey, K. R., & Zimpher, N. L. (1989). *Profiles of preservice teacher education, inquiry into the nature of programs*. Albany: State University of New York Press.

Hubbard, L., Mehan, H., & Stein, M. K. (2006). *Reform as learning*. London: Routledge.

Huberman, M. (1983). Recipes for busy kitchens. *Knowledge: Creation, Diffusion, Utilization, 4*, 478–510.

Huberman, M. (1988). Teacher careers and school improvement. *Journal of Curriculum Studies, 20*(2), 119–132.

Huberman, M., & Miles, M. (1984). *Innovation up close*. New York: Plenum.

James, C., Connolly, M., Dunning, G., & Elliot, T. (2006). *How very effective primary schools work*. London: Paul Chapman.

Jeffery, B., & Wood, P. (1999). Feeliing deprofessionalized. *The Cambridge Journal of Education, 23*, 325–343.

Jellison, J. (2006). *Managing the dynamics of change*. New York: McGraw-Hill.

Johnson, S. M. (1996). *Leading to change: The challenge of the new superintendency*. San Francisco: Jossey-Bass.

Johnson, S. M. (2004). *Finders and keepers: Helping new teachers thrive and survive in our schools*. San Francisco: Jossey-Bass.

Johnson, S. M., & Kardos, S. (2005). Bridging the generation gap. *Educational Leadership, 62*(8), 8–14.

Kanter, R. M. (2004). *Confidence: How winning and losing streaks begin and end*. New York: Crown Business.

Katz, E., Lewin, M., & Hamilton, H. (1963). Traditions of research on the diffusion of innovation. *American Sociological Review, 28*(2), 237–252.

Kearns, D., & Harvey, D. (2000). *A legacy of learning*. Washington, DC: Brookings Institute.

Kruse, S., Louis, K., & Bryk, A. (1995). *Building professional learning in schools*. Madison, WI: Center on Organization and Restructuring of Schools.

LaRocque, L., & Coleman, P. (1989). Quality control: School accountability and district ethos. In M. Holmes, K. Leithwood, & D. Musella (Eds.), *Educational policy for effective schools* (pp. 168–191). Toronto: OISE Press.

Lasch, C. (1991). *The true and only heaven: Progress and its critics*. New York: W.W. Norton.

Leithwood, K. (2005). *Teacher working conditions that matter*. Toronto: Elementary Teachers Federation of Ontario.

Leithwood, K., Bauer, S., & Riedlinger, B. (2006). Developing and sustaining school principals. In B. Davies (Ed.), *Sustaining and developing leaders* (pp. 120–145). London: Sage.

Leithwood, K., Louis, K., Anderson, S., & Wahlstrom, K. (2004). *How leadership influences student learning*. New York: Wallace Foundation.

Levin, J., Mulhern, J., & Schunck, J. (2005). *Unintended consequences: The race for reforming the staffing rules in urban teachers union contracts*. New York: New Teacher Project.

Levine, A. (2005). *Educating school leaders*. Washington, DC : Education Schools Project.

Lighthall, F. (1973, February). Multiple realities and organizational non-solutions: An essay on anatomy of educational innovation. *School Review*, pp. 255–287.

Lindblom, C. (1959). The science of muddling through. *Public Administration Review, 19*, 155–169.

Little, J. W. (1981). The power of organizational setting. Paper adapted from final report, *School success and staff development*. Washington, DC: National Institute of Education.

Little, J. W. (1990). The persistence of privacy: Autonomy and initiative in teachers' professional relations. *Teachers College Record, 91*(4), 509–536.

Little, J. W. (1993). Teachers' professional development in a climate of education reform. *Educational Evaluation and Policy Analysis, 15*, 129–151.

Lortie, D. (1975). *School teacher: A sociological study*. Chicago: University of Chicago Press.

Lusi, S. (1997). *The role of the State Department of Education in complex school reform*. New York: Teachers College Press.

Marris, P. (1975). *Loss and change*. New York: Anchor Press/Doubleday.

Marzano, R., Waters, T., & McNulty, B. (2005). *School leadership that works*. Alexandria, VA: Association for Supervision and Curriculum Development.

Maurer, R. (1996). *Beyond the wall of resistance*. Austin, TX: Bard Books.

McAdams, D. (2006). *What school boards can do*. New York: Teachers College Press.

McLaughlin, M., & Mitra, D. (2000). *Theory-based change and change-based theory: Going deeper, going broader*. Unpublished paper, Stanford University, Stanford, CA.

McLaughlin, M., & Talbert, J. (2001). *Professional communities and the work of high school teaching*. Chicago: University of Chicago Press.

McLaughlin, M., & Talbert, J. (2006). *Building school-based teacher learning communities*. New York: Teachers College Press.

McNeil, L. (2000). *Contradictions of school reform*. London: Routledge.

Micklethwait, J., & Wooldridge, A. (1996). *The witch doctors: Making sense of management gurus*. New York: Random House.

Miles, M. (1993). Forty years of change in schools: Some personal reflections. *Educational Administration Quarterly, 29*, 213–248.

Minthrop, H. (2004). *Schools on probation*. New York: Teachers College Press.

Mintzberg, H. (1994). *The rise and fall of strategic planning*. New York: Free Press.

Mintzberg, H. (2004). *Managers not MBAs*. San Francisco: Berret-Koehler.

Mintzberg, H., Ahlstrand, B., & Lampei, J. (1998). *Strategy safari: A guided tour through the wilds of strategic management*. New York: Free Press.

Morgan, G. (1989). *Riding the waves of change*. San Francisco: Jossey-Bass.

Mortimore, P., Sammons, P., Stoll, L., Lewis, D., & Ecob, R. (1988). *School matters: The junior years*. Somerset, UK: Open Books.

Munby, S. (2003). *Broad and deep: A whole authority approach to motivation and learning.* Mersey, UK: Knowsley Local Education Authority.

Murphy, J., & Datnow, A. (Eds.). (2003). *Leadership lessons from comprehensive school reforms.* Thousand Oaks, CA: Corwin Press.

Murphy, J., Yff, J., & Shipman, N. (2000). Implementation of the interstate school leaders licensure consortium standards. *International Journal of Leadership in Education.*

National Academy of Education. (2005). *A good teacher in every classroom.* Washington, DC: Author.

National Board for Professional Teaching Standards. (1993). *What should teachers know and be able to do?* Detroit, MI: Author.

National College for School Leadership. (2005). *Charting a course.* Nottingham, UK: Author.

National Commission on Excellence in Education. (1983). *A nation at risk.* Washington, DC: Author.

National Commission on Teaching and America's Future. (1996). *What matters most: Teaching for America's future.* Washington, DC: Author.

National Commission on Teaching and America's Future. (2003). *No dream denied.* Washington, DC: Author.

National Research Council. (1999). *Improving student learning.* Washington, DC: National Academy Press.

National Staff Development Council. (2005). *Standards of practice for professional development.* Oxford, OH: Author.

NBPTS upgrades profession, most agree, despite test-score letdown. (2006, June 14). *Education Week,* p. 1.

New Teacher Center. (2006). *Understanding New York's groundbreaking induction initiative.* New York: Author.

Newmann, F., King, B., & Youngs, P. (2000, April). *Professional development that addresses school capacity.* Paper presented at the annual meeting of the American Educational Research Association, New Orleans.

Newmann, F., & Wehlage, G. (1995). *Successful school restructuring.* Madison, WI: Center on Organization and Restructuring of Schools.

Noddings, N. (2005). *The challenge to care in schools* (2nd ed.). New York: Teachers College Press.

Noguera, P. (2003). *City schools and the American dream.* New York: Teachers College Press.

Nonaka, I., & Takeuchi, H. (1995). *The knowledge-creating company.* Oxford, UK: Oxford University Press.

Nye, B., Konstantopoulos, S., & Hedges, L. (2004). How large are teacher effects? *Educational Evaluation and Policy Analysis, 26,* 237–257.

Oakes, J., & Lipton, J. (2002). Struggling for educational equity in diverse communities. *Journal of Educational Change, 26,* 383–406.

Oakes, J., Quartz, K., Ryan, S., & Lipton, M. (1999). *Becoming good American schools.* San Francisco: Jossey-Bass.

Odden, A. (1996). Incentives, school organization, and teacher compensation. In S. Fuhrman & J. O'Day (Eds.), *Rewards and reform: Creating educational incentives that work* (pp. 226–256). San Francisco: Jossey-Bass.

Odden, A. (2000). New and better forms of teacher compensation are possible. *Phi Delta Kappan, 8*(5), 361–366.

Office for Standards in Education (OFSTED). (2003). *Inspector report: Knowsley LEA.* London: Author.

Ontario Institute for Studies in Education, University of Toronto. (2005). *Inital teacher education programs.* Toronto: Author.

Pekrul, S., & Levin, B. (in press). Building student voice for school improvement. In D. Thiessen (Ed.), *International handbook of student experience in elementary and secondary schools.* Dordrecht, The Netherlands: Springer.

Perkins, D. (2003) *King Arthur's roundtable.* New York: Wiley.

Peters, T. (1987). *Thriving on chaos: Handbook for a management revolution.* New York: Knopf.

Pfeffer, J., & Sutton, R. (2000). *The knowing–doing gap.* Boston: Harvard Business School Press.

Pfeffer, J., & Sutton, R. (2006). *Hard facts, dangerous half-truths and total nonsense.* Boston: Harvard Business School Press.

Pincus, J. (1974). Incentives for innovation in public schools. *Review of Educational Research, 44,* 113–144.

Policy focus converges on leadership. (2000, January 12). *Education Week,* pp. 3–4.

Popham, J. (2004). *America's "failing" schools.* London: Routledge.

Pressure drives heads to drink. (2000, July 14). *Times Education Supplement,* p. 5.

Reeves, D. (2006). *The learning leader.* Alexandria, VA: Association for Supervision and Curriculum Development.

Rohlen, T. (1999). Social software for a learning society. In D. Keating & C. Hertzman (Eds.), *Developmental health and the wealth of nations* (pp. 251–273). New York: Guilford Press.

Rolheiser, C., & Evans, M. (2006). *Creative connections: School university partnerships.* Toronto: Ontario Institute for Studies in Education.

Rosenblum, S., & Louis, K. (1979). *Stability and change: Innovation in an educational context.* Cambridge, MA: ABT Associates.

Rosenholtz, S. J. (1989). *Teachers' workplace: The social organization of schools.* New York: Longman.

Ross, S., Wang, L., Sanders, W., Wright, P., & Stringfield, S. (1999). *Two- and three-year achievement results on the Tennessee value-added assessment system for restructuring schools in Memphis.* Unpublished manuscript, University of Memphis, Memphis, TN.

Rudduck, J. (in press). Student voice, student engagement, and school reform. In D. Thiessen (Ed.), *International handbook of student experience in elementary and secondary schools.* Dordrecht, The Netherlands: Springer.

Rudduck, J., Chaplain, R., & Wallace, G. (1996). *School improvement: What can pupils tell us?* London: David Fulton.

Sammons, P. (1999). *School effectiveness.* Lisse, The Netherlands: Swetz & Zeitlinger.

Sanders, M., & Epstein, J. (2000). The national network of partnership schools: How research influences educational practice. *Journal of Education for Students Placed at Risk, 5*(1–2), 61–76.

Sarason, S. (1971). *The culture of the school and the problem of change.* Boston: Allyn & Bacon.

Sarason, S. (1982). *The culture of the school and the problem of change* (2nd ed.). Boston: Allyn & Bacon.

Sarason, S. (1995). *Parent involvement and the political principle.* San Francisco: Jossey-Bass.

Sarason, S. B., Davidson, K. S., & Blatt, B. (1986). *The preparation of teachers: An unstudied problem in education* (Rev. ed.). Cambridge, MA: Brookline Books.

Schön, D. (1971). *Beyond the stable state.* New York: Norton.

Scott, C., Stone, B., & Dinham, S. (2000, April). *International patterns of teacher discontent.* Paper presented at the annual meeting of the American Educational Research Association, New Orleans.

Senge, P. (1990). *The fifth discipline.* New York: Doubleday.

Senge, P., Cambron-McCabe, N., Lucas, T., Smith, B., Dutton, J., & Kleiner, A. (2000). *Schools that learn.* New York: Doubleday.

Senge, P., Kleiner, A., Roberts, C., Ross, R., Roth, G., & Smith, B. (1999). *The dance of change.* New York: Doubleday.

Shanker, A. (1990). Staff development and the restructured school. In B. Joyce (Ed.), *Changing school culture through staff development* (pp. 91–103). Alexandria, VA: Association for Supervision and Curriculum Development.

Sharratt, L., & Fullan, M. (2006). Accomplishing districtwide reform. *Journal of School Leadership, 16*(5), 583–595.

Simms, J. (1978). *The implementation of curriculum innovation.* Unpublished doctoral dissertation, University of Alberta, Edmonton, Canada.

Slavin, R., & Madden, N. (1998). *Disseminating success for all.* Baltimore: Johns Hopkins University.

Smith, L., & Keith, P. (1971). *Anatomy of educational innovation: An organizational analysis of an elementary school.* New York: Wiley.

Smylie, M., Bay, M., & Tozer, S. (1999). Preparing teachers as agents of change. In G. Griffen (Ed.), *The education of teachers* (pp. 29–62). Chicago: University of Chicago Press.

Snipes, J., Doolittle, F., & Herlihy, P. (2002). *Foundations for success.* Washington, DC: Council of the Great City Schools.

Snyder, J. (1999). *New Haven unified school district: A teaching quality system for excellence and equity.* New York: Teachers College, Columbia University, National Commission on Teaching and America's Future.

Spillane, J. (1999, April). *The change theories of local change agents: The pedagogy of district policies and programs.* Paper presented at the annual meeting of the American Educational Research Association, Boston.

Spillane, J. (2004). *Standards deviation.* Cambridge, MA: Harvard University Press.

Stacey, R. (1996a). *Complexity and creativity in organizations.* San Francisco: Berrett-Koehler.

Stacey, R. (1996b). *Strategic management and organizational dynamics* (2nd ed.). London: Pitman.

Steinberg, L. (1996). *Beyond the classroom: Why school reform has failed and what parents need to do.* New York: Simon & Schuster.

Stiggins, R. (2005). New assessment beliefs for a new school mission. *Phi Delta Kappan, 86*(1), 22–27.

Stigler, J., & Hiebert, J. (1999). *The teaching gap.* New York: Free Press.

Stoll, L., Bolam, R., McMahon, A., Thomas, S., Wallace, M., Greenwood, A., & Hawkley, K. (2006). *Professional learning communities: Source materials for school leaders and other leaders of professional learning.* Nottingham, UK: National College for School Leadership.

Stoll, L., & Fink, D. (1996). *Changing our schools.* Buckingham, UK: Open University Press.

Storr, A. (1997). *Feet of clay: A study of gurus.* London: HarperCollins.

Supovitz, J. (2006). *The case for district-based reform.* Cambridge: Harvard Education Press.

Surowiecki, J. (2004). *The wisdom of crowds.* New York: Doubleday.

The Teacher Training Agency. (2005). *The teacher training agency corporate plan 2005–2008.* London: Author.

The Teaching Commission. (2006). *Teaching at risk: Progress and potholes.* Washington, DC : Author.

Thiessen, D. (Ed.). (in press). *International handbook of student experience in elementary and secondary schools.* Dordrecht, The Netherlands: Springer.

Thiessen, D., & Howey, K. (Eds.). (1998). *Agents provocateur.* Washington, DC: American Association of Colleges of Teacher Education.

Time on his side. (2006, June 7). *Education Week,* pp. 30–32.

Times Education Supplement. (1997). Times Education Supplement survey. London: Author.

Timperley, H., & Parr, J. (2005). Theory competition and the process of change. *Journal of Educational Change, 6*(3), 227–251.

Togneri, W., & Anderson, S. (2003). How poverty districts improve. *Educational Leadership, 33*(1), 12–17.

Tomlinson, C. (1998). *The differentiated classroom.* Alexandria, VA: Association for Supervision and Curriculum Development.

Urbanski, A., & Erskine, R. (2000). School reform, TURN, and teacher compensation. *Phi Delta Kappan, 81*(5), 367–370.

Waller, W. (1932). *The sociology of teaching.* New York: Russell and Russell.

Werner, W. (1980). *Implementation: The role of belief.* Unpublished paper, Center for Curriculum Studies, University of British Columbia, Vancouver, Canada.

Wigginton, E. (1986). *Sometimes a shining moment: The Foxfire experience.* New York: Doubleday.

Wilkinson, R. (2005). *The impact of inequality.* London: New Press.

Wilson, K., & Barsky, C. (2006). *Education fiction: A new scenario for education.* Unpublished paper, Ohio State University, Department of Physics.

Wise, A. (1977). Why educational policies often fail: The hyperrationalization hypothesis. *Curriculum Studies, 9*(1), 43–57.

Wise, A. (1988). The two conflicting trends in school reform: Legislative learning revisited. *Phi Delta Kappan, 69*(5), 328–333.

Index

About the Author

Michael Fullan is professor of policy studies at the Ontario Institute for Studies in Education of the University of Toronto. Recognized as an international authority on educational reform, he is engaged in training, consulting, and evaluating change projects around the world. His ideas for managing change are used in many countries, and his books have been published in many languages.

Fullan led the evaluation team that conducted a 4-year assessment of the National Literacy and Numeracy Strategy in England from 1998 to 2002. In April 2004, he was appointed special advisor to the premier and the minister of education in Ontario. His widely acclaimed books include *Leading in a Culture of Change*, the *What's Worth Fighting For* trilogy (with Andy Hargreaves), the *Change Forces* trilogy, *The Moral Imperative of School Leadership*, *Leadership and Sustainability: Systems Thinkers in Action*, *Breakthrough* (with Peter Hill and Carmel Crévola), *Learning Places* (with Clif St. Germain), and *Turnaround Leadership*.